DHSS

Studies in Deprivation and Disadvantage 11

The Money Problems of the Poor
A Literature Review

Pauline Ashley

Heinemann Educational Books · London

Heinemann Educational Books Ltd
22 Bedford Square, London WC1B 3HH

LONDON   EDINBURGH   MELBOURNE   AUCKLAND
HONG KONG   SINGAPORE   KUALA LUMPUR   NEW DELHI
IBADAN   NAIROBI   JOHANNESBURG
EXETER (NH)   KINGSTON   PORT OF SPAIN

© Crown copyright 1983
First published 1983

British Library Cataloguing in Publication Data

Ashley, Pauline
  The money problems of the poor.—(DHSS/SSRC studies
  in deprivation and disadvantage; 11)
  1. Poor—Economic aspects—Great Britain
  2. Poor—Social aspects—Great Britain
  I. Title   II. Series
  362.5   HC79.P6

ISBN 0–435–82023–0
ISBN 0–435–82024–9 Pbk

Typeset by Inforum Ltd, Portsmouth
Printed in Great Britain by Biddles Ltd, Guildford, Surrey

Contents

Preface

This review forms part of the larger Programme of Research into Transmitted Deprivation which was organised from 1972 to 1982 by a Joint Working Party of the Department of Health and Social Security and the Social Science Research Council. The initial concern of the Joint Working Party, to test the cycle of deprivation hypothesis, developed into an extensive inquiry into the extent, persistence and cause of deprivation in Britain. The completed programme consisted of over thirty pieces of work from short review papers to major empirical research studies. Its principal findings are currently appearing in the Heinemann series Studies in Deprivation and Disadvantage and are summarised in the final report *Despite the Welfare State*.

As the programme evolved the approaches taken by researchers to the whole question of deprivation tended to diverge. Some workers concentrated their attention on the processes within families that seemed likely to influence for good or ill the development of the individual. Other researchers sought to elucidate the influence of social and economic factors on the determination of patterns of disadvantage. This increasing polarisation of approach reflected profound divisions, ideological rather than methodological, among those involved on the programme and at times it was difficult to find the middle ground of the inquiry.

In this context it seemed appropriate to focus some attention on the place of money itself in both the genesis and the transmission of deprivation. Few could doubt its importance: lack of money is obviously a major deprivation and many factors from the psychological to the structural are involved in both its availability and its use. It was hoped that a study of the significance and use of money would help to link the concern with personal and family factors to that for structural factors in understanding the process of deprivation.

The overall concern of the programme with transmitted deprivation limited the inquiry to questions about the lack rather than the abundance of money and focused attention on the handling rather than the getting of it. Although it has often been argued that wealth and privilege should be studied as consistently as poverty and deprivation they are still not widely regarded as social problems. In justification of this narrow approach it is clear that although money has enormous significance and power at all income levels, the handling of it becomes the more critical the less there is of it. Plain shortage of money for basic requirements is a major element of poverty and actual poverty is unequivocally regarded as a depriving condition. But poverty lines, wherever they are drawn, are only crude measures of the true extent of the deprivation involved in living on low incomes. Careful budgeting, as Mr Micawber knew, can make for happiness even on a low income. Careless spending, however, can lead to debt and the consequences of debt can be grim to the point of disaster. So it was felt to be important to consider why some people manage their limited resources well and others badly and to examine some of the consequences of difficulties in money management.

Not everyone on the programme agreed with this concern. Some members of the Joint Working Party felt strongly that any exploration of money management among poor families would serve to condone the low incomes on which many people have to survive. This is an important point, and it was very fully considered, but in the end it was rejected by the majority. Most members indeed felt that a study of budgeting problems could be used to attack rather than defend the persistence of low incomes. Evidence of the problems associated with and deriving from low incomes could be added to the arguments put forward in support of improved family income maintenance. Moreover, it was argued, that because some people manage better than others need not weaken the general case against extreme inequalities of income. Most importantly, it was felt to be consistent with the pragmatic approach of the programme as a whole to consider *any* ways in which the impact and persistence of deprivation might be understood and reduced. To share the wisdom of those who do manage remarkably well on slender resources amongst those who become hopelessly entangled by debt appeared therefore a reasonable, albeit modest ambition. And to draw the attention of policy-makers to the vulnerability of low income families to particular problems, such as fuel debts and disconnections, appeared a perfectly proper step.

A small consultative group was accordingly established, under my chairmanship, to consider how the significance of money in transmitted deprivation might be explored. The members were Sally Baldwin, Kay Carmichael, Hazel Houghton, David Piachaud and Barbara Rodgers. They brought much knowledge and insight into money problems from a variety of perspectives from academic research to social work practice.

The group only met a few times but its discussions were valuable. The initial proposal that was considered suggested that a literature review would be needed to cover existing work on the following topics: living on low incomes; the costs of child rearing; the differential impact of price rises on families at various income levels; the availability of credit; the distribution of insurance; and problems around the take-up of benefits. Further work could be pursued on questions of handling money – budgeting, saving, credit, etc. – and on the issue of how people learn about money management. The prevalence of money problems was also raised, in particular the extent and impact of debt, and, finally, some evaluation of existing interventions such as money advice centres and consumer protection legislations, was proposed.

In discussion of these areas the consulting group explored various issues. It is not possible here to summarise all that was said but one or two points deserve special mention. There was unanimous support for the need to demolish myths about money and money management. It was agreed that little was known about the acquisition of skills in handling money – beyond the paradox that the less of it one has the more skill is required in its handling. It was probably impossible to disentangle the emotional aspects of handling money from the purely practical ones. Fluctuations in income levels might well cause more problems than low incomes as such – poverty surveys tend to overlook the dynamic nature of the budgeting task. The equitable distribution of income within the family should not be taken for granted; many wives and children might suffer deprivation through an inadequate share of an adequate family budget.

There was a lot of interest in interventions. It was agreed that both low incomes and money problems could disadvantage a family and lead to the persistence of problems across generations. It was, therefore, important to consider how income deprivation could be prevented or reduced. Apart from the basic question of adequacy of benefit levels questions on the mechanics of payments were seen to be relevant and it was agreed that the appropriateness of different kinds of budgeting advice should be examined.

Not surprisingly, the group produced more ideas than it could follow up. There was alas neither the time nor the money for new empirical work but it was agreed that the detailed review of the existing literature should examine work relating to three main areas: the nature and management of the cash flow; financial problems – crises and crisis management; and the impact of money problems on the life chances of families and on their utilisation and under-utilisation of opportunities. Other reviews, on the programme by Berthoud, Fuller and Stevenson and Land, which had already been started, would concentrate on the prevalence of low incomes, the role of income maintenance and the distribution of income within the family.

The group was fortunate in obtaining the services of Pauline Ashley to undertake the review. She came to it with considerable general knowledge of the field from previous work and experience, and with a specialist interest in the issue of equivalence scales. She covered an extensive literature very thoroughly and succeeded both in putting it into a coherent form and in summarising it clearly and succinctly. Inevitably the actual availability of the literature directed the shape of the final review which deviates to some extent from the group's initial concept. But the essence of the enterprise – the concern with the problems of living and handling money on low incomes – has been retained as the review has progressed. And the numerous factors involved – affecting the resources and requirements of those at risk of low incomes and the money environment in which they operate – have been separated out for examination with great care.

What has emerged is a clear, painstaking and sobering account of the qualitative side of poverty. The reality of life on low incomes is detailed and the appalling vulnerability of poor families to budgeting problems, including debt and disconnections, is carefully and dispassionately revealed. The impact of money problems on the life chances of the poor is discussed though in this area, alas, the literature was disappointingly thin. Policy implications are drawn out with due care and a thoughtful consideration both for the complexity of the problems and the constraints on social action.

Readers must judge for themselves the usefulness of this review, but I am confident that it admirably fulfils at least one of the original aims of the consultative group – that of reducing the myths around money problems. Notions about the improvidence and extravagance of the poor die hard and complacency about the current income maintenance system is widespread. The sober evidence assembled in this review should help to dispel ideas that the poor have only themselves to blame for their difficulties, or that living on social security is an easy ride.

On the question of the precise transmission of deprivation the review can only offer tentative conclusions, as the evidence is relatively weak. But it does clarify the relationships between poverty and deprivation and problems of money management. For example it shows that the difficulties of the stereotypical problem family, though they exist, are fairly insignificant compared with the extensive problems of shortages and debts and stress experienced by large numbers of ordinary families on low incomes. And it is clear that children brought up in deprived and stressful circumstances are likely to suffer the kind of damage that can mar the development of all but the most resilient.

To understand and explain the phenomenon of deprivation many approaches are needed – and many have been pursued on the overall programme of research. This review of the significance of money itself is one fairly original approach. Although it is limited, not least by the limitations of the literature, it adds to our understanding of the dynamics of poverty and deprivation and is an important contribution to the programme. I hope it will help to move discussion of these problems on to a more informed and realistic plane and contribute to the development of more effective policies in this area.

Muriel Brown

Acknowledgements

The originator of this review is Muriel Brown. The first ideas were hers alone, and her enthusiasm led to the Joint Working Party on Transmitted Deprivation supporting their development. I am delighted that I was then able to become involved. Muriel has freely given me invaluable advice and guidance, while at the same time encouraging a wide-ranging exploration of the literature.

I am also greatly indebted to Barbara Rodgers. Her thorough assessment of my work as it progressed stimulated me to develop my ideas in many areas. I am grateful also to the other members of the consultative group whose deliberations gave me the first brief for this review. In particular, Sally Baldwin, Hazel Houghton, and David Piachaud provided many interesting and relevant suggestions.

An early draft was read by Brian Abel Smith, and I appreciated his sagacious comments. At a later stage, Sue Duncan gave me a most helpful detailed critique, while her colleague at the Department of the Environment, Keith Kirby, kindly aided me with the section on rent arrears. My thanks also to Betty Low who scrupulously tidied up my script. Members of my family have given me their less specialised views, and their common-sense approach has been of great assistance.

Many people have contributed to the development of this review. I am grateful to them all, but I take sole responsibility for the selection of the literature, the views expressed, and any inconsistencies or errors that may have slipped in.

Pauline Ashley

1 Introduction: Money Problems

Money! For a brief instant he was appalled by its significance and potency. Its influence on his life was immense. Why it was everything! He was as he was simply because he had no money.

W. Greenwood, *Love on the Dole*, 1933

Money is a unique multipurpose good which all societies need. Simple closed communities such as prisons may use something like tobacco for money. In sophisticated economies, money takes many forms, and bank deposits and credit facilities are as important as the coin of the realm.

Money has many uses as well as many forms, but the original and the most common is to facilitate exchange. As banking systems have developed the facility had grown. The development of credit has given a new dimension to the usefulness of money. It permits delay between purchase and payment, gives value to money not immediately required, and provides governments with tools of economic management.

For the individual, money has many roles. Used or unused, it is an obvious potential source of status and power, conditioning relationships, affecting attitudes and even personalities. It lubricates the business of living and prevents or resolves many of the problems that daunt those with little of it. But the prime importance of money to the individual lies in the claim it gives to goods and services. Money is the crucial determinant of living standards and of the extent to which an individual can participate in the society to which he or she belongs. Its importance here was described by the American sociologist Rainwater (1974) who wrote that people not 'protected by some cultural enclave cannot fail to define themselves most basically in terms of access to all that money can buy'.

The object of this review is to look at the process of getting and spending money, and consider where and how it appears to aggravate or reduce deprivation. It seeks to examine topics such as the availability of money to different groups of people, how it is obtained, the way it is spent, and the value derived from it. It also examines the effects of money shortage and its relationship to deprivation.

Discussion of deprivation is bedevilled by the difficulties of definition. Hawthorn and Carter's (1977) description of it as a state in which an individual is without something which it is believed that he should not be without is a mere starting point. The dispute arises over what the individual should not be without. What goods and services should be considered? At what level is provision deemed to be inadequate? Is it a relative or absolute level? Who should make the value judgements – the deprived, those who task it is to attempt to remedy deprivation, or external observors? Does the theoretical view differ from the practical reality?

Deprivation is frequently discussed in relation to various aspects of living, many of them closely linked to money shortage, but significantly money deprivation *per se* is rarely mentioned. Situations where there is a shortage of money are more commonly described as 'poverty', a milder word which does not imply the same need for remedial action as the word 'deprivation'.

The public response to poverty is one of apparent sympathy but not genuine widespread concern. Cash payments to those who have paid contributions are readily supported. But there is reluctance to approve them for others unless they are in urgent need and also considered 'deserving'. This attitude contrasts oddly with a readiness to provide for those deprived in other ways. For example, it is generally accepted that there should be full and virtually free medical facilities available for the sick, even though the ideal is not always realised. One reason for the difference in attitude may be that poverty is considered blameworthy but sickness is not. Another is that while medical treatment is obviously not needed or wanted by the healthy, money is in general demand.

Hawthorn and Carter's description of deprivation, while simple and clear, is not of great practical use. Although a precise definition is not feasible for a literature review, some indication of the interpretation used here is desirable. This review interprets deprivation as a state of 'being without' relative to accepted current standards of society, and to such an extent as to impose hardship.

The review is concerned with money deprivation and its long term effects, although inevitably these are difficult to analyse. One can rarely be certain that the current predicament of an individual is a result of some particular earlier circumstance, and still less that a particular circumstance will lead to a future predicament. Nevertheless it is useful to speculate about factors causing deprivations that have long-term effects. This review focuses on families with children because it is here that social policy, if it can reduce the long-term effects of deprivation, is most likely to be effective.

For the purpose of this review families suffering serious difficulties because of money are described as having money problems. Serious difficulties may be indicated by a standard of living much below that of the rest of society, help being sought from outside sources, or default on debt repayments. A rigid definition is impracticable, but these are the types of situations, indicating the existence of money problems, which are examined. However it is recognised that factors related to money are unlikely to be the only ones involved in money problems and they will interact with others.

Most individuals are closely involved with money. A high proportion of personal activity is associated with either getting or spending it; and that is carried out in a great variety of ways. Nevertheless there are common patterns which tend to be followed. Money is conveniently discussed in terms of people's resources and requirements. The former includes all sources of money, and the latter, all demands upon it. In a formal accounting sense, every financial unit eventually has to balance its resources and requirements. But how it is done affects people's welfare. Extensive borrowing or excessive economising undertaken only to achieve a balance are indications of money problems. When the necessary balance is achieved only with difficulty, it can be a fragile one, easily disturbed by relatively small changes in any of the elements that make up the amalgam of resources and requirements. Disturbance is more likely in some families than in others, and low income and a large number of dependent children are two factors which increase vulnerability. Chapter 2 of this review considers these crucial factors. The various causes of low income are examined, and also the ways in which the additional costs of children have been assessed. The subject matter in this chapter inevitably has a statistical bias. A balance has been sought between oversimplification and the complexity of detail, but those with an aversion to statistics may omit the chapter without impairing their understanding of later ones.

When income is low or demands upon it great, small changes in resources and requirements have enhanced importance, and become potential triggers of money problems for vulnerable groups. Chapter 3 examines factors modifying the level of basic income such as additions and irregularity of flow and possession of assets.

Factors affecting requirements such as social pressures on consumption, personal tastes and inclinations are considered in Chapter 4. Fuel and housing are looked at separately in Chapter 5. They are of particular interest because of their importance in many budgets and because their effective price is determined not only by market forces but also by government intervention.

The major financial concern of low income families is to satisfy their demand for goods and services, and money is the tool which enables them to do it. But it is not a tool which operates with automatic, regular efficiency. A variety of factors can give money a kind of elastic quality whose value changes in terms of the goods and services it can provide. The cost of credit is an obvious factor expanding or reducing value. So also do variations in the price structure facing different groups of consumers. Variations can be just the reflection of market forces. Other influences of a different kind may operate subtly in ways difficult to analyse. For example, marketing pressures can mould the pattern of demand. In addition, poverty and environmental pressures can interact, producing what are conveniently called 'poverty induced costs'. The summary term, 'the money environment', is used to describe these external factors that affect the value derived from money, and the relevant literature is discussed in Chapter 6 of this review.

The getting and spending of money are dynamic processes and they can have irregular fits and starts. There is no automatic mechanism matching income and expenditure in terms of either amounts or intervals of time over which each occur. If a family can do the matching competently, it can ease or relieve a potential imbalance of resources and requirements. Budgeting skills and a family's general attitude to money are very relevant to the avoidance of money problems, and the available literature is examined in Chapter 7. Styles of budgeting, although affected by external factors, are primarily matters of individual taste and the process of allocating money for the joint and individual needs of different members of a family – which is what budgeting is about – can be a very personal affair in which others hesitate to intervene. Sometimes the imbalance between resources and requirements can be so severe that not even the most skilful budgeting could close the gap. Nevertheless budgeting is not a topic which can be ignored. The tighter the constraint of income, the greater the importance of effective money management; for if money is short there is less flexibility and a reduced margin of error. It may be unreasonable and perhaps a vain hope to expect those on low incomes to budget more skilfully than others. But for them, the consequence of not budgeting proficiently is more likely to be serious.

The relevance of money problems to deprivation and its transmission hinges on the nature of the consequences of money problems. One direct consequence is debt and this is considered in Chapter 8. In this and other areas, it is unrealistic to expect strong evidence of causal links because most of the literature does not focus on links between money and deprivation. Indications or hints of relevant effects are more likely. Hence they are best termed repercussions rather than the consequences of money problems. Almost certainly they will relate to deprivation but the nature of the relationship may well be obscure. Literature relevant to the repercussions of money problems is discussed in Chapter 10. The most visible is a standard of living so low as to indicate hardship. Although difficult to analyse, the less visible personal effects may be equally important. Lack of money may result in stress or anxiety. Apathy, depression or ill health may follow. The relationship of money problems to fertility and to deprivation, although controversial is another important subject. Some suggest that high fertility is a cause of deprivation while others regard it is a consequence.

This review is wide-ranging, covering many apparent disparate subjects, but all are in some way related to money and deprivation. The object is not so much to probe deeply into each one but to try to give an overall view of possible interrelationships. In some sections of the review, where the information is fairly familiar, little detail has been given, but in other parts, where the works are new or less well known, brief résumés are attempted. Sources include government reports, large and small surveys, descriptive case studies, articles and, on occasions where there is little other evidence, press cuttings are used as indicators of the nature of the problem. Most of the literature is British, but where British coverage is slight, reference is sometimes

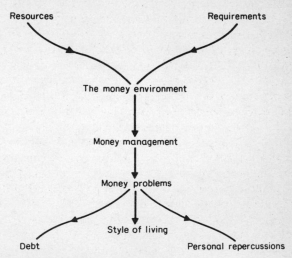

Figure 1.1 The development of money problems

made to pioneering studies carried out in other countries. The literature coverage is not uniform, because in some areas there is a large amount of firmly based information, whilst in others it is such that only an impressionistic picture can be given. Throughout the review, the literature is referred to by the name of the author and the date, but the full title and other details, in particular those relating to surveys, are given in the annotated bibliography.

The evolution of a family's money problems is illustrated by the flow diagram (Figure 1.1). The money resources and requirements of a family interact and their interaction is affected by the external money environment in which a family spends its money, and by its internal skills at money management. Following the interplay of all four factors, money problems may arise. The family may go into debt or its living standards fall. The personal repercussions on members of the family will vary, but for some they will be significant.

2 The Resources and Requirements of Those at Risk

People in all classes and at all levels of income have financial difficulties. Some may cause temporary inconvenience and a few, financial disaster. By no means all poor people have such difficulties, but poverty can be a catalyst, permitting and stimulating them. It may do so to the extent that financial difficulties become intractable money problems. The resulting hardship, debt, or inability to cope can create problems for society as well as for individuals; and where poverty leads to inflexible circumstances, the relief of money problems is the more difficult. The form poverty takes and the ways in which it creates vulnerability to money problems and inhibits solutions to them are very relevant to this review. But a full consideration of the large literature on poverty is not attempted.

Money problems arise when pressures on resources and requirements threaten an imbalance. For the purposes of this review, 'resources' is used as a summary term encompassing all available money from whatever source, while 'requirements' is a similar summary term covering all items wanted by a family which have to be paid for. Those with low incomes are inevitably at greatest risk of having money problems, but the risk is most unlikely to be directly proportional to the money level of income. Much more probable is an association with the level of equivalent income. This is a measure of income related to the variation in need that derives from family size and composition.

The Royal Commission on the Distribution of Income and Wealth (RCDIW) assembled and assessed much information about the circumstances of those with low incomes. People in the bottom quarter of the equivalent income distribution are of particular interest to this review because they are likely to have a precarious balance of resources and requirements.

Table 2.1 shows that in 1976, of those under pensionable age, one-parent families and those with three or more children were the type of family unit most likely to be in the bottom quarter; while the least likely were married couples without children.

The RCDIW also noted that in 1976, of the 12.8 million children in the population, 4.5 million (35%) were in the bottom quarter – more children than there were elderly people. Sixty per cent of all individuals in this quarter were in families with children. These figures are not surprising, for the increased pressures which dependent children bring are a familiar aspect of the family life cycle. The dynamic nature of the cycle is a reminder that the number of families who will have at some time lived at low levels of income, because of the pressures of children, will be much greater than the number doing so at any particular time. The statistics show that becoming old and having children are the two most likely demographic causes of depressed living standards.

Table 2.1   Total population by types of family units and numbers of people in lowest quarter of equivalent net family income distribution, 1976

Estimate of numbers of people in the lowest quarter of the equivalent net family income distribution divided according to the family units they are in, together with those not in households and comparable numbers of people in the total population, 1976

United Kingdom   millions

Type of family unit	Number in the lowest quarter				Total population	Percentage of total in lowest quarter
	Men	Women	Children	All		
The elderly	1.3	2.5	—	3.8	10.0	38
Single-parent family	0.1	0.4	0.8	1.3	2.6	50
2 parent family with						
3 or more children	0.6	0.6	2.2	3.4	8.1	42
1 or 2 children	0.8	0.8	1.5	3.1	19.1	16
Single adult below pensionable age	0.9	0.9	—	1.8	6.9	26
Married couples without children	0.4	0.4	—	0.8	8.4	10
All in households	4.1	5.6	4.5	14.2	55.1	26
Persons not in households	0.2	0.2	(0.03)	0.4	0.9	44
All in lowest quarter	4.3	5.8	4.5	14.6	56.0	26
Total population	20.7	22.5	12.8	56.0		
Percentage of total in lowest quarter	21	26	35	26		

Notes: This table takes the estimated number of family units (about seven million) which make up the lowest 25% of income recipients and divides them up in accordance with the sample numbers in the 1976 FES. The individual figures in the table should therefore be treated as orders of magnitude and for comparison with one another, rather than precise estimates.

No data about incomes of people not in households are available. However, for the purposes of illustration, it has been assumed that about half of such people would be in the lowest quarter of the net income distribution.

Source: Reproduced from RCDIW, 1978a, with permission of the Controller of HMSO.

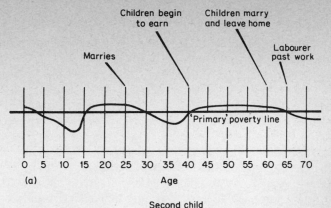

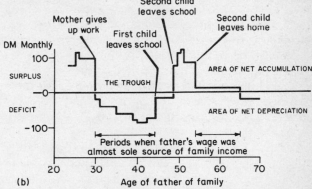

Figure 2.1 (a) Life cycle of Rowntree's labourer, 1901 (b) Life cycle of a Bavarian industrial worker, 1961
Source: Wynn, 1970. Adapted from Professor H. Schmucker, 1961.

The cost of children

A reasonably accurate estimate of the cost of children is important for two reasons. First, discussion of poverty is not meaningful without a measure of the effect on living standards of the presence of children. Second, estimates of the cost of children are necessary for assessment of the equity of state help for families in and out of work and with and without children. However, despite the simplicity of the concept of the cost of a child, obtaining acceptable estimates is surprisingly difficult.

An early account of the effect children have on living standards was that of Rowntree (1901) in his study of poverty in York at the beginning of the century. Many years later Wynn (1970) reproduced Rowntree's diagram of the life of a labourer which shows the depth of the poverty trough that occurred when he had several children and which lasted until they began to earn. Wynn compared it with a more modern version by Schmucker which considered the families of Bavarian industrial workers.

The more contemporary picture showed that the sharp drop in family prosperity that occured with the arrival of a child is accentuated if the working wife became a non-earning mother. An attempt to qualify in money terms the resultant change in life style was made by the Consumers' Association *Which? Book of Money* (1980). The loss of net take-home pay of a wife, with an average woman's earnings who gave up work completely, was estimated to be around £2800 p.a. (1980 figures). This far exceeded the cost of the child, estimated to be perhaps £375 p.a. for the child's first two years. On the assumption that the mother returned to work when the child started school, the Consumers' Association calculated that the overall net cost of supporting a child until it is 18 was £32,000 (1980 figures), of which £14,000 was the estimated loss of the mother's take-home pay for five years. The assumptions made were inevitably somewhat arbitrary, but they gave a useful indication of the costs involved. A similar type of calculation was made by Espenshade of the Urban Institute in Washington (*Guardian*, 27 October 1980). He estimated that it cost the average American family £42–£58,000 to support a child from birth and through four years of college, of which £19,000 arose because the wife was not working.

In their calculations, the Consumers' Association rightly made allowance for the cash benefits received from the state. It is the net cost of children that is important for it is this which affects families' living standards, and enables meaningful comment on relative hardship. The extra income obtained by a family because of the presence of a child is easily calculated but the extra cost has been found to be extraordinarily difficult to estimate. There are conceptual difficulties as well as methodological complexities; and these arise even when no attempt is made to allow for the loss of the wife's earnings, as is the case with most estimates made by governments and their agencies. One probable reason why such an allowance has not been made is that social security provision for dependent children, requiring assessment of the cost of a child, developed during the first half of this century, and that happened to be a time when relatively few wives were working. Hakin (1981), principal research officer at the Department of Employment, noted in a talk to the British Association for the Advancement of Science, that only one in ten married women worked between 1901 and 1931, compared with a quarter of wives and two-thirds of widows in 1851 and a quarter of all married women, aged from 15 to 59, in 1951. More recent figures show that by 1980 nearly 60% of all married women, aged from 16 to 59 were working, about half of them doing so part-time (*Social Trends*, 1981).

Early assessments of the costs of children were based on expert estimates of various 'needs', in particular the nutritional ones. These were costed and aggregated. Rowntree (1901) was one of the first to consider the varying needs of different size families in this way. This type of analysis was used by Beveridge (Treasury, 1942) and later became the basis of the National Assistance scales. However, as Wynn (1970) noted, Beveridge did not have available any detailed assessment of the total needs of children comparable with those that have been obtained from large-scale budget studies in other countries. Wynn commented on the extensive research and the thoroughness of the West German work, and drew attention to the low relative cost of adolescents assumed in the British Supplementary Benefits scheme in comparison with the allowance made for adolescents in other countries such as Germany and the United States which make greater use of budget studies. Studies such as these have the advantage of giving detailed expenditure and the level of the standard of living they are intended to reflect is generally made clear. Isherwood (1978) in an unpublished paper for a DHSS seminar, acknowledged their strong intuitive appeal, but he pointed out that the use of such methods in this country would require considerable investment in both methodology and data collection.

Using expenditure from budget studies to estimate the cost of children at different standards of living presents a fundamental difficulty. The amount of money spent on children varies with the standard of living, but that in turn is affected by the presence and cost of children. To overcome the circularity of argument the concept of equivalence has been developed. Equivalence scales are the ratios of the different levels of income required by families of different size and composition for them to have the same standard of living. The validity of the concept depends on whether it is possible to say that the standards of living of families of different composition are equal. To do so, an acceptable measuring rod of standard of living is needed.

Various ones have been used, including the amount spent on adult clothing (Nicholson, 1949), and the percentage of income spent on food (US Bureau of Labor Statistics, 1960). More recently, and partly because of the development of computers, equivalence scales have been derived from expenditure on a wide range of goods using the data from expenditure surveys. It is assumed that similar patterns of expenditure imply equivalent standards of living. McClements (1975), Muellbauer (1974) and the National Institute of Economic and Social Research (Fiegehen, Lansley and Smith, 1977) are amongst those who have obtained equivalence scales in this way.

In theory it is possible to assess whether the cost of a child varies with such factors as its age, its position in the family, and the total number of children. In practice, the range of information depends upon the sophistication of the method used. Details of the general method were described by McClements (1978) and by Isherwood (1978) in an unpublished paper from the DHSS Economic Advisers Office. Appendix E of the Sixth Report of the Royal Commission on the Distribution of Income and Wealth (1978a) discussed the concept and the problems that arise. There are two fundamental difficulties. One is that the standards of living of those with and without children cannot be validly compared by using the measuring rod of expenditure, whether it be in absolute or proportional terms, and whether it relates to one or more goods. This is because, as many writers have pointed out, preferences change when people become parents (Bagley, 1969; Nicholson, 1976). Secondly it is not necessarily true that the standard of living falls by the full cost of rearing children. Having children may be considered to be a chosen form of expenditure (Bagley, 1969).

Bagley's view is supported by the findings of the American writer Rainwater (1974). Rainwater adopted a subjective approach and obtained estimates from a sample of 600 people in Boston (USA) of the amounts of money they felt would be required for five different living levels for six family sizes. By comparing amounts for families with children with those for childless couples, subjective child equivalence scales were calculated for the different income levels. Rainwater found that, on average, a two-child family was thought to need a quarter more income than a childless couple. By comparison, the British SB system provides over 50% more (excluding housing costs). Rainwater suggested that his scales were much lower than those objectively obtained because his questions related to what he termed 'well-being', and his respondents appeared to feel that children, by their presence, add to 'well-being', and so they discounted a part of the extra material costs that appear in expenditure surveys.

Appendix E of the RCDIW Sixth Report (1978a) and Isherwood's paper (1978) gave the equivalence scales used or proposed in various countries. Generally they vary with age, but taking average values they range from 0.19 to 0.35 per child assuming a married couple is 1.0. Supplementary benefit rates for children are not based on assessments of equivalence scales, but the average for a child implicit in them is 0.27, and this is the ratio that is used by the RCDIW in its calculations of equivalent income distribution.

Levels of social security
All social security benefits, including those for working families, are relevant to money problems because they affect the balance between money resources and requirements. But supplementary benefit (SB)

has been the one which has received most attention. Because it is the safety net for those not in work, it has become the standard by which low incomes are judged. In addition many families with low incomes are dependent on it. For example, in December 1980, 4,864,000 people comprising 3,118,000 claimants with 621,000 dependent wives and 1,125,000 children had their standard of living determined by the complexities of SB regulations (Hansard, 21 December 1981, vol. 15, col. 295W).

The amount of benefit is related to defined requirements of the families and in particular to family size. In principle, resources and requirements are equal. However SB is a complex scheme, and as the Supplementary Benefits Commission (SBC) (1977b) pointed out in its evidence to the RCDIW, 'Whatever else the scale rates may represent they do not represent the actual incomes of the majority of claimants.' Despite these reservations the SBC concluded that 'the fact remains that for many claimants they [the scale rates] do in practice determine the amount of money left each week after paying the rent'. The standard of living of those on SB is affected by a variety of factors such as the presence of others in the household, the length of time on SB, previous levels of savings, income and material possessions, and whether or not there is disregarded earnings or other income.

The SBC (1979) discussed two methods by which benefits might be judged 'right' or adequate. Comparative measurements can assess whether people are getting 'a fair share of the cake', and the absolute approach, used by Beveridge, can attempt to build up an income 'adequate for subsistence'. The SBC rejected both these methods and called for an income that gives some differential between those on benefit and the great majority of those in work. This should be approved by Parliament at a level decided by 'the sensitive use of the subjective test that beneficiaries must have an income enabling participation in the life of the community'. The SBC did not discuss the compatibility of these criteria. Nevertheless it was clearly its intention that SB levels should be such as to avoid the deprivation of non-participation.

However the SBC's (1977b) summary of the information on the living standards of SB recipients, given in the four DHSS surveys by Marshall (1972), Knight and Nixon (1975), Calderbank et al. (1977), unpublished) and Clark (1978), indicated that its intention had not been achieved. It concluded that the scheme provided, particularly for families with children, incomes that are 'barely adequate to meet their needs at a level that is consistent with normal participation . . .'

SBC's concern for families with children implies that it regards the children's rates as being too low and hence the implicit equivalence scales as wrong. This view is also held by Hermione Parker (1979) who argued strongly for the calculation of family budgets, claiming that the children's SB rates are of doubtful validity. Piachaud (1979), after assessing and aggregating the various costs of a child, also argued that SB rates were too low. For a child aged 11 he found that the rate covered only 74% of the cost of providing what Piachaud felt were modern minimum requirements. Later (1981c) he updated the requirements and reported that the overall reaction to his subjective view of modern requirements indicated that they were not 'overgenerous, rather the opposite'. Acknowledging the wide variation in opinion on the needs of teenagers, Piachaud also gave an estimate of their minimum cost, basing it on the needs of a small (116) sample of young people. Finding that the minimum cost per week (£21.90) was twice as much as the current SB scale rate (£10.90), he concluded that many teenagers living in families on SB must 'suffer severe deprivation'.

Further criticism of the level of SB rates for children came from Walker and Church (1978) who suggested that they did not permit the proper nutrition of some children. By combining DHSS and the American Government's HEW tables of recommendations for the number of calories required daily for children of different heights and ages with estimates of efficiency in food purchasing, they concluded that '. . . even with the most efficient purchasing, 62p (child's daily SB rate) is inadequate to cover the cost of the food needs of the largest 8–10-year olds'. Wheeler (1979) referred to a difficulty in all arguments based on nutritional requirements when she pointed out that the UK recommendations are based on Widdowson's 1947 study, and Widdowson found 100% variation in the energy intake of healthy children. The argument rests in part on whether SB rates should cover only average costs or the maximum which can reasonably be expected.

In their Sixth Report the RCDIW (1978a) noted that if the SBC increased the benefit rate for children, but not the adult rate, there would be no clear evidence one way or the other about whether families would change the proportion of their income that they spend on children. However the major obstacle to an improvement in the SB children's rates has been the SBC's other criteria for benefit levels, which is the need for a differential between those on benefit and the great majority of those in work (SBC 1979). This consideration has been a crucial one as the SBC (1977b) admit, 'Wage rates for unskilled work have constituted a ceiling which it has always been felt . . . [should not be exceeded] . . . except in a small minority of cases'. In the same report the SBC gave a useful summary of the evolution of SB rates, making it clear that they are not based on 'precise calculations of subsistence needs'. The reality is that SB benefits are complicated, somewhat arbitrary, and result in varied levels of income, which for many does not permit participation in the life of society. The levels have evolved rather than having requirements, and hence resources, determined by any principles. An inflation-proof minimum level seems to have operated, but in practice the actual level is determined by the Government of the day and as the SBC (1977b) point out, 'is appreciably lower than that of the great majority of wage earners even amongst the lowest paid'.

The unemployed

Unemployment is an increasingly important circumstance creating vulnerability to money problems. Yet it is by no means a uniform one. People are unemployed for very varied lengths of time and, at least initially, their resources differ widely. The unemployed are commonly treated as a 'stock' with the numbers measured at a moment of time. Daniel (1981a) suggested that they are better regarded as a 'flow'. At times of high and low unemployment, thousands every month flow on and off the unemployment register. At times of average unemployment, about half of those going on to the register leave it within a month. In 1981, when unemployment was fairly high (approximately $2\frac{1}{2}$ million), Daniel estimated that the median time on the register was about three months.

Even those who are transiently unemployed find the drop in income unpleasant (Daniel, 1981b), and the ending of earnings related benefit from January 1982 is certain to intensify the feeling. Nevertheless it is the long-term unemployed who have the more serious and intractable money problems. Although only a minority of those who become unemployed, they are a considerable proportion of those unemployed at a moment of time and the number of people involved can be high. By 1982, the figure had risen to over one million, equivalent to one in three of unemployed. An unpublished MSC study (*New Society*, 12 August 1982) forecast that the figure could soon rise to as many as 1.5 million, and it noted the increase from 1 in 250 workers ten years previously to 1 in 25 in 1982.

As their resources are used up and the twelve-month eligibility for national insurance is exhausted, the long-term unemployed have no option but to fall back on supplementary benefit, and for them it is at a low level.

In 1973 the long-term addition to SB was dropped and two SB rates emerged. The policy afterwards was to make the same cash increase in these as in the corresponding national insurance rates. From 1975 to 1980, increases in long-term rates were linked to whichever was the highest of expected increases in prices or earnings. The lower rate was normally linked with expected price increases only. As a result by November 1981 when the previous links were broken, the long-term rate (£47.35 for a married couple) was 25% higher than the short-term rate (£37.75). People on the long-term rate are old age pensioners, and those who have been on SB for two years (one year from 1980) – except for the unemployed. All the unemployed were excluded from qualifying for the long-term rate. But in 1981 those over 60 who were willing to withdraw permanently from the labour market were made eligible (Hansard, 20 July 1981, vol. 9, col. 34W).

A major objective of social security provision is relief of hardship, and the major constraint is shortage of resources. But with the unemployed there is an additional constraint. Although certain categories of people, such as the sick, the retired, married women, and those with unearned income, are not expected to work, there is a strongly rooted expectation that others should either work or be seeking work; and the strength of that expectation varies little with whether or not jobs are available. The logical accompaniment is that people should not be better off without a job than they are with one. If they were, it would be unfair to those who work for the same or less money, and, if financial reward is seen as the only reason for working, it would deter people from seeking work.

The policy of having two SB rates has ensured that the felt need to preserve work incentives has kept down only the SB rate for the unemployed and not that for other claimants. But it has also placed the long-term unemployed in an increasingly unfavourable position in relation to others on SB. The SBC itself has been a frequent critic of the differential between the two rates mainly because of its detrimental effect on the living standards of the long-term unemployed. It noted (1978a) that the findings of the inspectorate suggested that the 'margin provided by the long-term rate does not go to meet any particular need or needs which grow longer or more urgent with the passage of time'. The main effect is to give a higher standard of living. The SBC compared the low level of benefits for the unemployed with the higher entitlement of the long-term sick. The following year, the Commission (1979) detailed the development of the differential and it criticised the rationale behind it. The successor to the SBC, the Social Security Advisory Committee (1982) strongly endorsed the views of the SBC and described the denial of the long-term rate to the unemployed as being 'wholly unjust'. However no government of either party has been persuaded, and it remains to be seen whether reduced job opportunities will lead to a greater weight being given to the hardship argument and so to a change of policy.

Many writers have reported on the low incomes of the unemployed. Layard, Piachaud and Stewart (1978) in their background paper for the RCDIW, *The Causes of Poverty*, reported that 28% of all male unemployed had incomes below that provided by long-term SB. Their analysis of the 1975 GHS led them to conclude that the longer the period of unemployment, the lower does income relative to needs fall. Clark (1978) in her 1974 national survey of 0.6% of the unemployed on SB found, not surprisingly, that the vast majority had incomes very close to SB level. But in this case, the SB level used was the short-term rate, which, as already noted, is the only one for which the unemployed are eligible: 12% were below it and only 8% more than 10% above it.

A striking illustration of the adverse position of the unemployed comes from the DHSS Family Finances Survey, a study of low income families (OPCS, 1981). The income measure used in the survey was relative net resources (RNR). This was the name given to net income less housing costs and work expenses expressed as a percentage of SB. The low income sample was divided into three groups of roughly equal size. Those with lowest purchasing power had incomes of up to 100 RNR; in the middle range, RNRs were above 100 and up to 120; and in the higher range RNRs were above 120 and up to the survey's cut-off point of 140. The unemployed were only 18% of the low income group as a whole but they made up 34% of the families with lowest RNRs, i.e. incomes just up to SB levels. The disproportionate increase is certainly attributable to the fact that virtually all the unemployed never get the long-term rate of SB.

The standard of living of those on the lowest rate of SB was examined by Piachaud (1981b) in his discussion paper *The Dole*. He revalued at 1981 prices the cost of the items that Rowntree, in 1936, felt were necessary for a family with three children if physical efficiency was to be maintained. Piachaud found that such a family living on SB in 1981 would get only 27% more in real terms than Rowntree felt was necessary in 1936. By contrast the average material standards of those in work had approximately doubled since the 1930s.

People suffering lengthy unemployment tend to be those whose characteristics make them both more likely to lose their jobs, and less likely to get another one quickly. In his study of two unemployed samples of white and ethnic minority groups in 18 areas of England, Smith (1980) found that for the white unemployed, the lower occupational groups were more likely to become unemployed, and within each occupational group, those unemployed the longest tended to be the ones who had had poorly paid jobs. Hence those likely to remain unemployed for a lengthy period were already relatively poor when they lost their jobs. Even so, Smith found that, in the great majority of cases, unemployment made them substantially poorer. On average, unemployment led to real income declining to 44% of the previous level. Only 3% received more in benefits than they had previously earned.

Daniel and Stilgoe (1977) found that hardship was greatest for men with dependent children. This finding agreed with that of Smith who (1980) reported that despite the larger benefits they received, men with an above average number of dependants suffered most because 'the gearing of social security benefits is insufficient to meet the needs of those with large families'. These men were the most likely to be actively seeking work, although they found it more difficult to get as they sought a reasonably high level of earnings in order to support their dependants. The statistical analysis of Smee and Stern (1978) showed that although there tends to be a disproportionate number of single men and of married men with no dependent children amongst the unemployed, there is also a disproportionately high incidence of large families. In the years they analysed, the unemployment rate of heads of families with five or more children was about three times the average, and for unskilled family heads it was about six times. For those unemployed and on SB, there was an even greater disproportionate increase in the proportion with children and in particular in those with large families (Clark, 1978).

As might be expected, several studies have indicated a relationship between class and unemployment. Layard, Piachaud and Stewart (1978) found that unemployment was heavily concentrated amongst unskilled manual workers and nearly half of the unemployed when they worked, were in the bottom 20% of weekly earnings. A structured survey by Colledge and Bartholomew (1980) emphasised the importance of occupational and health factors. Nearly three-quarters of the 16,989 long-term unemployed people studied had formerly been manual workers; only a minority had any formal education or vocational qualifications; and more than one-third had some handicap or illness affecting their activities. The SBC (1980) reported similarly on the unemployed heads of large families using information from the DHSS cohort study – a nationally representative sample of men who became unemployed at the end of 1978.

The general position of the unemployed was aptly summarised by the RCDIW (1978a) when it commented that low earnings and unemployment are 'to some degree concentrated upon the same individuals'. 'They are frequently associated with ill health, low skill, lower than average education, and having a father who was a manual worker.'

The SBC (1980) argued that this concentration of unemployment on those who are already poor and disadvantaged was 'neither inevitable nor desirable'. In the United States and Canada 'no more than one-third of unemployed men came from the lowest fifth of the weekly earnings distribution'. The North American experience merits investigation, as does the SBC claim that the present concentration is not inevitable. Past experience and the growth of technology, with its enhanced demand for highly skilled labour, make it seem likely if not inevitable that, with the British economic system, the low paid unskilled worker will be the one most vulnerable to unemployment however undesirable that may be.

Fortunately from the point of view of transmitted deprivation, relatively few (27%) of the unemployed on SB are heads of families, as Table 2.2. shows. In comparison with the 4.5 million children in the bottom quarter of the equivalent income distribution (in 1976), the 153,000 children with long-term unemployed fathers (in 1980) comprised a relatively small group, but the incomes for their families were particularly low. Writing in 1978 when there were 170,000 such children, the SBC (1979a) commented, 'The prospect of so many children being raised in the atmosphere of social and material deprivation that unemployment so often brings is intensely discouraging'. However rising unemployment generally leads to a rise in the proportion of younger men amongst the long-term unemployed thus leading to an increase in the number of dependent children (Smee and Stern, 1978).

Table 2.2   Numbers unemployed and their children, December 1980

thousands

	Unemployed getting SB	Unemployed getting SB heading families		Children in families with an unemployed head getting SB	
		one-parent	two-parent	one-parent	two-parent
All durations	854	11	221	15	494
Over 52 weeks	245			153	

Source: Hansard, 21 December 1981, vol. 15, col. 295W.

One-parent families

One-parent families are a large and growing group with a high risk of having a low income. The National Council for One-Parent Families (NCOPF) (1980) estimated that the number of such families had been increasing by 6% per year since 1972, and it calculated that there were

850,000 one-parent families in 1978, and, by 1980, 920,000 lone parents would be bringing up over 1,500,000 children. On the Council's analysis, at least one in eight families in Britain was headed by a lone parent, a figure confirmed by the General Household Survey 1978. In parts of London the incidence was one in three.

The chance of a child living at some time in a one-parent family is thought to be very high. Rimmer (Study Commission on the Family, 1981) considered long-term trends, and she estimated that of the children born in 1980, one in five will have divorced parents before his or her sixteenth birthday. Many of the children will grow up in reconstructed families, since 80% of those who divorce before they reach 30 marry again within five years. Rimmer also reported a growth in the number of illegitimate children – 11% of all children in 1980, compared with 6% in 1961. The increase was partly due to more illegitimate births to divorced women and partly to the growing number of couples who wished to remain legally single.

The Finer Report (DHSS, 1974), which looked at the overall circumstances of one-parent families, found, as would be expected, that with only a few exceptions, fatherless families, lacking a male wage, were considerably worse off financially than two-parent families. The overall picture remained unchanged in the years following the publication of the Report, although the analysis was strengthened by relating income to family composition.

Every relevant survey has shown that lone parenthood brings with it a high risk of poverty. The RCDIW (1978a) reported that lone parents had a 50% chance of being in the bottom quarter of the equivalent income distribution. The DHSS Family Finances Survey (OPCS, 1981) calculated that one-parent families comprised 38% of those with low incomes although they represented only 12% of all families. Townsend (1979) found that nearly half of the one-parent families in his 1968–9 survey had incomes below 140% of SB. Analysis by Layard, Piachaud and Stewart (1978) of the later 1975 GHS data gave a comparable figure of 58%. Of those not working, 87% had net incomes below 140% of long-term SB, while for those in work, the figure fell to 37%. Of all families, those with only one parent were the ones most likely to be poor.

Layard and his colleagues also found a disproportionate degree of severe poverty amongst lone parents. They comprised 15% of the very poorest, those having incomes below the long-term SB level, although they represented only 4% of the population. The degree of poverty was assessed by Beckerman (RCDIW 1978a). He estimated that the difference between the average net disposable income of lone parents and the appropriate level of SB, which he termed the 'poverty gap', was £7.10 on an equivalent income basis, and this was higher than for any other type of family.

More recent confirmation of the extreme poverty of one parent families came from the DHSS Family Finances Survey (OPCS, 1981). Lone parents were 27% of those whose income fell in the lowest of the three low income ranges, the proportion being exceeded only by that for the unemployed (34%).

Despite the overall concentration of lone parents in the lower ranges of the equivalent income distribution, some have higher incomes. However the incidence of average or above average income varies amongst the different categories of lone parents as Table 2.3 indicates. As would be expected, lone fathers tend to be the most comfortably off, followed by widows.

Table 2.3   Family income relative to SB by type of parent
One-parent families
(Two-parent families)   percentages

Type of parent	Under 100	100–	120–	140–	200–	250–	500+	All	N
				Family income as percentage of SB					
Single woman	58	5	9	21	2	5	—	100	43
Widow	18	18	20	18	16	12	—	100	51
Separated woman	43	19	7	22	5	5	—	100	88
Divorced woman	51	18	10	13	3	5	—	100	67
Lone man	12	2	7	33	24	21	—	100	42
All one-parent families	38	14	10	21	9	8	—	100	291
All two-parent families	4	6	9	38	22	20	1	100	2,284

Source: Layard, Piachaud and Stewart, 1978. Reproduced with permission of the Controller HMSO.

The distribution of family income for lone fathers has been found to be noticeably different from that of lone mothers, and Layard and his colleagues (1978) found it was not dissimilar to that in two-parent families: 86% of the fathers worked and they earned on average as much as other men. The Finer Committee (DHSS, 1974) held a different view, reporting that lone-father families, although better off than lone-mother ones, were worse off than two-parent families. The difference is perhaps because the Finer Committee did not look at equivalently adjusted income.

The more comfortable position of lone mothers who are widows, confirmed by Marsden (1969), Marshall (1972) and Townsend (1979), arises for several reasons. They are more likely to be older and so perhaps with a firmer financial base; having older children gives a greater freedom to work if necessary; and their pension is not means tested and can be supplemented by earnings. Townsend found that no widows in his survey were on SB. The other lone mothers lacked pensions and those he studied received little support directly or indirectly from the children's fathers, the average amount per family being £2. However the situation of divorced mothers was particularly varied with the better off having fewer dependent children and working full time. In Townsend's survey, the poorest lone mothers were separated wives having large families and living on SB. On the other hand Marsden found that the poorest in his sample of 86 lone mothers were the unmarried mothers and others with illegitimate children. But as Marsden stressed, lone parenthood is a complex and variable situation, with movement between one marital status and another.

Provision for lone parents has undoubtedly improved since the Finer Report, but in some respects only marginally. The introduction of child benefit brought a special payment, called Child Benefit Increase (CBI), of £2 a week (£3 by November 1980) for the first or only child in one-parent families. But for a non-means tested benefit, take-up of CBI has been surprisingly low. Those on SB do not benefit by claiming since the increase is deducted from their SB child allowance. By November 1979, 40% of those who stood to gain by claiming, had not done so (National Council for One-Parent Families, 1980). Partly as a result of pressure from the National Council for One-Parent Families, the Government changed the name of this payment to 'One-Parent Benefit' in April, 1981 so that lone parents might more readily realise that the additional payment was for them. Provisional figures for December 1981, given in April 1982, indicated that the percentage who would gain but were not claiming had fallen to 30% (Hansard, 7 April 1982, vol. 21, col. 404W). Single parents with high enough incomes also benefit from having tax allowances equivalent to that of a married couple. *The Green Paper on the Taxation of Husband and Wife* (Treasury, 1980) discussed whether this should be converted into a cash benefit in the form of a higher rate of one-parent benefit.

Family income supplement (FIS), introduced in 1971, was intended in part to counterbalance the lower earnings of women heading one-parent families compared with that of male heads of two-parent families. Lone parents get extra help from it because the needs allowance for one parent is the same as for a married couple (as is the case with housing allowances). The 1979 reduction in qualifying hours for FIS led to one third more lone parents getting FIS. By August 1981 the number benefiting had reached 55,000, about half of all FIS families, and about 6% of all one-parent families (Hansard, 21 December 1981, vol. 15, col. 294W).

Dependency on SB is more common than supplementary help from FIS. In December 1980, 37% got SB (Hansard, 21 December 1981, col. 295W). For SB claimants, the only concession to lone parenthood has been a special disregard of earnings. Before November 1980 this was £6 a week in comparison with £4 for other claimants. Subsequently this became a £4 disregard for all claimants with the addition that lone parents could keep half of any earnings between £4 and £20 a week.

A low level of earnings is a major factor keeping most lone mothers at or near poverty levels of income. In Townsend's (1979) sample 57.7% worked, 40% of them full-time, but with one or two notable exceptions they could not earn enough to take them very far above the poverty level. Townsend attributed their economic disadvantage to men's higher wage rates and greater access to high paid jobs, while the lone mother's earning power was curtailed by obligations to care for a family. These obligations can also result in extra expense, in particular that of having to pay for the care of children during working hours (RCDIW, 1978a).

Families with disabled members
Disablement is a condition not easily analysed because of the difficulties of definition and the variety of effect. It can be considered from many viewpoints, and Townsend (1979) described five concepts of disability. The traditional operational definitions, related to unfitness for work and loss of faculty, are used by the Department of Employment and the Department of Health and Social Security respectively. More recently the emphasis has shifted to imperfections in the mental or physical state which prevent normal functions and thus restrict normal activity.

The number estimated to be disabled varies with the definition. Harris's (1971) OPCS survey found three million aged 16 or over living in private households had a physical, mental or sensory impairment. Townsend (1979) calculated that there were six million people who, on their own estimate, had a disabling condition which prevented them from doing things normal for their age. He also questioned those surveyed in his sample about their capacity to perform various activities, and estimated that the number in the population who were severely or appreciably incapacitated was nearly two million. Harris gave a figure of just over a million for the number disabled, defined in a similar way.

Townsend concluded that disability, because it restricts access to resources, is responsible for a substantial proportion of poverty.

Nevertheless it is not very relevant to this review because the majority of the disabled are elderly and hence relatively few children are likely to live in disabled families. Of the three million disabled in Harris's survey 85% were aged 50 or over, and Layard and his colleagues (1978) reported that, of adults under pensionable age, only 1.7% of men and 0.9% of women were permanently unable to work because of disablement.

The presence of disabled children in a family may reduce its living standards because it may restrict opportunities for work of both the mother and the father, and because additional costs arise because of disability (Bradshaw, 1975; Baldwin, 1977).

Layard, Piachaud and Stewart (1978) analysed the incomes of families with one adult permanently disabled. They found a clear difference between families according to whether it was the man or the woman who was disabled. For married men below pension age, 58% had incomes less than 140% of SB. For married women, the comparable figure was 33%. In general, families with a sick or disabled bread-winner who are on social security benefit will have higher long-term incomes than the unemployed because they are not restricted to the level of short-term benefits, and they may be eligible for invalidity allowance as well as invalidity benefit, and possibly also attendance and mobility allowance. But they may not be better off because if they are sufficiently disabled to be eligible for the latter two benefits, it is certain that they will be facing extra costs.

The additional costs of disability effectively reduce the income available for normal expenditure and, as the Royal Commission noted, these should be 'borne in mind when considering the GHS analysis' (RCDIW, 1978a). The burden of additional costs is regularly detailed by the Disability Alliance and the Disablement Income Group. Attendance and mobility allowance are intended to meet some of them, but Townsend (1979) argued that although helpful, they are available to little more than a minority.

Large families
The economic disadvantage which generally accompanies large family size has been shown in many surveys. Table 2.1 reproduced from the RCDIW (1978a) indicates that, in 1976, 42% of all two-parent families with three or more children were in the bottom quarter of the equivalent income distribution, a percentage exceeded only by that for one-parent families (50%). More children in this bottom quarter lived in large families than in any other types of family. Numbering 2.2m, they were nearly half of the total of 4.5m in the bottom quarter.

Similarly the DHSS Family Finances Survey (OPCS, 1981) showed that large families were disproportionately vulnerable to low income (incomes of up to 140% of SB). Those with three children formed 20% of all families receiving child benefit, but they were 36% of low income families. Larger families, those with four or more children, were found to be even more vulnerable. Although they represented only 5% of all families, this group comprised 14% of those with low incomes. In addition, the Family Finances Survey showed that having four or more children rather than three or fewer affected not just whether a family was poor, but also how poor it was. The smaller sizes of family were distributed roughly equally between the three different poverty ranges in the survey. Those with four children were weakly represented in the top, slightly better off, range and were strongly represented in the bottom one, i.e. the very worst off.

Many other studies, e.g. the Ministry of Social Security *Circumstances of Families* (1967), Coates and Silburn (1970), and Land's (1969) study of 86 families in London having five or more children, have reported a very high incidence of poverty amongst large families. One of the more detailed statistical studies was made by Layard, Piachaud and Stewart (1978). Like the DHSS (OPCS, 1981), they used an equivalent measure of net income, but they compared it with the long-term rate of SB and did not deduct work expenses.

Table 2.4   Distribution of family income relative to SB by number of children

Couples with children						percentage
Family income as percentage of SB	Number of children					
	1	2	3	4	5+	All
100 or less	2	3	5	10	20	4
100–	4	5	9	17	26	6
120–	7	8	14	15	22	9
140–	34	41	40	43	31	38
200–	25	24	17	7	—	22
250–	28	18	14	7	2	20
Over 500	2	1	1	1	—	1
All incomes	100	100	100	100	100	100
N	1041	1260	473	145	65	2984

Source: As Table 2.3.

Table 2.4 shows how, as the number of children in the family increased, income as a proportion of SB fell: 16% of two-children families had incomes below 120% of SB compared with 42% of four-children families, and 68% of those with five or more. Analysis of the

GHS data showed that the major reason was the difference in requirements of the two sizes of families, as measured by their SB entitlement. The adverse effect of increased requirements was over twice the beneficial effect of the increased amount of transfers and tax savings received by the larger family so it was not surprising that families tended to get poorer as they got larger. In addition the earned incomes of both fathers and mothers were less in larger families. The proportion of husbands and wives in paid work was a good deal lower, and they tended to have lower hourly earnings although not shorter hours. Compared with SB (which varies with family composition) the average income was 25% lower for four-children families than it was for those with two children. Layard and his colleagues concluded that this was not because they earned an unduly low total income but because the enhanced requirements of large families were not matched by an enhanced net income.

Families with low earnings
Table 2.5, from the *Sixth Report of the RCDIW* (1978), indicates that, except for one-parent families, a high proportion of the income of families with children in the lowest quarter of the equivalent income distribution comes from earnings, not social security.

The subject of low pay has a large literature which is not being reviewed here. But some indication of the main points of interest to this review is required. Low pay can be defined in several ways: in relation to 'needs', by comparison with a certain percentage of average earnings, or by comparison with the level of earnings at some particular point in the income distribution. Townsend (1979) discussed the conceptual difficulties of definition and expressed a preference for a comparison with a percentage of average earnings. The RCDIW (1978a) used the definition of low earnings as being at or below the lowest decile of the earnings distribution of full-time manual male workers aged 21 and over in the New Earnings Survey whose work was not affected by absence. Using the same definition for men and women, the RCDIW noted that in April 1977 9% of all men and 50% of all women had low earnings.

The RCDIW (1978a) provided a useful summary of relevant aspects of low pay. It noted that over a run of five years, one-fifth of all male manual workers in the New Earnings Survey matched sample had been in the lowest decile of male manual earnings for at least one year and that in the 1970–4 matched sample, 2.9% were in the lowest decile in all five survey years. Hence there appears to be a small core of long-term low paid and a much larger proportion who are low paid intermittently.

Table 2.5   Main sources of income of families in the lower quarters of the equivalent net income distribution, 1976

Percentage of gross income of families in the lower quarters of equivalent net income distribution coming from employment or State benefits, 1976

United Kingdom   percentages

Family type	Employment and self-employment income as percentage of total gross income		State benefits as percentage of total gross income	
	Lowest quarter	Second lowest quarter	Lowest quarter	Second lowest quarter
Elderly				
Man aged 65 or over	0	6	86	64
Woman aged 60 or over	0	4	90	62
2 adults, 1 or both over retiring age	3	21	79	51
Single adult				
Man aged under 65	66	93	22	4
Woman aged under 60	60	88	27	6
Adults with no children				
2 adults both below retiring age	72	88	13	4
Single parent families				
1 adult and 1 child	21	69	69	13
1 adult and 2 or more children	10	12	66	22
Families with children				
2 adults and 1 child	77	90	17	5
2 adults and 2 children	82	87	12	3
2 adults and 3 children	80	89	14	6
2 adults and 4 or more children	74	89	30	6

Source: RCDIW, 1978a. Reproduced with permission of the Controller HMSO.

Townsend (1979), in his poverty survey, found a higher proportion of relatively low paid workers than is obtained from the New Earnings Survey. He attributed this to the fact that the New Earnings Survey does not obtain information about 20% of the sample, and this would be likely to include a disproportionate number of the lowest paid.

Many women are low paid and although between 1970 and 1977 the percentage of them in the low earning group fell from 77 to 72%, women still represent nearly three-quarters of the low paid. Of all female manual workers 68% had low earnings and even for non-manual workers, the percentage was 46% in 1977. The general low level of women's earnings is the reason why many lone parents, most of whom are women, find they are better off on social security than they are working, particularly if allowance has to be made for child care costs.

The high proportion of women amongst the low paid explains why many of those who are low paid by the Royal Commission's definition are not members of families with low incomes. Most low paid women will have working husbands, and the additional income will raise the family above the lowest levels. Moreover low earnings are related to age. The young and the old are disproportionately represented, and they are less likely to be in families with dependent children. For these reasons, as the RCDIW pointed out, the correspondence between low earnings and a place in the bottom quarter of the equivalent income distribution is not close. Layard, Piachaud and Stewart (1978) calculated that only one in five of the workers with wages in the bottom decile lived in households that had incomes also in the bottom decile.

Townsend (1979) similarly found that, although the lower individual earnings, the more likely it is that income units and households will be living in or on the margins of poverty, there is no strong correlation between them. However he found 2,760,000 working men were living on the 'margins of poverty' in 1968–9, 'margins of poverty' meaning 140% of SB scale rates plus housing costs. Of these 1,450,000 had no interruptions of work for sickness or unemployment.

From a poverty viewpoint, it is the relationship between low pay and requirements that is relevant. Despite their deficiencies, SB levels are the most commonly used measure of requirements. The DHSS Family Finances Survey (OPCS, 1981) showed that employees formed a large proportion of those with low net incomes in relation to SB. But half were in the upper range of low incomes while only 14% were in the lowest of the three poverty ranges considered.

Although families with working heads form a large proportion of those with low incomes, this is because the total number is large. Overall, and as would be expected, they are not as vulnerable to low income as other groups. However, as Layard et al.'s analysis showed, the risk is greatly affected by whether the wife works and the number of children. In the most adverse circumstances, where there are three or more children, a non-working wife, and a husband working less than 40 hours a week, 72% of families had household incomes below 140% of SB; when the husband worked more than 40 hours, the figure fell – but only to 40%.

The RCDIW Sixth Report (1978a) noted that the study of the 1975 GHS by Layard, Piachaud and Stewart (1978), and the investigation of the 1972 Nuffield Mobility Study (for the main features of the study see Goldthorpe and Llewellyn, 1977), undertaken for the Royal

Commission by Goldthorpe and Ridge, indicated that low earnings are more likely for those with least qualifications and skill levels and for the elderly and the young. However, the Royal Commission pointed out that the question of causation is open to argument and the studies found that these variables explained only 40 to 50% of the variation in earnings.

For those people who move in and out of unemployment and low earnings situations, it is worth noting that low earnings depressed the level of the unemployment benefit when this was earnings related. (Earnings related benefit ended in January 1982.) In addition unemployment may affect the growth of wages following a return to work because, as some research has shown, the job opportunities of the long-term unemployed are likely to be diminished according to the length of time they are out of work (SBC, 1980).

State help for working families is important for two reasons: its value to the families getting it and its implications for others on benefit. The view that there should be a differential between the incomes of those on benefit and those at work has already been discussed. State social security help for working families consists of child benefit and family income supplement (FIS). Child benefit is for all children, is fully claimed, and is non-means tested. Were it to be at a level which would eliminate the need for any other state provision for children, the problem of maintaining differentials between the working and non-working poor would be greatly reduced. But because of the high cost, this level has not been obtained. Instead, the means-tested benefit FIS has been introduced for working families with children. The numbers benefiting are small, only 110,000 families in July 1981 as the Social Security Advisory Committee (SSAC, 1982) pointed out, but its importance has been recognised by its value being increased by more than the rate of inflation. Although FIS was conceived as a temporary benefit, the SSAC urged that it should 'now be viewed as a crucial integral part of the social security safety net . . .' (SSAC, 1982).

The problem with FIS has been take-up and there has been controversy over the size of the percentage of those eligible who fail to claim. The RCDIW (1978a) reported that the DHSS claimed a 75% take-up by 1975. Townsend (1979) argued that the Government's estimate of eligible families had been too low and therefore 'take-up' overestimated. A parliamentary reply (Hansard, 10 June 1981, vol. 6, col. 133W) reported that new estimates, obtained from the Family Finances Survey carried out from October 1978 to September 1979, showed 'take-up' by only half of those eligible. It also admitted that revaluation of early estimates indicated that previous take-up was also only about one-half rather than three-quarters as previously estimated.

The Social Security Advisory Committee (1982) recognised the difficulties in the take-up of FIS and expressed interest in action by employers and trade unions to increase it.

The two FIS studies by Knight and Nixon (1975) and Knight (1976) suggest that those low earners who are receiving FIS, although badly off, were not quite as badly off as those on SB. They found that 4% had incomes below SB levels in both of the years of the FIS study. For the years 1972 and 1973, the percentages were 8 and 12 respectively. In addition Knight and Nixon (1975) found that 35% on FIS had been unemployed during the past three years, a finding which supports the contention of the RCDIW that it is often 'the same individuals' who suffer low earnings and unemployment.

Net disposable income
Vulnerability to money problems depends on net disposable income, not gross earnings. Recognition of this has become more necessary in recent years as falling tax thresholds have led to families simultaneously paying tax and receiving benefit. Table Q3 in the *Sixth Report of the RCDIW* (1978a) showed how the tax threshold for a family with two children aged between 11 and 16 dropped sharply from 97.4% of average gross earnings in 1955/6 to 48.8% in 1976/7. Interest in the net disposable income has also been stimulated by the growth of means tested benefits, of both cash and kind. An annual series of articles in *Economic Trends* on the effects of taxes and benefits on household incomes (e.g. *Economic Trends*, January 1980) has encouraged discussion of the subject.

The RCDIW (1978a) noted that although tax changes and falling thresholds have had a more severe impact on families with low earnings than on those with median ones, the combined effect of taxes and benefits has been that earnings after tax and benefits as a proportion of earnings before tax and benefits had increased between 1970 and 1977 for families with children, and especially so for large families. The introduction of FIS was particularly important. The other means-tested benefits considered by the Royal Commission were rent and rate rebates, free school meals and free welfare milk. However it needs to be remembered that taxes are nearly always imposed whereas means-tested benefits are not always taken up.

The effect of the increased number of means-tested benefits has been to heighten the effect of what is commonly called the 'poverty trap' and to compress the range of net incomes that families actually receive in the lower income groups.

Figures 2.2a and 2.2b taken from *Social Trends* (1981), show the position in 1981. Although increasing the level of a family's income is

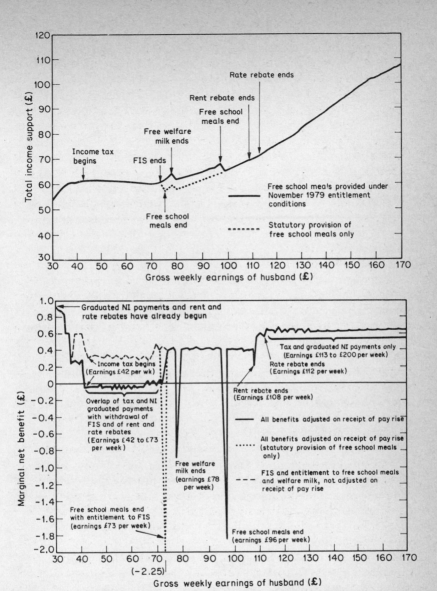

Figure 2.2 Marginal net benefit from increases in earnings
(a) The relationship between total income support [a] and gross earnings of the husband as at April 1981, for a married couple with two children aged 4 and 6, with the wife not earning.
(b) Marginal net benefit from £1 increase in gross earnings as at April 1981, for a married couple with two children aged 4 and 6, with the wife not earning.
Note: [a] Total income support is the income of the family from earnings and benefits, after deduction of tax, NI contributions, net housing costs, and work expenses (DHSS).
Source: Social Trends, 1981.

the main way a family can lift itself clear of the poverty levels, Figures 2.2a and 2.2b show that until a certain level of income is reached, the various means-tested benefits, if claimed, result in a relatively unchanged amount of spending power over quite a wide range of gross income. In some circumstances net spending power actually decreases with an increase in gross income. The charts show the narrow but sharp dips which occur when eligibility for free welfare milk and free school meals is lost, and the less sharp ones which occur when eligibility for rent and rate rebates goes. If the benefits were reassessed immediately when income rose there would be a substantial range of income (approximately £42 to £73 per week in 1981) over which there is an effective marginal tax rate of over 100% because of the loss of means-tested benefits. However the policy of granting FIS, free school meals and free welfare milk for one year greatly reduces the poverty trap, as the dotted line shows.

Social Trends reported that the DHSS analysis of the Family Expenditure Survey showed that out of 6.3m families with a parent in full-time employment or self-employed in 1977, about 50,000 would, in theory, have gained no marginal benefit from a £1 increase in earnings. A further 60,000 would have gained less than 25p. In addition 150,000 would have gained between 25p and 49p. (Social Trends, 1981). However this theoretical discussion assumes that means-tested benefits are taken up, whereas in practice complex benefit schemes are often not understood, even by experts; eligibility is frequently not appreciated; and stigma, dilatoriness and even indifference, when the amount of benefit due is small, all play a part in reducing take-up. The practical position is likely to be rather different from the theoretical picture of means-tested benefits raising the living standards of those who would otherwise be the very poorest, so that large numbers of families are living at approximately the same minimum standard.

The overall picture
For effective analysis poverty has to be looked at from two distinct viewpoints, as Layard et al. (1978) pointed out: examination of which groups are most likely to be poor and of which constitute the largest number of poor families. These two aspects have been considered in this review in the discussion of the circumstances of the separate groups. The overall picture is given by Layard and his colleagues' two diagrammatic trees reproduced as Figures 2.3 and 2.4. These show how important it is to make the distinction. Those at greatest risk of being in poverty such as one-parent and large families tend to be only a small proportion of those in poverty.

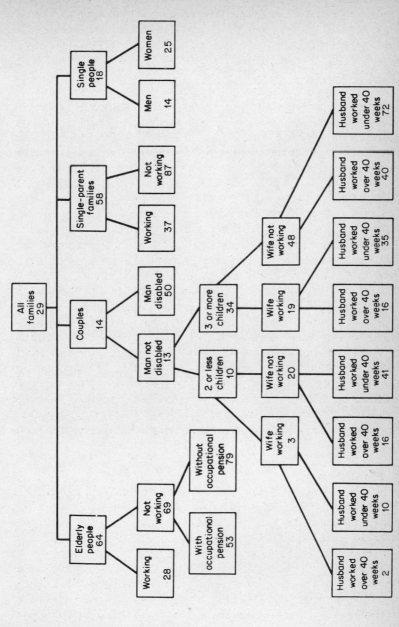

Figure 2.3 Families in each category having household income below 140% of SB (%) Source: As Table 2.3.

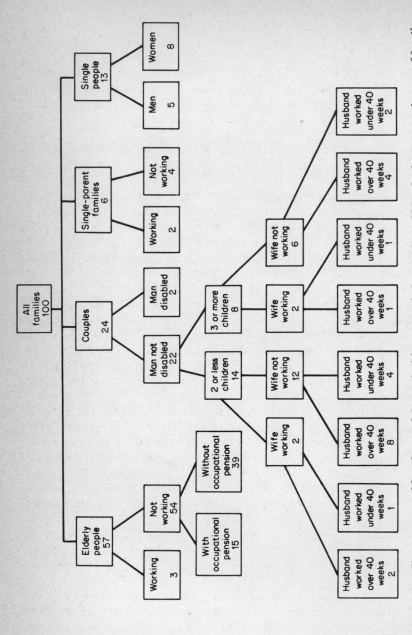

Figure 2.4 Percentages of families with household incomes below 140% of SB which are in each type of family
Source: As Table 2.3.

Most poverty studies, once having defined a poverty level, do not distinguish between poverty of different levels. Tables 2.6 and 2.7, taken from Hansard, provide a useful summary of the distribution of different types of families at various poverty levels in 1979. Of the approximately 2.36m children included because they lived in families with incomes of less than 140% of SB, 880,000 were in families receiving supplementary benefit. Of these, 570,000 lived in one-parent families and 280,000 in two-parent families where the head had been unemployed for more than three months. More than a million other children were in families whose head was in full-time work or was self-employed.

In Table 2.8 the number of children in 1979 living in families with incomes of less than 140% of SB, is categorised according to the status of their parents.

As income levels range from below the SB rate to 40% above it, there is an approximate 50% difference in the living standards of the poorest and the best off of the families included in Table 2.8. The variation in hardship felt by the families is likely to be wide.

Aggregating Tables 2.6 and 2.7 produces Table 2.9. It indicates, very approximately, the number of children living in 1979 at different poverty levels according to the employment category of their parents. Only an approximation is possible because some of the smaller figures included in the aggregation were noted by the DHSS as being subject to very considerable proportionate statistical error. In addition, Table 2.9 assumes that those receiving SB have an income between the SB level and 110% of it. Because of disregards, which are particularly significant for lone parents, some of the SB families may in practice have higher incomes.

All but one of the poverty categories are dominated by the children of those in full-time work or self-employed. Over half of these children are in the topmost of the poverty categories with the remainder being relatively evenly distributed amongst the other three categories. Nearly half of the children of the sick and disabled are also in the top category and none are recorded in the bottom one. By contrast children of the unemployed and of lone parents (who form the bulk of the category 'other families') are concentrated in the bottom half, and around SB level. Of those below SB level, nearly two-thirds are children with parents in full-time work or self-employed, just over a tenth have unemployed parents and a quarter live in one-parent families.

There is a great deal of literature on the circumstances of the different groups generally considered to be in poverty or on the margins of it. By selecting from it, this section of the report has attempted to give an

Table 2.6 Families not receiving supplementary benefit, Great Britain 1979 average

Employment category Families with	Below supplementary benefit level		Above supplementary benefit level but within 10 per cent of it		Above supplementary benefit level but within 20 per cent of it		Above supplementary benefit level but within 40 per cent of it		Total below supplementary benefit level and above supplementary benefit level within 40 per cent of it	
	Families	Children	Families	Children	Families	Children	Families	Children	Families	Children
In full time work or self-employed										
One parent	[*]	[*]	[*]	[10]	[*]	[10]	[10]	[10]	[10]	[10]
Two parents	90	180	[40]	[100]	120	320	390	960	480	1140
One and two parents	90	180	[50]	[110]	130	330	400	970	490	1150
Sick or disabled for more than three months										
One and two parents	[*]	[*]	[10]	[10]	[20]	[40]	[40]	[90]	[40]	[90]
Unemployed for more than three months										
One and two parents	[10]	[30]	[10]	[20]	[20]	[30]	[30]	[40]	[40]	[70]
Others										
One parent	[†]	[†]	[†]	[†]	[†]	[†]	[†]	[†]	90	150
Two parents	[†]	[†]	[†]	[†]	[†]	[†]	[†]	[†]	[20]	[20]
One and two parents	[50]	[70]	[10]	[10]	[10]	[30]	[50]	[100]	100	170
Total numbers of families and children										
One parent	[40]	[60]	[10]	[20]	[20]	[60]	70	130	110	190
Two parents	110	220	60	130	150	370	450	1070	570	1290
One and two parents	160	290	70	150	180	430	520	1190	680	1480

Notes: * Indicates that the number in the group is below 10 000; † Indicates that the sample is too small for a reliable estimate to be made.

The figures shown in square brackets are subject to very considerable proportionate statistical error.

Table 2.7 Families receiving Supplementary benefit, Great Britain, 1979 average

Employment category	One-parent families		Two-parent families		One and two-parent families	
	Families	Children	Families	Children	Families	Children
Sick or disabled for more than three months	[†]	[†]	[10]	[20]	[10]	[20]
Unemployed for more than three months	[†]	[10]	110	280	120	280
Others	310	570	[†]	[10]	320	580
Totals	320	580	130	310	450	880

Notes: * Indicates that the number in the group is below 10 000.
The figures shown in square brackets are subject to very considerable proportionate statistical error.
Source: Hansard, 20 July 1982, vol. 28, cols. 145–8

Notes on tables 2.6 and 2.7

1. The estimate of those in receipt of supplementary benefit is derived from the annual statistical inquiry of supplementary benefit claimants. The estimates of those with incomes below and above supplementary benefit level have been based on the DHSS analysis of income and other information recorded by respondents to the family expenditure survey – FES – 1979.

2. These estimates, which have been rounded to the nearest 10 000 relate only to people living in private households, as people in institutions are not part of the FES sample. The figure for supplementary benefit claimints has been adjusted as to be based on similar assumptions.

3. Income refers to net income less net housing costs and work expenses where appropriate. The supplementary benefit level has been taken as the scale rate(s) appropriate to the family, using the long term rates for pensioners only, but with heating additions for people of 75 years and over, and children under 5, where the head is a householder.

4. The estimates for families with incomes above and below supplementary benefit level include examples where the head of the family had been off work due to sickness or unemployment for less than 13 weeks at the time of the survey. In these cases, the family's normal income when the head was in work was used in determining the level of income. Correspondingly the figures derived from the annual statistical inquiry exclude those who had been in receipt of supplementary benefit for less than 13 weeks.

5. The estimates are subject to statistical error.

6. The estimate of the number of families with income below the supplementary benefit level does not indicate unclaimed entitlement to supplementary benefit. For example, those who are in full-time work or undertaking full-time education would not normally have entitlement to supplementary benefit. Furthermore, no regard is had in these estimates to factors such as disregarded income, treatment of capital or exceptional circumstance additions, each of which can affect payment of supplementary benefit.

Table 2.8   Children living in families with household income below 140% of SB

Parent's status	Number of children		
	Parents not on SB	Parents on SB	Total
			thousands
In full-time work or self-employed (one and two-parent families)	1150	—	1150
Sick or disabled for more than three months (one and two-parent families)	90	20	110
Unemployed for more than three months (one and two-parent families)	70	280	350
Other one-parent families	150	570	720
Other families	20	10	30
	1480	880	2360

Source: Tables 2.6 and 2.7.

Table 2.9   The number of children in poor families according to the employment category of the head of the family and the level of income of the family

1979 average figures   **thousands**

Employment category of head of family	Balow SB level	At SB level and within 10% of it	Above 10% of SB and within 20% of it	Above 20% of SB and within 40% of it	Total number of children
In full-time work or self-employed	180	110	220	640	1150
Sick or disabled for more than three months	—	30 (of which 20 get SB)	30	50	110
Unemployed for more than three months	30	300 (of wich 280 get SB)	10	10	350
Other (mainly one-parent) families	70	590 (of which 580 get SB)	20	70	750
Total number of children	280	1030	280	770	2360

Source: Tables 2.6 and 2.7.

indication of how the groups get on to what might be called the poverty map, of their position on it, and of the nature of the pressures that keep them there.

Although only an approximate cost of children can be established, the literature shows that the cost bears heavily on many working families. For those on social security the standard of living is theoretically unchanged by the number of children. But there are strong indications that this may not be so in practice, and in addition, by most definitions, such families will be living in poverty.

An obvious response to money problems is to try to get more money; and pressures that prevent this need investigating. For each of the groups under discussion, the pressures have been found to be different. The SBC reports show that the living standards of the unemployed are reduced by the alleged incompatability of giving adequate state benefits and maintaining work incentives. Some surveys have shown that when families are large, there is no reduced inclination to work but there is greater difficulty in finding work that pays sufficient to provide adequately for the family. Research has indicated that the disabled have additional costs arising from their disability which are not always allowed for. Lone parents are not a homogeneous group but the low earnings potential of lone mothers makes it difficult for many of them to lift their living standard much above that of SB. Working families have to bear the additional cost of children which, analysis has shown, is not covered by additional state benefits even when income is low. The larger the family, the greater is the pressure. The relatively extensive provision of means-tested benefits can, if the benefits are claimed, help those with the lowest incomes, but it also means that living standards rise only slightly over a wide range of earned income.

3 Factors Varying Resources

Families with a low overall income tend to get most of it from one major source. But the regularity or otherwise of the income, and the presence or absence of additions to it, affect the likelihood of money problems.

Additions to income
There are many potential sources of income, and they provide useful additions to basic income. In his poverty survey, Townsend (1979) identified 42 different sources of income. The familiar ones – wages, salaries, self-employment, pensions and social security payments – provided most income. The only other payments that in aggregate accounted for more than 1% of the total income of all those surveyed were interest on savings (1.5%), stocks and shares (1.5%), holiday pay (3.87%), and windfalls (1.1%). However the analysis was of total figures and Townsend did not investigate the importance to individuals of income from sources that were of minor importance to the population as a whole.

For people on the margins of poverty, additions to income of any kind can be important. In an American study of female households Rein and Rainwater (1978) drew attention to the additions to earnings assembled by women who had claimed welfare money. Describing them as 'bits and pieces', Rein and Rainwater commented, 'Welfare recipients seem to be able to contrive elaborate and complicated packages of income that defy generalisation.'

In the United Kingdom only incidental attention has been paid to 'bits and pieces' additions to income. The main interest has been in national and local authority means-tested benefits, such as rent and rate rebates, free schools meals, family income supplement (FIS), and the additions to supplementary benefit – exceptional circumstances allowances (ECAS) and exceptional needs payments (ENPs). The discretionary nature of SB additional payments gave them a particular importance until they were restricted as part of the changes made in the supplementary benefit scheme in 1980. The DHSS review of the scheme, *Social Assistance* (1978), which preceded the change, re-ported that 34% of the sick and disabled, 30% of lone parents and 19% of the unemployed were receiving ECAs at the end of 1976. A special survey of ENPs was carried out for the review. Over a two-year period ending in November 1976, 26% of the sample was awarded one or more ENP, the average amount being £21.56. Lone parents received over a third of them, although they were only 10% of the sample. The incidence of ENPs was over twice as high for families with children compared with those without, and the number of ENPs was higher in large families. One-half (52%) of the ENPs awarded were for clothing, and 18% for furniture and household equipment.

The 1980 Social Security Act replaced much of the discretion, which the Supplementary Benefits Commission possessed, by regulations for which Ministers are directly responsible to Parliament. Although the establishment of firm clear rights was welcomed, the SBC (1980) and pressure group organisations were apprehensive about the effects of the likely reduction in the number of ENPs granted. Some items such as clothing are supposedly covered by the weekly scale rates, but in practice many claimants had also been getting ENPs. Restricting the availability of these was expected to cause hardship.

Marsden's (1969) study of 116 lone mothers illustrated the im-portance of additional income. He found that additional sources of income in cash and kind, such as free school meals, private cash receipts, gifts and occasional state or local authority payments, totalled nearly one-fifth of the original income. The pattern of help was very varied: some mothers getting a lot, others, very little. Some of the young, separated or unmarried mothers got relatively large board subsidies from their families, but they were likely to be of short duration. About one-quarter were helped by their parents, although with some loss of independence, and two-thirds got substantial gifts at Christmas and birthdays. Help from outside the family was slight. In Townsend's (1979) survey, all the unmarried mothers lived with relatives, and to some extent they were protected or, as Townsend commented, had their poverty 'concealed'. Other indications of the nature of help came from Marshall (1972) who found, in her DHSS survey of 348 families on SB, that two-thirds of fatherless families and a half of two-parent families got help from relatives. However in another DHSS survey, Knight and Nixon (1975) reported that the majority of families getting FIS preferred to do without family help rather than ask for it. Only 10% had had help from relatives even though 21% were having to cut back their expenditure.

The study by Marsden and Duff (1975) of twelve unemployed families showed that although in some instances hardship was eased by help from relatives, families could become completely estranged. In the North East, help in the form of a cash flow from those in work to the workless was thought to be probably small and confined to the man's world, being used mainly to subsidise drinking. Of the unemployed on SB surveyed by Clark (1978) 39% had been helped by relatives in the preceding month. Over half received money, a quarter, food, and a further quarter, new or second-hand clothes. Clark commented that since well over 90% were manual workers 'it is interesting that more were not being helped out by their families'. She noted a marked decline in family help the longer the men were on benefit, which supports Marsden's observation that family disapproval was common, particularly as the time unemployed lengthened. Alternatively it may merely indicate that relatives, likely also to be manual workers, could not continue to give indefinite support.

A Wife's Earnings
An additional source of income for many households is the wife's earnings. Piachaud (1982) argued that 'The most important single change in the economic circumstances of families since the war has not been any change in benefits for children but rather the growth of the two-earner family.' The change is particularly important for families on the fringe of poverty because, as Layard, Piachaud and Stewart (1978) found, from their analysis of GHS data, whether a wife works is a 'crucial determinant' of whether a family is poor. Even when the husband had very low earnings, only 18% of families they studied had incomes below 140% of SB if the wife worked compared with 76% if she did not.

Research confirms that some wives work because of necessity rather than choice. The first survey of families receiving FIS, by Knight and Nixon (1975), reported that 8% of the wives were working. A year later, the second survey by Knight found that the percentage had risen to 20%. Knight suggested that this was a coping response to inflation, and for these families it was the only remaining option.

Piachaud (1982) drew attention to the extent of the change that had occurred when he noted that between 1961 and 1979 the percentage of wives with dependent children in paid work had more than doubled, rising from 25 to 52%. Hamill (1978), in a DHSS paper, reported that analysis of FES data showed that, on average, working wives contributed one-quarter of the total of the family's income. Two million wives contributed between one-third and one-half and a further five million contributed something.

For some families, the earnings of wives may be an unreliable source of additional money. In her study of 86 large families Land (1969) found a quarter of the mothers worked, but childbirth, illness and accident caused interruptions.

Ironically the poorest families who most need the benefit of secondary earnings are, in some circumstances, the least likely to have them. Smee and Stern (1978) from the DHSS Economic Adviser's office commented on the lack of a 'cushion' for many unemployed families because of no secondary earnings. Their analysis of the 1971 Census and the GHS, which was supported by the findings of Layard and his colleagues (1978), showed that wives were less likely to be working if their husbands were unemployed. This tendency was strongest in Class V and it increased with the number of children in the family. Layard *et al.* (1978) drew attention to the disincentive effect of SB regulations which, after disregards, reduce the benefit payable pound for pound by a wife's earnings. However they added that the disincentive to a wife working may be lessened by the relatively short average duration of unemployment (at that time less than 20 weeks). The strength of this argument is weakened by the fact that no family knows initially how long their own unemployment will last.

The Earnings of Dependent Children

The earnings of dependent children appear unlikely to be significant additions to family income. In Piachaud's (1981c) study, approximately half of a small sample of 91 teenagers worked, but they earned, on average, only £2.40 a week (at 1981 prices). Expenditure on teenagers, by themselves and their parents, was wide-ranging, with the average amount being £18.45 a week. Teenage earnings are likely to be divided between additional teenage expenditure and relieving the pressure on the family budget but where the emphasis generally falls is unknown. However the scope for any significant effect on the family budget appears to be limited. Nevertheless there may be individual cases where a teenager's earnings are high enough for them to have an important effect, even if it is only to ease the difficulty poor families often have in affording clothes.

'Fiddling'

An important source of income, but one of unknown size and importance, is that arising from 'moonlighting' or 'fiddling'. It is a part of what is commonly called the unofficial or black economy. This includes undisclosed earnings, however small or infrequent, as well as systematic deliberate fraud. Its size is unknown for, by definition, its activities are undisclosed to officialdom. Sir William Pile, when Chairman of the Inland Revenue, provided the first official 'guestimate' of size in evidence he gave to the Commons Public Accounts Committee on 26

March 1979. He and senior colleagues thought it was 'not implausible' that undetected incomes could amount to 7.5% of GDP, whereas 15% would be implausible. The derivation of Sir William's figures, to which much attention has been paid, was surprisingly simple. Sir Lawrence Airey, his successor as chairman, told the Commons Public Accounts Committee on 4 June 1980 that the Inland Revenue had calculated that if the black economy amounted to 15% of GNP, it would imply a figure of £720 per annum in 1979 for each member of the working population. This seemed too high a figure to be at all plausible. Working back through various components of total GNP, Sir William came to the view that a figure of about half that would not be implausible. In other words 7½% was 'simply not an implausible figure'.

Since Sir William's guestimate, many other figures, some based on extensive calculation, have been produced. They range from just over 2 to 15%. The variation is not surprising. O'Higgins (1980), in his study of the methodologies used in this country and abroad, concluded that most estimates relied more on faith than on fact. One obvious reasons for this was well expressed by A. Smith (1981) when he wrote that in this field 'information is by defection or desire, hidden, submerged or camouflaged in some form or other'.

The Central Statistical Office estimate of 3½%, obtained by Macafee (1980), was based on a comparison of discrepancies between the income and expenditure measures of the gross national product. An even lower estimate of no more than 2 to 3% was put forward by Dilnot and Morris (1981) of the Institute of Fiscal Studies (IFS), albeit 'with little confidence'. But they also claimed that other estimates were 'almost without value'. IFS used the FES to find a representative sample of people whose expenditure diverged from their income. Their use of FES was criticised by Feige (1981) on the grounds that as many as 40% of self-employed people, thought to include a high proportion of tax-dodgers, do not respond to the FES. A similar criticism of the methodology was made to the Commons Public Accounts Committee (6 April 1981) by Sir Lawrence Airey.

Feige's own estimated figure of 15% was twice as high as that of the Inland Revenue, but the Revenue, in their evidence to the Commons Select Committee on the Treasury (1982), dismissed it as 'not a plausible estimate'. It would imply that on average, each taxpayer had an undisclosed income of over £1000. Feige's calculation was based on the amount of money people used in buying and selling. Another approach, used by the Taxpayer Compliance Measurement Programme in the US, was to subject a sample of 50,000 taxpayers to a detailed and comprehensive tax audit. The figure they obtained, of between 6 and 8%, broadly agreed with the 7½% British Inland

Revenue figure. Despite its somewhat unscientific origins, this last figure was the one which O'Higgins felt that the data supported.

Interest in the black economy grew in the years following 1979 primarily because of economists' concern about the depressed economic situation. One economist, A. Smith (1981), warned that uncertainty about the size and rate of growth of what he called the informal society could lead to unsuitable economic policy remedies being taken. He postulated that a shift from a formal economy to an informal one is part of economic evolution and can be regarded as a natural reaction to events.

The Inland Revenue had understandably been more concerned over lost tax revenues, estimated to be as much as £4 billion in 1981 (House of Commons Public Accounts Committee, 6 April 1981). In its 123rd report (1981), it defined two broad categories of tax evasion. In one, the source of income is acknowledged but the amount understated; in the other, there is no reporting at all of the source of income. Self-employment presents the greatest opportunities for understatement of income and O'Higgins (1980), using data from the 1975 FES, made a 'crude calculation' that the degree of understatement was about 12%, equivalent to £13 per week per self-employed household in 1977. O'Higgins quoted the 1976 comment of the General Secretary of the Inland Revenue Staff Federation: 'The low incomes to which the self-employed admit deny belief!'

Those who do not disclose a source of income are commonly described as 'moonlighting', and this part of the black economy is the one most relevant to this review. If the income is a second one, the person is unlikely to be on the fringes of poverty. But in the case of those who moonlight whilst on social security, their poverty is not as great, if it exists at all, as is officially assumed. DHSS estimates of the revenue lost to the state have ranged from £50m to £170m and the so-called social security scroungers have attracted much publicity and media attention. By contrast, a high degree of public tolerance towards the £4 billion lost through tax evasion was shown by a survey carried out by Ilersic, Christopher and Mydelton (1979) for the Institute of Economic Affairs. Commenting on the survey, the IEA said that it revealed a degree of tolerance which would probably not exist for most forms of illegal activity. Feige described the black economy as causing a massive redistribution of income from taxpayers to tax avoiders. An article in *The Sunday Times* (15 August 1982) argued that although many appeared to feel that evasion was basically the working man's illegal version of the professional man's legal tax avoidance or perks, the point at issue was that having millions operate outside the law sapped respect for it.

As with other aspects of the black economy, the degree of social security scrounging is difficult to establish. The DHSS report *Payment of benefits to unemployed people* (1981b) suggested that at least 8% of those claiming SB because they were supposedly unemployed were actually working, although in some cases it was part-time or casual work. One in ten was estimated to be a trivial offence. In 1979 benefit paid to the 8% would have totalled about £108m. The estimate was based on investigations in two out of twelve DHSS areas. The Government, who in the previous year had been heavily criticised by pressure groups and trade unions for its estimate of £50m lost through scrounging, responded to the report with caution, taking note rather than endorsing the estimates, and it referred to considerable doubt about their accuracy. But in a later parliamentary reply, a figure of approximately £170m was given as the amount saved in 1980/81 by the detection of improper claims (Hansard, 20 October 1981, vol. 10, col. 150).

The large-scale benefits fraud investigation in Oxford in September 1982 illustrated the complexity of the scrounging issue. Many of the 172 people, who were arrested outside a bogus benefit office, had no proper homes. The case showed how a landlord willing to provide inadequate accommodation or an address for SB claimants could get a substantial income from organised fraud. The Campaign for the Homeless and Rootless (CHAR) claimed that some landlords were charging £10 or more for the use of their address, and it quoted one case where five people shared one room, paying the landlord £25 a week each, the money coming from Social Security. CHAR called for a inquiry into the administration of board and lodgings benefit.

There has been less interest in the nature of the black economy than there has been to its size. Gershuny and Pahl (1980), two of the few academics currently (1982) working in the field, based their analysis on a division of the informal economy into three areas, the household, black and communal economics. *Can I have it in cash?*, edited by Henry (1981) is one of the few published studies of the activities that make up the black economy. Henry's book puts forward some explanations for fiddling, suggesting that in addition to raising income, moonlighting is done for enjoyment of the work or to help someone out. Explanations of activities such as fiddling have to be treated with caution, and it is not surprising that few poverty studies refer to the subject. An exception is that of Marsden and Duff (1975) which reported that some of the twelve unemployed families studied had undetected income of £5 to £10 above SB levels. In this narrative, Marsden admitted that he could say nothing about the extent of fiddling, but he suggested that it was policed informally by local public

opinion and anonymous letters. From the point of view of the unemployed, Marsden felt that fiddling fulfilled a number of needs,
giving a sense of control over their lives, and a freedom to spend again,
particularly in male company. He felt that it kept alive an individual's
self-respect.

Irregularity of income

Irregularity can be interpreted in a variety of ways. Some of the
additions to income already discussed such as help from the family and
money obtained by fiddling are likely to be of an irregular or inter-
mittent nature. A different type of irregular income is that of a wife
who never knows how much money her husband will give her. This
aspect of irregularity is dealt with more fully in a later section in this
review, on distribution of income within the family.

The extent of medium-term variation in earnings has been studied
using data from the New Earnings Survey (Department of Employment *Gazette*, January 1977; Thatcher, 1974). But the effects of
short-term irregularity of income on a family have been little investigated and only an indication of its possible importance can be obtained
from the literature. Some jobs inevitably result in a variable level of
weekly earnings, for example the self-employed or industrial workers
whose wages are related to levels of production. If the irregularity is
expected and the basic level is adequate, one would expect some
degree of adaptation. To permit this, an adequate level of basic income
is important. Brown (1964), in a small-scale study of ways of helping
homeless families in Manchester, found that these families, who
presumably did not have a high level of basic income, found it harder to
manage on irregular incomes than on ones which were low but steady.

Fluctuation of income appears to be a common but not invariable
feature of those requiring help. In his study of families being helped by
the Family Service Units (FSU), Philp (1963) noted that 54% were
judged to have regular incomes and 38% fluctuating ones. However
Wilson and Herbert (1978), who made a careful study of the circumstances of 56 inner city large families dependent on social service
departments, found that income fluctuated for many families even
amongst those who were on social security. Sometimes the benefits
varied even within one spell off work. In other studies, the regular
payment of social security has been noted with appreciation. For
example, some of the lone parents studied by Marsden (1969) compared unfavourably the uncertainties of budgeting during marriage
with the regular income they got from the National Assistance Board,
the precursor of the Supplementary Benefits Commission. Coates and
Silburn (1970) estimated that only 5% of the cases of poverty in a

deprived area of Nottingham were caused by sickness. Those with chronic ill health at least had a secure income. Much more seriously affected were those whose illness was intermittent. Each bout of illness could mean two or three days when they were neither earning nor eligible for sickness benefit. Twenty-six years earlier Stephens (1946) writing about problem families commented, 'More important than even the size of the income is its regularity.' The irregularity, he observed, arose from ill health which caused intermittent unemployment. Ill health may in the future lead to increased fluctuation of income once the proposals set out in the DHSS Green Paper *Income during initial sickness: a new strategy* (1980a) are adopted. As the Low Pay Unit (1980), amongst others, have argued, the payment of sickness benefit unrelated to family size, payable by the employer for the first eight weeks will lead to disproportionate hardship for low paid and part-time workers with families.

In proportion to the numbers involved, complaints about delay or irregularity of payment of social security in the UK have been relatively few. However Van Ginneken, Join-Lambert, and Lecaillon (1979), in their report of an ILO seminar on persistent poverty in the industrial market economies, commented on administrative delays and irregular payments of some social insurance benefits, describing them as 'chaotic income flows'. These are situations particularly likely for those termed the 'persistent poor'. If they do work, they do not have steady jobs and insecurity leads to frequent changes in the composition of households and of address. Van Ginneken and his colleagues pointed out that the handicap of irregular and unpredictable income arising from not having a steady job is compounded by the irregularity of payments from public assistance or social security. However there is little evidence that these criticisms of social security apply to Britain.

Of those in the UK with low earnings many appear to have fairly stable ones. Knight and Nixon (1975) reported that two-thirds of families receiving FIS had wages which did not vary from week to week. The higher were the wages, the greater the probability of a variation. The most common reasons for variation were overtime and bonuses. As has been noted, FIS has been claimed by only half of those eligible. Little is known about the nature of the income of those who have not claimed, nor of the 20% who fall through the net of the New Earnings Survey. Townsend (1979) quoted the Department of Employment's suggestion (*New Earnings Survey*, 1968) that the missing 20% included people who only take employment intermittently or at particular times of the year, those temporarily incapacitated by sickness or injury, and those attending courses, in addition to others registered as wholly unemployed. Many of these would have inter-mittent employment and hence irregular income, but, as Townsend noted, no estimates have been made of the different categories, and there is no information about their circumstances.

Land (1969) observed that in the sample of London large families she studied those with the highest regular incomes had the largest irregular additions. Overtime was very important for a large propor-tion of the families. Nearly one-third worked more than 50 hours a week. Holidays, when there was no overtime money, were times of particular difficulty. Land's findings show that although in the context of poverty it seems absurd to suggest that overtime and bonuses are anything but welcome, if they are irregular, they need to be reserved for expenditure that is itself not a frequent regular commitment. If the family budgeting does not adjust to their insecure nature, they, or rather their absence, can lead to money problems. Land also drew attention to financial windfalls. Twenty-seven out of 86 families had received one in the past year. Betting was reported by Land as being one way of financing clothes and household goods. However, it seems unlikely that betting is a generally reliable source of finance.

A little discussed form of irregularity of income is that which arises from strikes. Those involved in the 1980 steel strike had been earning approximately £100 a week, and for most, the strike brought a very sharp drop in income. Newspaper articles written at the time referred to unpaid HP and fuel bills and curtailed leisure activities. The long-term effect of strikes will depend in part on the duration and extent of the loss of income, and the accumulated resources of the family. A *Guardian* article (6 March 1980) commented that experience of other strikes has shown that recovery from the financial effects is fairly quick, with debts being paid off after four or five months and life returning to normal even earlier. If this comment is correct, it illus-trates how a temporary loss of income can be uncomfortable rather than disastrous. The payment of bills can be postponed if there is a reasonable certainty of income returning fairly soon to at least its former levels. In addition, subsistence living may be more acceptable in a group situation than in an individual one, particularly when there is involvement in a common cause.

The importance of fluctuations of income in relation to poverty was stressed by Liffman (1978). As part of the Family Centre Project in Melbourne, Australia, an income supplement scheme was introduced to give the families a degree of stability. It saw the families through the weeks when there was no income. Liffman commented, 'These occasions had in the past constituted the most crippling and destructive aspects of the families' poverty leading to desperate financial crisis –

evictions, termination of gas and electricity, massive debts and so on.'
His views underline the value of the immediacy and regularity of most
of the British SB provision. Liffman went on to say, 'The effectiveness
of any scheme of income support will reside as much in its ability to
meet need at the time it occurs as in the overall level of payments it
provides.'

Assets and savings

Marketable assets and savings are obviously relevant to money problems. Townsend (1979) outlined four ways in which they affect living
standards. They can be realised to meet expenses; ownership of some
assets such as television sets or houses obviates the payment of rent;
assets can be used as security for loans which can smooth uneven flows
of income; and assets give security which can have beneficial effects
such as arousing expectations in others. For example relations may be
more willing to care for a wealthy old person than for a poor one. But,
of course, low income families with children rarely have assets. Official
statistics show that ownership of wealth has been minimal for about
half the population as well as for those at the bottom of the income
distribution. In 1975 the bottom 50% of the population had approximately only 6½% of the marketable wealth, based on Inland Revenue
figures; and more than half of the UK adult population had an
estimated total net wealth of less than £1000 (RCDIW, 1979). In an
earlier report (1978a), the Royal Commission noted that of those in
the bottom quarter of the gross household income distribution (not
equivalently adjusted) for 1976, households with two adults below
retirement age had, on average, 2% or less of their income coming
from investment. Where there were children in the household, the
figure fell to 1% or below according to the number of children. Apart
from financial assets, those on lower incomes were less likely than
others to own material ones.

Townsend's poverty survey (1979) collected extensive information
on assets. He considered those which were readily realisable and others
less so. Thirteen per cent of all households had no assets, or were in
debt, and a further 18½% had ones worth less than £200 in 1968–9
when the poverty survey took place. Many people's only asset was part
or full house ownership. If only readily realisable assets were considered, 58% of all the households had either none or some worth less
than £200 at the time of the survey. Of the types of assets held by
households, Townsend found that the most common were owner-
occupied houses, cars, personal possessions, premium bonds and
money in the Post Office Savings Bank and bank deposit accounts. The
most common form of debt was hire purchase but the average amount

was only a seventh of the average overdraft or loan. Townsend analysed net total assets according to different types of household at different percentiles of income distribution. His figures showed that at the 75th percentile, assets averaged £112. In households without children, debt was not sufficient to be recorded even at the lowest percentiles. But households with four or more children were, on average, in debt at the 75th percentile. For other families with children, there was debt, on average, only at the 95th percentile. Townsend found that the assets of lone parents were particularly varied. Between a quarter and a third of lone fathers, widowed and divorced mothers in his survey had assets in excess of £5000, compared with none of the separated or unmarried mothers. But as a group, divorced people had the widest range of inequality of assets. Townsend's survey showed a low level of assets for most families, but it was particularly low for those with children and these families also had more debt.

One view of the attitudes of poor people towards their financial future was provided by Hoggart (1957). His observation of working class life led him to comment that forms of saving or paying in advance were traditionally for specific purposes. There was a 'mistrust of a more general kind of saving . . . you might get knocked down tomorrow'. Hoggart's writing was largely based on the pre-war experience of his own childhood, but the reluctance or, more likely, the inability of poor people to save still seems to exist. Clark (1978) reported that 42% of unskilled workers never saved, and, perhaps not surprisingly, she found, in her DHSS survey, that 86% of the unemployed on supplementary benefit had no savings, and 66% of them had none before they went on SB. Other statistical surveys such as the Ministry of Social Security's *Circumstances of Families* (1967), Knight and Nixon's (1975) study of families receiving FIS, and Land's (1969) study of large families have presented the same predictable pattern. The lower the income and the greater the number of children, the less likely the families are to save. Marsden's (1969) study of lone mothers showed a similar but more complicated picture. Only four of the mothers had any capital and they were spending it. Ten had houses of varying quality and the need to continue repayments led to a form of enforced savings.

The difficulty, if not the impossibility, of saving when on a low income relative to needs was noted by Clark (1978). The inability to accumulate applied not only to savings but also to clothing and household equipment. Her findings were supported by Bradshaw (1974). In an article written about the Rowntree Trust's Family Fund, which provides payments to families with handicapped children, he

suggested that Family Fund payments were a response to the deprivation that exists in the ownership of assets. He contended that 'even
with a substantially increased income, they [families with handicapped
children] would have difficulty in finding the capital sums or raising the
credit needed to accumulate possessions'.

Evidence from Cartwright's (1976) large-scale study of family size
and spacing suggests that the low level of savings may not be because
there is no wish to save. Cartwright asked those interviewed what they
would do with another £5 a week. Fifty per cent replied that they would
save it. Lack of capital was the reason Marsden (1969) gave for lump
sums and other gifts being so important to lone mothers. They had a
small effect on living standards but an important effect on morale.

There are no major studies that focus directly on the factors that vary
resources. Information is available about such matters as level of
assets, amount of overtime worked, or number of ENPs paid to those
on SB, but there is no research that directly assesses the importance of
these in families' budgets. However the literature provides a few
pointers. The large number of ENPs received by SB claimants before
1980 suggests that even relatively small capital sums are particularly
difficult to accumulate on low incomes. Lump sum additions to income
which meet these needs may be particularly helpful.

There is little firm evidence on the objective value to families
or their subjective appreciation of either regularity of income or
additions to it. Lump sums that are rare or unexpected may give
particular pleasure because they are not already spoken for in the
budget, although their real value may be slight. More regular additions
such as overtime are normally of greater value but dependence on
them may diminish appreciation.

A further finding of interest from the literature is the hint – and it is
no more than that – that families in serious difficulty because of
irregularity of income may include those about which virtually nothing
is known, because their irregularity of work enables them to slip
through the net of the New Earnings Survey.

4 Factors Influencing Requirements

Social pressures and personal inclinations

Requirements show individual variation yet, on the whole, they conform to a relatively uniform pattern. A high proportion of a family's expenditure can be put into categories such as food, clothing, accommodation and fuel. Within the categories, external pressure and personal inclination interact to determine an individual's requirements. The interaction has not been extensively analysed and there is little relevant literature.

The pressure coming from society has been most stressed by Townsend (1979) who described needs as arising 'by virtue of the kind of society to which individuals belong'. The concept of relative poverty, of which he has been the foremost exponent, is an acknowledgement that requirements are more than basic needs. In his book, *Poverty in the United Kingdom* (1979), he discussed the concepts of relative poverty and deprivation in detail and stressed the importance of society which 'imposes expectations through its occupational, educational, economic and other systems and [it] also creates wants through its organisation and customs'. For example he suggested that a man's dietary needs are determined by work and activities. But, 'Society determines what foods he should look for, produce or buy and eat.' Television was used as an example of needs changing with expectation. 'Within a generation, the possession of a television set . . . has changed from being a doubtful privilege of a tiny minority to being the expected right of 95% of the population.' He emphasised that social pressure does not eliminate individual preference. 'People engage in the same kind of activities rather than the same specific activities.' Implicit in Townsend's work is the belief that, in so far as income permits, there will be active participation in a style of living. In an earlier article Townsend (1974) made the pertinent comment, 'Any attempt to define this style and represent it in some form of operational index is bound to be rough and ready.'

While it is readily acceptable that society creates a general style of living, movement away from generalities and attempts to specify the style are bound to be controversial. When Townsend (1979) used indicators in the form of a deprivation index to define a style of living he hoped that measureable divergences from it would provide an objective measure of poverty. One criticism of his index came from Piachaud (1981a) who argued that it did not offer a solution to 'the intractable problem of disentangling the effects of differences in tastes from those of differences in income', and it rested on the belief that poverty could be seen as the outcome of choice whereas it was really related to the constraints upon choice. In reply, Townsend (1981) countered that the items in the index 'correlated strongly with diminishing income'. Piachaud is clearly right in his view of poverty, while the validity of Townsend's index rests on whether there is a pattern of spending closely associated with incomes declining to deprivation levels. The disentangling, Piachaud referred to, is undoubtedly difficult and yet some attempt to do so is necessary because hardship will be felt most keenly when low income limits the influence of taste on expenditure. Without a greater awareness of what matters to the individual, any description of circumstances as deprived can only be an external judgement.

Fiegehen, Lansley and Smith (1977) noted that the behaviouristic concepts used by Townsend to define poverty were not entirely novel. The first studies of household budgets had shown that the poor had a distinctive expenditure pattern, spending a significantly larger proportion of their income on food. Fiegehen and his colleagues analysed the 1971 Family Expenditure Survey to see if there were any relatively abrupt changes in expenditure which might distinguish the poor from the non-poor. Despite fairly involved analysis, there was no evidence of this, and the authors concluded that there was a rather unstable relationship between income and proportional changes in expenditure on particular goods and services. This suggests that other factors, such as social pressures and individual tastes, have an effect on expenditure that varies with income level.

The motivation underlying expenditure on different goods and services has been little researched by academics, although various surveys of people living on low incomes contain statistical and descriptive accounts of the goods people do not possess and the activities in which they cannot participate. Fiegehen, Lansley and Smith (1977) produced the chart reproduced as Figure 4.1 showing the expenditure of poor people (the fifth percentile of the equivalent income distribution) as a percentage of the expenditure of the median household on various goods and services. The analysis does not distinguish between the elderly poor and the poor with children, which is unfortunate as the two groups are known to have very different expenditure patterns.

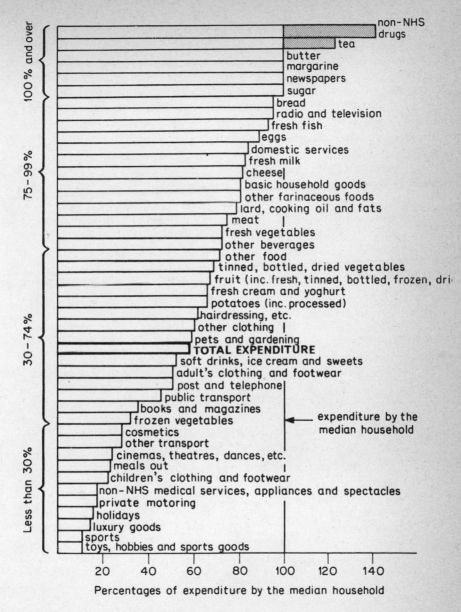

Figure 4.1 Comparative equivalent expenditure on individual items by the fifth percentile household, 1971

Source: Fiegehen, Lansley and Smith from printed tabulations of the 1971 Family Expenditure Survey

Nevertheless Figure 4.1 provides a detailed and, in some ways, surprising picture of the priorities of poor people compared with those with average income.

On the whole little is known about the priority which individuals attach to the things they have or have not got nor about the extent to which they are influenced by social pressures. It cannot readily be assumed that the differences between the expenditure patterns of the poor and not so poor show what the poor would buy if only they had the money, because the two groups consist of different people.

Concern for children

One persistent theme emerging from the literature is the concern that many in poverty feel for their children. In its written evidence to the RCDIW the SBC (1977b) commented that 'families with children are likely to be especially anxious not to deny them the higher standards enjoyed by their peers'. Marsden (1969) in his study of 116 lone mothers reported one-third as saying that they were 'most sharply pierced' by feelings of deprivation through their children. The wants of older children were wide-ranging. They were influenced by advertising and the competition of other teenagers. Fashion and pop records were particularly important. Marsden's observations indicate that peer group pressure was affecting these teenagers.

In another study with Duff (1975), Marsden looked at the problems of twelve unemployed men and their families. Again parents were found to be sensitive to the problem that their children might be excluded from the general pattern of spending and they usually mentioned giving children priority. An ex-grammar school skilled worker commented that the social pressures were very strong. 'This suburban estate here that we live in, we live by a set rule . . . The kid's got to have various things. You've got to keep up with it, you've got to keep a face on.' The expressed greater concern for the children may arise from genuine parental feelings, or it may be that those interviewed were reluctant to mention their own frustrated aspirations. Possibly the school friends of the children provided a strong comparative reference group, whereas many parents with low incomes tend to lead more restricted and isolated lives.

Extravagances

Most people get more enjoyment from the purchase of what they see as luxuries than they do from buying day-to-day essential requirements. For families on low incomes, purchases of so called luxuries are likely to be difficult to afford, and their cost can force the exclusion of other items which outsiders feel should have preference. But there is some evidence that luxuries are particularly valued by poor families.

The classic 1930s study of mass unemployment in an Austrian village, by Jahoda, Lazarsfeld and Zeisel (1933) described how although women were preoccupied with working out how to spend the little money they had, equally significant were 'the traces of irrational spending, splurges . . . sometimes signs of disintegration, sometimes last links with richer experiences of the past'. The absolute standard of living in Marienthal was lower than that considered as poverty in Britain in the 1970s, yet the people planted flowers in the allotments and bought curling tongs for their hair and picture books for the children.

Nearly 40 years later, Land (1969), in her study of large families in London, reported that all families had television and many little treats. Mothers, bringing up their children alone, studied by Marsden (1969), were defensive but determined about the possession of a television, feeling 'entitled to a bit of something'. Marsden commented that television became a 'symbolic reward for other deprivations'. He described the mothers as being unable to keep up the 'steady scrimp and scrape, the constant vigilance'. Buying something extra even though they knew they would regret it was a kind of 'emotional release'.

Hoggart's (1957) descriptive account of the 'full rich life' of working class people provided a rationale for working class expenditure and extravagances. Although it related to a period of time when working class living standards were generally lower, many of those currently in poverty may be similarly motivated. When poor people purchased goods perhaps not strictly needed, Hoggart described them as 'having a go', making a splash 'because most of the rest of life is humdrum and regulated'. A gesture is needed 'even though finances do not reasonably permit it'. The extras add 'variety or colour or some quality to life'.

Goldring (1973), writing about the work of the Family Service Units, quoted the suggestion of Bob Purves, Glasgow Unit organiser, that there should be 'an extravagance fund' for 'fun and frivolity once in a while'. He added, 'Few of us can conceive the dreadful monotony of being poor week after week with no future and no prospect of change.'

Morris (1965), in her study of prisoners and their families, gave a different reason for splurging. Describing a woman who spent £40 on special white 'Whit week clothes' for her children, Morris said, 'Since there were so many emotional problems in this family, debt seemed almost a minor difficulty.' In a related vein, Philp (1963), writing about problem families, observed that 'much unwise expenditure arose from parents trying to show love for their children by over-lavish gifts'.

Addictions and obsessions

Addictions and obsessions are common throughout society and some people undoubtedly gamble, smoke or drink to an unacceptable extent in relation to their income. But the evidence tends to be anecdotal and although there has been some analysis of the incidence, there has been little of where it occurs, or of the severity of the financial problems that may arise.

Estimates of the number of alcoholics show wide variation which probably arises from differences in definition. The *General Household Survey 1978* found that a quarter of all men over 18 are heavy drinkers defined as consuming seven pints of beer twice a week. Of these, about a third are married. A Report of a Special Committee of the Royal College of Psychiatrists (1979) gave a 'conservative estimate' of at least 300,000 people in the country with drinking problems of such severity as to merit the concentrational label of 'alcoholism', and the report added 'this may well be a gross underestimate'.

The DHSS publication *Drinking Sensibly* (1981a) quoted the OPCS as reporting that 240,000 people were dependent on alcohol in 1976, and three-quarters of a million had a serious drinking problem in 1977 – an increase of 50% over the preceding ten years. The 1980 OPCS *Survey on Drinking in England and Wales* found that 5% of men and 2% of women had drinking problems.

In expenditure surveys, it is known that people understate the amount that they spend on drink and tobacco. Possibly some suffer genuine self-delusion or forgetfulness, while others try to conceal the true expenditure in case it is thought excessive.

Low income has been associated with lower absolute drink and tobacco and low income households spent a slightly lower percentage of their income on alcohol than the average household – 4% compared with 5%. For tobacco, the percentage figure, 4%, remains unchanged by low income (Van Slooten and Coverdale, 1977). The DHSS Family Finances Survey (OPCS, 1981) found variation in the percentage figures for different low income families. The overall figures were higher in this survey because housing costs were excluded. On average, low income families spent 7% of their relative net income on alcohol and tobacco, but the figure was 5% for one-parent families and 8% for two-parent families. The unemployed spent 9%, those off work because they were sick 8%, while the figure for employees was 6%. The higher figure for the unemployed probably reflects their lower average income rather than a higher cash expenditure. It also indicates that people may have difficulty in quickly reducing expenditure on alcohol and tobacco when income falls. This may be because of the addictive nature of smoking and drinking, or because unemployment enhances the desire to smoke or drink.

Financial aspirations may be a reason for gambling and Land (1969) described winning the pools or coming up with the horses as the only hope for poor large families of escaping from perpetual pinching and scraping. Coates and Silburn (1970) found that many in the poor area of Nottingham they surveyed had an occasional flutter but a very much smaller number gambled regularly and the sums were usually small. Overall a lower proportion of income than in general was spent on betting.

Hoggart (1957) referred to gambling in his description of working class life as being something people are 'fond' of; it was one of the 'few available outlets for self-expression'. But for almost all the people that Hoggart knew, taking part was a 'sort of throw, a gesture for luck'.

Social pressures affect all forms of consumption, restraining or intensifying personal inclination, and addictions and obsessions are no exception. Sometimes the pressure works in subtle ways. An example of this was given by Whyte (1943), in a detailed account of the pre-war street corner environment in an American city. He described how a corner boy who saved his nickels would have more money than if he bet on numbers, but 'he could not pursue that course without disagreeable social consequences. The corner boy who has money is expected to help his friends . . . Savings therefore is not a real alternative to gambling on the numbers. The small change would be dissipated in one way or another, whereas the large amounts occasionally won have real meaning for the corner boy.'

In many respects the literature relevant to factors affecting requirements is slight. The view that requirements or needs are not absolute is put forward strongly by Townsend, but the precise way in which society influences them is less discussed. Comment is sparse on the consumption pressures that arise through membership of groups such as the family or peer group. There are indications that, for some families, concern for children may be a strong motivation for expenditure but evidence is inadequate to assess how common it is. Addictions or obsessions such as gambling, smoking and drinking are well researched, but not from the point of view of the financial pressures they put on low income families. There is some evidence of a need for an occasional purchase of an extravagance, but in general information regarding personal motivation for expenditure is slight and only impressions can be obtained from occasional comments within the general literature.

5 Requirements Affected by Government Intervention

Housing and fuel are of particular interest to this review for several reasons. They are essential goods, each taking a sizeable share of the expenditure of most families. Their importance to low income families is shown by the DHSS Family Finance Survey (OPCS, 1981) which reported that low income families allocate 61% of total expenditure to housing, fuel and food compared with only 44% for families in general. If there are money problems, payment for these commodities is likely to contribute to or be affected by them. Because of their generally accepted importance, the extent to which they are possessed has not been left solely to the operation of market forces. In the case of housing there is a long history of government intervention, whereas for fuel it is of more recent origin.

Housing

Housing is a major item of expenditure for most households. The cost tends to vary with the nature of the tenure and, both overall and at a moment of time, it frequently bears only an approximate relationship to value. The many reasons for this include government regulations, the pattern of government subsidies, variation of house prices because of local demand, and the effect of inflation in reducing the real cost of mortgages over time.

As an essential and valued commodity, housing has been much subsidised, but by no means solely for the relief of poverty. Other political objectives have also been important. Home-buyers get their subsidy in the form of mortgage tax relief, which increases in value with the size of the mortgage and the level of income. Local authority housing has been subsidised directly by government, but the value to the tenant depends upon the composition of the housing stock belonging to the authority, its rent policy, and the attitude of the government of the day towards council housing and local authority expenditure.

In addition, low income families on SB have had the full amount of rent and rates taken into account when their benefit was assessed.

Alternatively they and other low income families have been able to claim rent and rate rebates or allowances. The calculations required to make the best choice were complicated because of the many differences in the criteria for the two-means-tested benefits. As a result it was estimated that 400,000 people would have been better off had they made a different choice, with 300,000 of these choosing rebates when the better choice would have been SB (Hansard, 18 May 1981, vol. 24, col. 24W). Because of its concern that poor tenants were failing to get the benefits to which they were properly entitled, the SBC called for a single housing benefit to provide 100 per cent of reasonable housing costs for all on SB and for others, including people in full-time work on comparable incomes. Ideally the new benefit would extend to the owner-occupier (SBC, 1978a).

Legislation in 1982 provided for a unified housing benefit to be introduced in two stages in November 1982 and April 1983. Local authorities were given the responsibility for administering the new benefit. Because the change was to be made at no additional cost, gains for some had to be met by losses for others. However the Government agreed to limit the losses during the transitional period to 75p per week.

The losses resulting from the introduction of the scheme would have been larger and more numerous had the Government not committed itself to a permanent 'topping-up' provision from the DHSS for an estimated 140,000 who would be left with a net income after the payment of rebated rent and rates that was below SB level. Under the old schemes these people would have been entitled to SB. However pressure groups feared that the previous so-called 'better off problem' would be replaced by a 'take-up' problem as local authorities would not have the resources to ensure that those who would benefit from 'topping-up' would be advised to claim the benefit. People failing to claim would lose not only the benefit but also the passport advantages of the SB scheme such as free school meals, and possible eventual entitlement to the long-term SB rate.

A major objective of the unification of housing was to cheapen and simplify administration but immediately prior to its introduction, many doubted that this would be achieved. The Director of the Institute of Housing was quoted as forecasting 'rent and rates chaos' and a 'bureaucratic labyrinth'. He claimed that one in three households would be affected by the new scheme, and one in ten would be worse off (*Guardian*, 27 August 1982). Possibly some may understand their individual position better because of the clearer identification given to money intended to pay housing costs; but others, who have to be 'topped-up' are likely to be more confused than before. A further disadvantage is that tenants who are heavily dependent on SB will lose control over a substantial part of their money. They will not be able to 'borrow' from the rent money however great the need, as it will be transferred directly from the DHSS to the local authority.

In the first few years of 1980, the pressures that increase housing costs have been strong, and in some respects seem likely to continue to be so. For the owner-occupier, house prices were stable in 1981, even falling in some parts of the country. But mortage rates at 14–17% were at or near their highest levels, although they declined to around 12% in 1982. For tenants, the average unrebated local authority rent rose in the two-year period April 1979 to April 1981 by 78% (Hansard, 18 November 1981, col. 172W), and the Environment Select Committee estimated that rents might be as much as 50% higher in real terms in 1983/4 than they were in 1979/80 (HC 714 1979/80, Appendix 1).

Table 5.1   Average proportion of expenditure allocated to housing analysed by tenure (%)

Local authority housing	Owner-occupier with mortgage	Private tenancy – unfurnished	Private tenancy – furnished	Owner-occupier without mortgage	Living rent free
20	24	18	26	6	3

Source: DHSS Family Finances Survey (OPCS, 1981).

The type of tenure has a significant influence on the percentage of expenditure allocated to housing as is shown by the figures in Table 5.1. Variation in cost over time produces a different pattern because inflation reduces the real cost of mortgages. Townsend's (1979) national poverty survey in 1968–9, showed that families buying their homes had, on average, annual costs just over twice as great as those of council tenants, but those owning their houses outright had costs only three-fifths of those of council tenants. Townsend's analysis of the complexities of the housing market led him to conclude that in any real meaning of 'cost', the average owner-occupier pays less absolutely, as well as relatively, for his housing than the council tenant. However a long-term balancing of expenditure and assets is irrelevant to low income families who cannot afford the high repayments required in the early years of a mortgage, nor are they likely to be able to obtain mortgages, as Townsend pointed out.

In the late 1960s and early 1970s, poor people had some difficulty in affording housing (Heywood and Allen, 1971; Coates and Silburn,

1970). More recently the advent of rent and rates rebates related to family size as well as income has led to a better match of expenditure on housing with ability to pay.

Figures for April 1981 show that the average unrebated local authority rent was £11.39, while the estimated rebate for England and Wales (excluding the New Towns) was £6.22, and the average rent allowances were £4.54 and £5.08 for unfurnished and furnished accommodation respectively (CIPFA [Chartered Institute of Public Finance and Accountancy], *Housing and Rents Statistics*, 1982). Take-up was estimated to be 75% for rent rebates and 55% for rent allowances (*Housing and Construction Statistics 1969–79*, 1980). Despite the provision for rebates Wilson and Herbert (1978) found much overcrowding amongst 56 large poor families living in deprived inner city areas because they could not afford housing commensurate with family size. However rent and rate rebates have enabled some FIS claimants to occupy houses of a standard they could not otherwise afford (Knight and Nixon, 1975).

In the post-war years, housing has generally been in short supply in relation to demand. People in accommodation have, to some extent, been protected from market forces, but some entering the housing market have faced considerable difficulties with prices rising faster than for other commodities (*Social Trends*, 1979) and with tenancies difficult to secure. Local authority housing lists have generally been long. Townsend (1979) found that 69% of those he surveyed in 1968–9 had waited for more than a year, with 46% having waited for three or more years. Since then the shortage has tended to ease but by no means uniformly.

For some families, private rented accommodation is a matter of choice. For others, it can be a necessity because of inability to buy or get a local authority tenancy. The RCDIW (1977) showed that in 1975 those in private rented unfurnished accommodation had lower mean and median incomes than owner occupiers with mortgages and local authority tenants; and, compared with the other two groups, they were disproportionately concentrated in lower income ranges. For example 12% had incomes of less than £1500 compared with 5% of local authority tenants and 1% of owner-occupiers with mortgages (Table 74). However Townsend's poverty survey found that 'contrary to impressions given in the media', families in council tenancies were poorer than those with other forms of tenure: 41% had net disposable incomes of less than 140% of SB scale rates plus housing costs compared with 27% and 37% for private tenants in furnished and unfurnished accommodation respectively. Possibly the difference between Townsend's figures and those of the RCDIW arises from

Townsend using an equivalently adjusted measure of income.

Rent controls have kept rents down thereby benefiting private tenants, but they have also reduced the amount of accommodation available. Between 1961 and 1971 there was a 30% decline in the number of households who were neither owner occupiers nor local authority tenants (RCDIW, 1977).

The housing difficulties of lone parents have attracted particular attention in poverty studies. The DHSS Family Finances Survey (OPCS, 1981) singled them out as a special group because, amongst other factors, their relatively higher housing expenditure distinguished them from other groups in poverty. Marsden (1969) found that, of the lone mothers he surveyed, the unmarried were in the worst accommodation and where it was excessively bad, the mothers were likely to be paying more because they were not statutory tenants. All the unmarried mothers in a small postal survey by Holman (1970), regardless of class, had similar difficulties in finding accommodation and it was the largest single item in most families' budgets. In Ferri's (1976) sample, derived from the National Child Development Study of children born in 1958, 17% were living in private rented accommodation; for unmarried mothers, the percentage was 26% compared with only 7% for two-parent families. She suggested that the differences arose because lone mothers couldn't get mortgages and in the past local authority regulations may have worked against them. The 1975 GHS analysed by Layard, Piachaud and Stewart (1978) showed that a higher proportion of lone parents lived in council housing than was the case with the rest of the population. This may be no more than a reflection of the fact that lone mothers are less likely to be owner-occupiers than other groups. Layard and his colleagues also found that single mothers were the group most likely to live in furnished accommodation and 78% of mothers in this type of accommodation had household income below SB level. The housing position of lone mothers such as these will be eased by the Housing (Homeless Persons) Act 1972 which put a statutory duty on local authorities to house families with children regardless of whether the parents were married or not.

The problems of owner-occupiers whose incomes subsequently fall causing difficulties in meeting their commitments were noted by Marshall (1972). Of the groups on SB she was studying, mortgage repayments caused about half of the owner-occupiers to have incomes below her definition of basic need, while only 2% and 20% of female and male tenants respectively had such low incomes. The SBC (1978a and 1979) discussed these difficulties, noting that they were being experienced by a small but growing group of claimants, typically elderly and living in older property. However Ferri and Robinson (1976) observed the same situation with lone parents. They also found that, over time, property repairs became an increasing problem.

Government intervention in the housing market has evolved over many years, and the general principles seem to be well accepted, although there is continuous political dispute about the details. Over the years there has been reasonable stability in the cost of housing for low income groups although shortages and market rigidities have consistently distorted the value for money obtained in different areas and from different forms of tenure. However housing expenditure is a significant proportion of many budgets, and with government subsidies being large but subject to political mood, housing is a potentially demanding and expensive requirement for low income families.

Fuel

Steeply rising prices for fuel put severe pressure on money requirements during the second half of the 1970s and in the early 1980s. As a result fuel debt became the subject of more interest, research, and controversy than any other form of debt. The attitudes and responses of debtors, creditors, government and campaigners are relevant to the study of money problems in general.

Difficulties in paying for fuel appear likely to persist. The Green Paper on Energy Policy (Department of Energy, 1978) estimated that energy prices will double in real terms by the year 2000. The extent to which this will perpetuate or intensify money problems depends upon how far real incomes rise in parallel, how uniformly they do so, and how easily low income families are able to make the necessary budgetary changes. Even when real incomes, including pensions, rose faster than the real cost of energy, as they did during the ten years up to 1978 (SBC, 1979), people with low incomes still had great difficulty in paying for the fuel they needed (SBC 1976, 1977a, 1978a, 1979). The difficulties arise because of the interaction of a number of factors.

Factors Causing Variation in Fuel Consumption and Expenditure

High fuel consumption relative to income obviously makes people vulnerable to fuel payment difficulties. FES data shows that expenditure on fuel as a percentage of total expenditure fluctuated from $5\frac{1}{4}$ to $6\frac{1}{4}$% between 1970 and 1977, but there were large variations in proportions of expenditure between different income groups and household types.

Table 5.2, calculated by McClements (1978) of the DHSS Economic Adviser's Office, shows that in every quintile of the equivalent

Table 5.2   Budget shares for fuel in households of different type classified by equivalent income, 1975

Household type	Equivalent income quintile					All households
	1	2	3	4	5	
Single adult	0.086	0.071	0.056	0.046	0.043	0.050
Two adults	0.080	0.061	0.064	0.053	0.042	0.050
Other adult households	0.066	0.054	0.051	0.046	0.036	0.044
One-parent families	0.100	0.074	0.060	0.063	0.064	0.079
Two adults 1–2 children	0.069	0.061	0.055	0.051	0.043	0.054
Two adults 3+ children	0.060	0.052	0.050	0.049	0.036	0.052
All other households with children	0.057	0.048	0.042	0.036	0.034	0.041
Single pensioner	0.133	0.110	0.091	0.078	0.076	0.108
Two pensioners	0.107	0.095	0.068	0.067	0.077	0.087
All households	0.084	0.065	0.055	0.049	0.042	0.055

Source: McClements, 1978.

income distribution, pensioners had the highest budget share for fuel, i.e. the proportion of the budget spent on fuel, with one-parent families second. In the bottom quintile, the fuel budget share of one-parent families at 10% was particularly high in comparison with a figure of 5.5% for all families.

Isherwood, also of the Economic Adviser's Office at the DHSS, in an unpublished paper (1979), showed that in 1977, 15% of households had fuel budget shares of more than twice the median figure for all households. Households that were more likely to have high budget shares (i.e. between two and four times the median figure) included those with one adult at home, those heavily dependent on solid fuel, those with slot meters, and those in the bottom two quintiles of the equivalent income distribution. Some of these circumstances are, of course, interrelated.

A detailed investigation into the single and combined effect of various factors on household fuel expenditure is currently (1982) being carried out by Hutton at the Social Policy Research Unit of York University. Hutton's disaggregation of 1978 FES data showed that income was not as directly related to fuel expenditure as were other variables such as the number of people and number of rooms in a household (Hutton, 1981). Overall she found that expenditure rose with income, and it did so sharply with incomes up to £70 a week. Hutton suggested that this could mean that increasing income was associated with more people or more rooms, or that the desired level of comfort could not be afforded at the lower income levels. Expenditure levelled off for incomes between £70 and £180 a week, but then rose even more sharply, suggesting that when income was high, fuel was treated more as a luxury-type commodity than as a necessity.

In his review of the electricity and gas industries code of practice, Berthoud (1981) compared fuel expenditure with income expressed in terms of SB levels (i.e. equivalent incomes). Expenditure was high at the lowest income levels, falling as income rose slightly, and then rising again as income rose further.

Any significant difference in the price of different fuels will affect levels of fuel expenditure in the short and medium term. Switching from using one fuel to another does not quickly follow price movements. It is often unjustified because of the high capital cost of central heating equipment; and, for tenants, it is often impossible because the landlord determines the heating system.

A Consumers' Association *Which?* report (September 1980) indicated that gas used in a central heating boiler then cost only about a quarter as much as full cost electricity to provide the same amount of heat. Not surprisingly the analyses of Hutton (1981) and Isherwood (1979) of the fuel expenditure of consumers using different fuel combinations for heating and lighting, showed that those using gas and electricity were in the most favourable position. They were less likely to have a high budget share for fuel (Isherwood) and they had the lowest average expenditure on fuel (Hutton). Central heating increases expenditure for all fuel combinations – although of course it also increases comfort. Hutton found that people with gas central heating had the lowest average expenditure and that having central heating increased expenditure most when electricity was the sole fuel. She felt this was a matter of particular concern because electric central heating is 'more commonly associated with low incomes, one-adult households, local authority housing and other unfurnished rented accommodation'. However, despite the general increased expense resulting from electric central heating, Hutton found that for the lowest income groups (less than £30 per week in 1978) those with central heating who used solely electricity spent only 10p a week more than those with central heating who used the cheaper combination of gas and electricity, even though they got less heat for their money. Average expenditure on fuels was very similar for people with low incomes, irrespective of type of central heating, or no central heating. Similarly Isherwood found that low income households that were very dependent on electricity were *not* more likely to have a high budget share for fuel (i.e. greater than twice the median figure for all consumers).

At first sight, these findings seem surprising, but as Hutton suggested, they are the predictable result of low income families having to keep their fuel expenditure within strict limits. Richardson's (1978) survey of two low income centrally heated council estates showed that 30% of the tenants did not use their central heating at all. Bowen (1980) in a survey for the Electricity Consumers' Council, reported that people who used electricity for heating, switch the power on for markedly shorter periods and heat fewer rooms than those using other fuels. Nevertheless this survey of all income groups found that the last bill for those living in all-electric homes was nearly double the average for people using other forms of heat.

The effect of differing fuel prices on expenditure, consumption and welfare is the fuel issue most likely to diminish in importance during the 1980s. The Government announcement (Hansard, 16 January 1980, vol. 976, cols. 1644–6) that domestic gas prices were expected to rise by 10% more than the rate of inflation and electricity prices by 5% more for a period of three years made it clear that the price advantage of gas would diminish. Whether it will disappear is less certain. Price changes are the responsibility of the industries, but they have to meet government-set targets for the annual rate of return.

The FES provides valuable data for sophisticated analysis of fuel expenditure. Hutton's work at York University illustrated this complex relationship with an ideogram (Figure 5.1). The number of persons has an effect in three ways on fuel expenditure: directly, through the size of the house and through incomes. Number of rooms is directly related to fuel expenditure as is central heating. Income affects fuel expenditure through number of rooms and central heating.

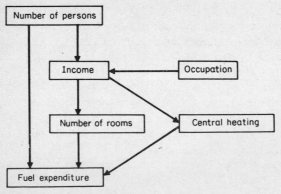

Figure 5.1 The money problems of the poor

The FES data does not permit analysis of all factors relevant to fuel expenditure. One of considerable importance is the type of accommodation. Richardson (1978) felt it was a crucial factor, perhaps more important than family composition. Bradshaw (1978), in his discussion of the effect of type of dwelling on fuel costs, found that sources giving variation in expenditure by type of dwelling are scarce. FES relates only to tenure, although the GHS gives a little more detail. Variations in effectiveness of heating systems depend in part on their internal efficiency, but also on the construction of the dwelling and the amount of insulation installed later. For these reasons rising fuel prices have a variable effect on consumers. A Fabian pamphlet by Gray *et al*. (1977) drew attention to the need to consider costs falling on other agencies. For example cost cutting by private developers or local government, either by installing low capital cost heating systems or by ineffective insulation, can create long-term higher running costs for householders. These costs may be more likely for those with low incomes. The need for help with fuel costs arises from low income and living in accommodation that is particularly difficult to keep warm. As the SBC (1980) pointed out, both need to be taken into account if fuel help is to go to those who most need it. The Commission called for an accommodation inventory despite its cost in staff. However the cost and effectiveness of an inventory have to be assessed before it can be considered a realistic option.

Fuel has traditionally been a necessity which was cheap and relatively easy to afford. Substantial fuel price rises of the mid-1970s transformed the situation. It quickly became apparent that the pressures of high fuel costs were not simple and uniform but complex and varied. Family structure, income, fuel used, and structure of accommodation were amongst the factors which had to be taken into account for a proper understanding of the new financial pressure on low income families which had suddenly emerged.

6 The Money Environment

The term 'the money environment' is used in this review to describe the financial structures, commercial practices and external pressures which people meet when they come to spend their money. It is a complex and even untidy environment with many loosely related factors affecting how people spend their money, the value they get for it, and the additional costs that poverty brings. The nature of the various forms of credit, their cost, availability and the pressures under-lining their use are an obvious part of the environment. A different and more subtle aspect is the marketing pressure exerted consciously by sellers but only dimly perceived by most consumers. A further large group of diverse factors directly diminish value or create additional costs. Some are the result of consumer circumstances, while others derive from the market. Of a different and unique nature are dif-ferential price increases. This chapter examines all these multifarious aspects of the money environment.

An adverse environment can lower living standards as effectively as a fall in income. Modifications to the environment are therefore a potential method of increasing welfare. The increases are unlikely to be large but then nor are many that are made in cash benefits; and for those with severe money problems, marginal gains are important.

The money environment of poor people can vary from that of others for a variety of reasons. For example charges for credit granted to those with insecure low incomes may reasonably be higher to allow for a greater risk of default. But they can also be higher because of prejudice and exploitation.

The foremost critic of the environment of poor consumers has been the American writer Caplovitz. In his book *The Poor Pay More* (1963), about the consumer experiences of poor families in a deprived area of New York, he wrote, 'The consumer pattern amongst the urban poor of sixty years ago is still with us today sustained by poverty and ignorance. The poor are subject to crass exploitation . . . Given some protection by the law, they are too naïve, too uninformed to know their rights or to exercise them when they do.'

British comment has been more restrained. Writing at a similar time as Caplovitz, the Maloney Committee on Consumer Protection (Board of Trade, 1962) referred to the disruption of the old established balance between buyer and seller by the emergence of radically different methods. Some years later the report of the Crowther Committee on Consumer Credit (Department of Trade and Industry, 1971a) and the Payne Committee on the Enforcement of Judgement Debts (Lord High Chancellor's Office, 1969) both showed a cautious awareness that problems had developed from the interplay between marketing and credit practices and the characteristics and circumstances of some consumers. A fundamental difficulty for poor people was put by Goldring (1973), in his study of the work of the Family Service Units, 'Life in Britain today is not only more affluent, it is also more complex and requires greater skill for survival.' It is those with the lowest incomes who most need to avoid getting poor value or incurring additional costs, but doing so requires knowledge and sophistication which they are the least likely to possess.

The credit society

Lending money is a centuries old procedure which has traditionally been viewed by society with some disapproval. In early years, payment of interest was illegal and later (1545–1854) interest rates were limited. In this century there has been a qualitative change. The development of hire purchase and other credit facilities has blurred the old distinction between the unwanted debts of the unfortunate needy and the credit deliberately sought by others (NCC, 1980).

Major surveys of credit use were carried out in 1969, 1977 and 1979. They were commissioned by the Crowther Committee (Department of Trade and Industry, 1971b), the Office of Fair Trading (1979b) and the National Consumer Council (1980) respectively. The OFT reported a rapid growth in the proportion of the population using credit during the 1970s. By 1977 over half the population was using credit (excluding first mortgages) compared with only a fifth in the earlier 1969 survey. But this growth was not matched by any large increase in the proportion of spending on clothes, durables, cars, etc. financed by credit. The percentage figure oscillated over the period but increased only slightly from 35% in 1970 to 39% in 1979 (NCC, 1980).

Despite its high level of use, attitudes to credit seem to be ambivalent. The NCC (1980) reported that, of those it surveyed, 29% felt it was 'never a good thing'.

The NCC (1980) comparison of the use made of the various credit facilities over the period covered by the three major surveys is shown

Table 6.1   The use of credit

Consumers currently using	1969 (%)	1977 (%)	1979 (%)
Mail order	10	22	24
HP, credit sale, etc	9	11	13
Bank credit cards	n/a		9
Shop credit cards	n/a	9	2
Other credit cards	n/a		*
Bank personal loans	*	6	7
Shop budget account	n/a	4	5
Shop ordinary credit account	n/a		5
Credit purchase from fuel board	n/a	n/a	4
Loan from finance company	1	2	3
Bank overdraft	*	3	2
Check or voucher trading	2	2	2
Second mortgage	n/a	1	2
Tallyman	n/a	1	2
Shop check	n/a	1	*
Moneylenders	*	n/a	*
Pawnbrokers	n/a	*	*

n/a – not asked
* very small numbers – always less than 1 per cent
Source: NCC, 1980

in Table 6.1. This illustrates the growing importance of mail order, hire purchase and credit cards. The percentage of consumers using mail order doubled over the period. It is noticeable also that credit sources, such as checks and tallymen, commonly used by the poorest in society, have overall a very low incidence of use. Loan finance companies are similarly little used, but there was a very large increase (300%) in that use over the decade.

The elderly use credit much less than others. The NCC (1980) found that 28% had never done so compared with around 10% for other age groups. The elderly generally have low incomes, and this is probably a partial explanation of the low incidence of use amongst all those with low incomes. Only 22% of those with incomes below £40 a week in 1979 were found to be using credit compared with 48.61% of those with higher incomes (NCC, 1980).

Ison's (1979) examination of marketing integrity has been an important contribution to the wider aspects of the use of credit. As part of his study, he interviewed a national random sample of 1540 British consumers who had purchased one or more household goods, many of whom had used credit. The study resulted in several reasons for the use of credit, and of course the most obvious was that the money was not available to pay cash. Other reasons included the retention of security and flexibility as a result of keeping savings intact, and economy, because the interest costs were offset by inflation. Major items were routinely bought on credit by many families. For some of them, Ison felt that 'the pressures of the moment are always stronger than the discipline or budgeting skill necessary for saving'. 'Paying instalments to a seller . . . may be perceived as demand that must be met, whereas savings can be deferred.'

This important characteristic of credit was stressed also by Caplovitz (1963) whose early pioneering work into credit and consumer practice, although old, is still of interest because it relates to consumers particularly vulnerable to severe credit problems even though they are atypical. He interviewed 464 poor families, with a response rate of 82%, in a deprived housing area of New York. A high proportion, 75%, were coloured, and there was an above average number of younger and larger families. Caplovitz described credit as providing 'a system of enforced savings with the discipline imposed from without'. Immediate gratification, a need for the discipline of required payments, and ease of use appear to be the main reasons for using credit, while an improved standard of living is likely to be the most beneficial result.

Caplovitz (1963) found that amongst the low income Americans he studied, those who bought always on credit owned more than those who paid only in cash. However this may merely reflect the fact that those who wished to own more had to use credit to do so. The Crowther Committee (Department of Trade and Industry, 1971a) saw credit as a means of giving the poor their only chance of buying necessities at a reasonable cost. Studies of poor British families suggest that hire purchase may be needed for the acquisition of a whole range of goods. An extreme example is the comment of a mother of a large family reported by Land (1969) as saying, 'without HP I wouldn't even have a mop'. Comment from other British studies indicates an awareness of the need for hire purchase but some aversion to its use. 'I have a check but I hate doing it that way because you pay so much more' (Marshall, 1972). Marsden (1969) found their background influenced spending behaviour amongst the lone mothers he was studying. Some did not 'believe in' hire purchase or checks. But he observed that 'when items of furniture or clothing were needed, these mothers would have to go short'. However, paying for the facility of credit takes up purchasing power and, as the NCC (1980) noted, using it makes people poorer in terms of what they can buy than they otherwise would have been.

Ison (1979) opposed limiting the use of credit because he felt credit had a beneficial effect on the standard of living. He argued that it encouraged the diversion of income from transitory pleasures to durables of more lasting benefit. However he did not discuss the possibility that the consumer might prefer transitory pleasures. He went on to suggest that it is 'a matter of moral value judgements and social policy to arrive at a point in the expansion of consumer credit when it is thought to achieve the optimum good'. The concept of an optimum point of credit use is helpful to discussion, although in practice the point is difficult to identify.

Past the optimum point of credit use, people are buying more on credit than their incomes can sustain. This can result in serious money problems and those with low incomes are obviously most vulnerable. Sellers want to sell and Ison pointed out that the practical ease of credit buying is heightened by the blandishments of the seller. More disturbing is his view that credit provides opportunities for 'predatory practices, deceit and other abuses'. He stressed that credit does not create these but it may aggravate them. Credit could well be the crucial factor in the crooked fringe of business. For example excessive pressure to buy unwanted encyclopaedias and faulty central heating would not have succeeded if customers had had to pay cash. In his study of debtors, Caplovitz (1974) expressed a similar view. He argued that the growth of credit has been a 'boon to deceptive and fraudulent marketing practice'. With cash transactions, if there is no cash, there is no transaction. Credit is different because 'affording' becomes less relevant, and the creditor knows he can force the agreement. Neither Caplovitz nor Ison suggested that all creditors are unscrupulous. Unfortunately it is the poorest consumers, because of their lack of creditworthiness, who are most likely to be exploited.

The major surveys have given an overall favourable endorsement of the credit society. The Crowther Committee (Department of Trade and Industry, 1971a) concluded that on balance 'consumer credit is beneficial'. The NCC (1980) found no evidence of widespread credit problems. However, its report noted that surveys of the population as a whole do not throw up the most serious problems and the NCC took further steps to investigate these. It commissioned in-depth interviews with a small sample who had been taken to court for debt; it organised discussions with special groups which included ethnic minorities and those living on a 'problem' estate; and it requested a report from G. Parker (1980) on the work of the Birmingham Settlement Money Advice Centre. The difficulty in getting evidence in the sensitive areas of debt is shown by the fact that the NCC succeeded in getting only seven in-depth interviews after sending out 161 letters to a selected sample of people who had been taken to court. Based on the evidence it obtained, the NCC commented that 'there were a few severe problems for a minority of people'. But its overall conclusion was ambivalent. For poor people, it felt that it was 'both an obvious refuge and an unduly heavy burden', and its report stressed the increase in anxiety which credit use could bring.

Those whose work brings them into contact with the problems arising from credit take a less benevolent view of it than did the Crowther Committee. One example is the comment of Katy Ritchie, the head of the New Cross Debt Clinic, who in a newspaper interview (*Guardian*, 13 March 1979), caustically described society as being 'oiled with credit' with a 'whole army of factors' conspiring to lead the poorly paid into the trap of being unable to meet commitments.

The dilemma for the poorest people living in a credit society was described by Caplovitz (1963). 'Americans . . . are trained to consume in order to win the respect of others and to maintain their self-respect.' 'Families with almost no claims to credit (i.e. no creditworthiness) are shunted to a special class of merchants who are ready to accept great risk.' There are two options for the poor – 'forgoing major purchases or being exploited'.

Availability of Credit

Credit is said to be both too readily available and too restricted in supply. The source of this paradox is that the credit industry has a commercial motivation but its activities have a personal impact. Finance companies are in the business of making money. For maximum return they need to balance the extra interest, derived from expansion, against the potential loss by default as they expand their business towards the boundaries of creditworthiness. They take account of the cost of preventing default, and, as most are commercial organisations, they will tend to use the cheapest method of doing so.

The extent to which credit is refused is difficult to assess. Only 3% in the NCC survey admitted to having difficulties in getting credit, but the report suggested that the low figure may be due to a reluctance to apply for credit which people felt they would not get (NCC, 1980). Alternatively people may be reluctant to admit to a refusal.

Doig and Millar (Scottish Law Commission, 1981c) in the Scottish Law Commission's survey of 56 credit granting agencies in Scotland found that the most thorough and sophisticated forms of credit checking were carried out by national retailers and money lending organisations. These were impersonal checks which contrasted to the subjective approach of local retailers, tradesmen, and commercial organisations who relied more on personal knowledge and judgement. Rock (1973) in his sociological study of debt collection noted that most mail order firms rejected 10% of would-be customers, HP companies rejected 10–20%, and moneylenders, 80–90%. He made the critical comment, 'Credit sanctioning is a manipulation of stereotypes based on social characteristics which are seen as causally linked with default.' Supporting evidence comes from Cranston (1978) who gave examples of restricted supply with some creditors refusing to grant credit to all those living on a particular street or council housing estate because in the past they had a disproportionate number of defaulters from the area. A specific example of 'red lining', as it is called, was provided by Clive Soley, the MP for Hammersmith, who complained that the whole of the White City estate in his constituency was 'red lined' by one company until the local newspaper took up the matter (Hansard, 16 March 1981, vol. 1200, col. 5).

Doig and Millar (Scottish Law Commission, 1981c) found that all the 56 Scottish credit-granting organisations they surveyed said that residence in specific areas was not a bar to the extension of credit, but a few said it would lead to caution. The NCC (1980) gave estates in Bradford and Finsbury as examples of credit ghettoes. The Director General of Fair Trading (1982b) criticised the red-lining practice and warned that creditors refusing credit because of it risked contravening sex and discrimination laws and could have their licence withdrawn. He also criticised 'credit scoring', a practice whereby points are allocated according to factors such as employment, marital status, etc. Credit is automatically granted if sufficient points are awarded. The Director General argued that under this system, some individual cases would be unfairly refused.

The opposite approach of individually assessing customers was criticised by the NCC. It queried the view of the National Consumer Council Federation that the agents of check traders have a truly accurate perception of customers' ability and will to pay, on the grounds that personal considerations affect collectors' willingness to go to some areas. High rise blocks are time-consuming, some areas have a reputation for muggings, one personal attack was known to have led to a collector never returning to the area again. The high incidence of credit refusal in some circumstances is illustrated by the statement of the Consumer Credit Association representing small credit tradesmen and money lenders that about half of all applications may be rejected. Quoting this statement, the NCC (1980) suggested that some people may be good payers but they are 'stamped'.

Credit refusal because of status also seems to be common and the NCC (1980) referred to difficulties experienced by single women with children and by the unemployed. People denied credit in these ways suffer unfair discrimination, for the denial is not because of their own lack of creditworthiness but because of that of their neighbours, their status, or because of the characteristics of the area where they live.

Denial may be justified if the individual risk is unacceptably high, and the customer is genuinely not creditworthy. But it is argued that this too may lead to unfair penalties. A Canadian Special Senate Committee on Poverty (1971) pointed out that society is geared to credit, in the sense that quality and price of goods are based on the assumption that they are paid for over time. The implication of this comment is that those forced back to cash only purchases suffer from the failure of the market to adapt to their needs.

The opposite criticism, that hardship is caused by some creditors granting credit too easily, is more common and more strongly held. The problem arises because debt collection is generally effective enough to produce some indifference about the establishment of creditworthiness. The Crowther Committee on Consumer Credit (Department of Trade and Industry, 1971a) blamed a small number of credit-giving bodies that granted credit without enquiring into credit-worthiness for being responsible for the majority of court cases involving debt. The Committee noted that a survey by British debt services of 3000 defaulting debtors showed 57.3% had a previous record of default. 'Sometimes the same creditor is issuing judgement summons against debtors while through its agents it is persuading that debtor to accept extra credit.'

The NCC (1980) showed how readily and almost unconsciously debtors, likely to get into difficulty, can take on additional credit. Checks on creditworthiness are not generally asked for by mail order firms nor by weekly credit callers. Mail order is easy and convenient; while a subtle relationship often develops between a family and a weekly credit caller, leading to the personalisation of transactions. The payments become a habit and the caller, a friend. Priority tends to be given to maintaining payments to the caller so as not to jeopardise the friendship nor the chance of getting help in times of need. Knowing this, callers are willing to make further loans even when it would normally not be prudent to do so.

Excessive credit may be encouraged by the payment of commission to the seller, a practice which was criticised by the Maloney Committee on Consumer Protection (Board of Trade, 1962), the NCC (1980), and by Morris (1965). In her study of prisoners and their families Morris was particularly interested in the effects of hire purchase, and she strongly criticised those in the credit industry who grant credit irresponsibly. She referred to the lot of the debtor as becoming 'increasingly wretched' . . . the community and the taxpayer 'becoming increasingly and expensively involved' and concluded that 'it could be reasoned that to encourage further indebtedness among the already

gullible and feckless is like plying an alcoholic with liquor'.
The situation may be little changed since Morris wrote in 1965. In
1981 the NCC complained that companies were leading the unemployed into debt by advancing them too much credit, and they quoted
the example of a mentally handicapped man with a very low wage
being allowed to run up a debt of £286 when he already owed over
£1500 (*Guardian*, 25 September 1981).

Types of Credit: their cost and use
The additional charge for credit is usually described merely as interest,
although it includes the cost of setting up the loan and takes account of
such factors as the availability of security, the period of the loan, and
the believed creditworthiness of the customer which could affect the
method and cost of obtaining repayment.

Since 6 October 1980 all credit has had to be expressed in terms of
an annual percentage rate (APR). This has to include all the extra costs
paid by a credit consumer. APRs will vary over time with movements
in the general level of interest rates, but the pattern of rate variation
changes little. Table 6.2 shows the pattern of typical borrowing costs in
1979 in terms of APR at a time when the banks' base rate was 14%:

Table 6.2   Typical borrowing costs, 1979

Type of loan	Annual percentage rate (APR)
Bank overdraft	16–20
Bank ordinary loan account	16–20
Bank personal loan	18.3–19.7
Bank budget account	variable
Revolving loan	19–27
Bridging loan	about 17
Bank card	up to 26.8
Insurance policy loan	9–15
Finance company personal loan	about 27; sometimes more, up to 50
Increasing the mortgage	12–13
Hire purchase	20–40
Credit sale	up to 60
Shop accounts	16–31
Trading checks	72.5
Trading vouchers	40
Mail order catalogues	
with commission	0 based on prices being 5–15%
without commission	47 higher than in the shops
Second mortgage	18–42.5
Money lender	20–73.5
Pawnbrokers	at least 26.8, normally more

Source: Consumers' Association, 1979; NCC, 1980

The Times (2 February 1980) noted how the more 'down-market' one goes, the higher the interest rates become. 'A company lending unsecured money for short terms and in small amounts, relying on manual collections as the only way of bringing its risks down to acceptable levels, will be charging an APR of more than 100%.'

For cash loans the cheapest form of credit is a bank overdraft, but lower social class families are less likely than others to have bank accounts, although the proportion that do so is increasing as is shown by the figures in Table 6.3.

Table 6.3   Percentage of the population with bank accounts

Social class	1971/2	1978/9
A/B	75	83
C1	58	71
C2	34	51
D/E	21	36

Source: Inter-bank Research Organisation figures quoted in NCC, 1980

Greater use of banks was one important way which the NCC (1980) felt could bring more informed use of lower cost credit. Masey (1977) commented that making loans at a reasonable rate of interest is a most 'valuable service for the poor'. But she made it clear that the greater use of commercial banks is not easily achieved. There are few banks in poor areas, and their hours of opening are restricted. The poor are not likely to be profitable customers. Bank charges would be high if their weekly wages went in on Thursday, and were drawn out on Friday. Low wages resulting in a low bank balance would not encourage bank managers to give bank loans. These would probably be required for fairly small amounts and the setting up costs might well exceed the interest charges. Masey reported in 1977 that the break-even point was £350, although at this time interest charges were relatively low.

Baldwin (1973) asked a small sample of banks if they were willing to lend money for the purchase of consumer durables to male manual workers. The majority replied that the bulk of their customers were salary not wage earners, and they would first require a deposit account for about six months with at least £75 in it before they would loan £200. More recently banks have tried to attract customers from all classes, and they have publicly advocated increased payment of wages through banks (as an example see the full-page Barclays Bank advertisement in *The Times*, 29 July 1979). In 1979, 54% of all British employees were still being paid in cash, usually weekly, compared with only 1% of

American workers and 5% of those in Germany. By 1981, the Inter-bank Research Organisation reported that the percentage figure in Britain had fallen to 44%. In 1969, it was 75%, and so it seems likely that the banks' campaign has successfully speeded up a long-term trend (*The Times*, 7 June 1982).

Changing to non-cash payments has been particularly slow amongst manual workers in Britain, with 78% paid in cash in 1979 in comparison with 89% in 1969 (Central Policy Review Staff, 1981). Large companies, who find it cheaper and safer to pay wages through banks, have supported the banks' campaign, although the 150-year-old Truck Act prevents companies from insisting on the non-cash payment of wages. By contrast, French workers earning more than a given indexed sum a month (about £280 in 1981) cannot be paid in cash. The cost of paying an employee in cash is estimated to be £30 per annum (CPRS, 1981). The financial benefit to companies and Government of cashless payments is clearly substantial but worker resistance to the loss of traditional wage packets appears to be fairly strong (*The Times*, 13 July 1981). The Birmingham Chamber of Commerce and Industry, in a response to the Central Policy Review Staff (CPRS) report on cashless pay (1981) pointed out that cashless payments would have to be accompanied by changes in banks' marketing practices for shop-floor workers (*The Times*, 14 August 1981). Although the poorest consumers may eventually benefit marginally by gaining greater access to bank services including loans, the breakdown of traditional attitudes is likely to be relatively slow.

In some countries, for example the United States, Germany, France, Ireland and New Zealand, credit unions are important cheap sources of credit. In the US they provide about one-sixth of loans granted each year, and 15 million people belong to French and German unions (*Guardian*, 21 August 1979). In 1979 there were only about 50 in England, but the 1979 Credit Union Act is expected to increase their numbers and importance. Credit unions are a form of money co-operative, owned and run by their members who must all share a 'common bond' such as a common occupation, workplace, or industrial locality. There is no restriction on the purpose of loans, but it must be accepted by a committee of the union, and the amount that can be borrowed is limited. The rate of interest charged is restricted to 1% per month on the reducing balance; and interest paid to depositors is correspondingly low – a maximum of 6% per annum in 1979. However the Act provides for the specification of other rates from time to time. In the US and Germany there are many middle class members. But in Britain credit unions have so far tended to be a working class organisation. The loans are unsecured but the incidence of default appears to be virtually negligible. In 1979 the 97 credit unions registered in Northern Ireland had assets of £16m and a membership of 85,000. By the end of 1977, there had been no loss of money whatsoever (Hansard, 12 February 1979, vol. 962, col. 801). The excellent safety record of credit unions is probably because they have personal knowledge of their members. They provide a club-like atmosphere with the committee trying to help to resolve financial problems whenever possible. For example it has been reported that occasionally more money is lent than was requested, so that HP debts, incurring a higher rate of interest, could be paid off (*Guardian*, 21 August 1979).

Those with no access to credit union or bank loans have to turn to other sources. The Crowther Committee (Department of Trade and Industry 1971a) found that licensed money lenders charged between 20 and 50%, depending on whether or not the loan was secured, although there were some much higher rates. In terms of APR, these rates would be higher. A 1975 NCC survey reported by Masey (1977) found that for small loans the true rates were much higher than the average given by *Money Which?* (Consumers' Association, 1979), ranging from 143 to an excessive 1706%. The Birmingham Settlement Money Advice Centre has said (1979) that many of the people who come to them for help made extensive use of finance companies, particularly to settle electricity bills. The true rates they charged were 40% or more.

The NCC (1980) suggested that some groups of people, commonly rely on weekly callers for cash loans, but the price paid is high. Parker (NCC, 1980) gave, as a typical example, a £20 loan paid back at £1 a week for 26 weeks, thus having an APR of 187.2%. 'Reloaning', as it is called, is another expensive but common practice. Halfway through, i.e. after 13 weeks, a further £20 is borrowed £13 of which is used to pay off the remaining instalments of the first loan. The net effect is a loan of £27 paid back at £1 a week for 39 weeks, giving an APR of 232.2%. However, Parker (NCC, 1980) warned against making the weekly caller type of business difficult because those using it probably could not get credit elsewhere. The NCC accepted that the prices of some forms of credit, based on weekly collecting, although high in APR terms, is 'very reasonable' when the cost of collection is taken into account.

The very poor and those desperate for cash may be forced to make use of illegal money lenders. The Crowther Committee (Department of Trade and Industry 1971a) reported that 'there is reason to believe that a certain amount of unlicensed money lending still goes on . . . not difficult to guess that the true annual rate of interest involved is very high'. As would be expected, information about illegal transactions is scarce, but there is some evidence from responsible sources. In 1982, the Cheshire controller of trading standards told the public protection committee of illegal creditors charging 'astronomical' rates of interest, in some cases 2400%. (*Sentinel* 4 November 1982). He added that the extent of malpractice was growing at an alarming rate, with pension and child benefit books being held as security, a practice described by Moore (1980) as leading to an 'ever more coercive financial relationship'.

The Annual Report for 1977/8 of the Head of Consumer Protection of the Strathclyde Regional Council (1978) gave some more colourful detail. It referred to 'heavies' being used to ensure the repayment of debt, of 'factory gate' collectors stationing themselves handily on pay-day, of family allowance books being used as security and of families so heavily in debt that there was no foreseeable release beyond something like a win on the football pools. Sutherland (1980) described money lenders in Scotland as 'shadowy criminals', and he referred to pressure for payment being exerted by individuals 'well known to social work departments for their violent criminal records'. Sutherland felt it would be the 'single parent, . . . the depressed, the "victim" of Scotland's rampant alcohol abuse and the growing army of unemployed' who would fall prey to the illegal money lender.

Many goods are purchased on credit, and as already noted, mail order is the most popular form. The NCC (1980) observed that this was partly because of its convenience and partly because of the general absence of credit vetting. Although there is no claimed interest charge, the higher prices are estimated by the NCC to result in an equivalent APR of 47% unless the customer is the agent who is paid a commission.

Interest rates charged for HP and credit sales vary considerably, as the *Money Which?* (Consumers' Association, 1969) figures indicate: Ison (1979) reported from his survey, carried out in 1969, an average interest rate of 21%, but over 30% was not uncommon and a few were as high as 50%. Some of the variations may be class-related. In September 1969 *Money Which?* (Comsumers' Association, 1969) found that the current rates charged for credit purchases of furniture in shops for the middle classes were lower than in those for manual workers, 22.9% and 32.4% respectively. The NCC (1975) claimed the differential was larger, namely that the rate of interest charged in shops for working class people was twice as high as in shops for the middle class. The extent to which this is justified by a higher rate of default is unknown, but it seems unlikely that it would justify a rate twice as high.

An unusual and little known form of hire purchase is hire purchase mortgage. As a way of buying a house it has numerous disadvantages.

The ownership of the property does not pass to the would-be purchaser until the payments are fully completed, so that if, for example, the property was compulsorily purchased, the compensation would go to the statutory owner and not to the person buying the property. In addition, purchasers are responsible for all repairs and do not get mortgage tax relief. In the event of arrears of payment, the recovery process is quick, for the purchaser, being neither a tenant nor an owner, has few legal rights.

One of the few public references to the system was made, by Gerald Kaufman MP, under the protection of parliamentary privilege. He described it as an iniquitous form of hire purchase, and called some landlords in his constituency 'a gang of crooks', who 'should be in gaol' (Hansard, 18 January 1980, vol. 976, part 2, col. 2090). The incidence of HP mortgages, commonly known as the 'drip', is uncertain, although the North-West housing policy officer for Shelter was reported as saying that he had come across it in Liverpool, London and Manchester (*Guardian*, 22 January 1980). Its nature, and the comments made about it, suggest that those who use it are exploited, and they are most likely to be poor, unsophisticated people.

There is no doubt that credit charges vary substantially, and the variation has been strongly criticised. The *Money Which*? (Consumers' Association, 1969) reported an 'unpleasant minority of grossly excessive rates' amongst those charged for HP and credit sales. The Crowther Committee (Department of Trade and Industry, 1971a) concluded that the differences in rates were greater than was justified by the risks involved. The report suggested that the poorer members of society, as a result of having less education and through ignorance, often pay more than is justified by their credit-rating. They are less likely to make informed decisions and 'not surprisingly higher social class groups are generally more knowledgeable than the rest'.

Both the Crowther Committee (Department of Trade and Industry, 1971a) and the earlier Maloney Committee (Board of Trade, 1962) emphasised inadequate information and lack of initiative in undertaking comparative shopping as the important factor leading to unnecessary rate variation. In the past, comparative shopping in the credit market has been particularly difficult for consumers because people offering credit were allowed to quote their terms, including the rate of interest, in any way they chose. As previously mentioned, rates of interest have had to be expressed in terms of APR since October 1980. This arose from a section of the Consumer Credit Act 1974 concerned with 'truth in lending'. APR should make comparisons of the cost of lending easier. However, it does not apply to goods with a cash price under £30, and 'typical' rates may be used in advertisements.

The credit market is an intricate one where lack of knowledge would be expected to be particularly detrimental. However the situation is complex as is shown by the findings of the NCC (1980). Very few of those involved in the group discussion the NCC organised, had considered any type of credit other than that actually used. This was usually introduced to them by personal contact, and there was then no thought of comparing credit facilities. People were 'propelled by habit, convenience, ignorance and diffidence about alternatives'. Yet at the same time, they were aware of their weaknesses and felt lack of knowledge was at the heart of their credit problem. They wanted protection from creditors and from themselves and to be given information so long as it was highly visible and understandable. The NCC drew attention to their diffidence and stressed the anxiety that asking for credit induced. These are likely explanations for an anomalous situation whereby people, saying they want help and information, remain passively inactive.

The situation is further complicated because cost in terms of APR is not always the one found most relevant by the consumer. The NCC (1980) suggested that four measures of credit cost are considered by the consumer: subjective feeling, percentage rate of interest, add on cost, and instalment amount. The evidence the NCC obtained indicated strongly that the cost that matters most, to those likely to have severe problems with credit, is the size of the weekly instalment, because it has to fit into the weekly budget. But outweighing all the measures of cost was convenience which was the dominant factor in determining peoples' choice of credit facilities.

Force of marketing
The selling of goods is a useful service, meeting the needs of those who want to buy. Marketing of goods is something different. The word 'marketing' implies that some extra effort is being put into the selling process which will increase sales above the level that would otherwise occur. Advertisers and economists argue that this stimulates the economy to the benefit of all. In so far as it leads to the dissemination of useful information, it will benefit the individual directly. But marketing is an activity undertaken by the seller in his own interest and not in that of the consumer, and the two interests do not necessarily coincide. In addition marketing can become overforceful and develop into excessive sales pressure or even misrepresentation or malpractice.

Adaptation of the Market
Low income consumers inevitably face difficulties in matching their desire to consume with their low incomes. Caplovitz's early (1963)

study of consumer practice in New York provided a striking example of how a vigorous market economy can adapt to meet their particular requirements. His research took place in a poor area of New York where there had been slum clearance and redevelopment. There were many furniture and appliance shops in the neighbourhood even though the local people generally had low incomes and poor credit positions. Unsophisticated and largely coloured, many of the families were anxious to purchase major durables. The shops contained goods generally of poor quality. Caplovitz noted that price tags were 'conspicuously absent' and every effort was made to 'catch the customer'. The stores personalised their services, using Christian names to make their customers feel at home, and peddlers and other devices brought the customers in. The prices, when revealed, were high because the law regulated the rate of interest for credit, and a high mark-up of 100–300% was needed to get around this restriction. The amount sold depended only on the merchant's willingness to grant credit to customers. The poor were enabled and encouraged to buy despite their poverty, but they were limited to mainly inferior goods at high cost and in a commercial atmosphere designed to generate such purchases.

Salmon (1974) used similar terms to describe the circumstances of poor families helped by the Brotherhood of St. Lawrence in Melbourne. Because of the families' untenable credit positions, systems were set up to exploit them, so that they bought at inflated prices with inflated credit terms. In Melbourne travelling salesmen collected money to pay off debts and induced further ones. Salmon stressed their power which included the use of threats. Families could elude them only by moving, and Salmon noted that 55% of the families had had one or more moves.

In Britain shopping markets vary in style according to the income level and class of their customers. At one extreme, working class street markets sell goods at low prices. Some of the goods are 'seconds' and 'end-of-the-range' items. With vigour and informality, salesmen encourage customers to buy. At the other end of the market, exclusive shops and stores sell top quality goods at high prices in a quietly luxurious atmosphere. However there is no evidence that the British style of market adaptation has exploited customers. For this to occur, it is probable that communities need to be more 'closed' than is common in Britain.

Sales Pressure

Although there is no British research into market adaptation comparable with Caplovitz's American study, there are a few descriptions of a style of marketing so vigorous that it could be described as excessive selling pressure. The Birmingham Settlement Money Advice Centre has spoken (1979) of salesmen turning up at houses on new estates with precise quotations for supplying carpets and curtains, having previously obtained the dimensions of the rooms and windows from the builder. The fact that some of the customers eventually went to the Money Advice Centre for help in sorting out their debts suggests that the purchases could not be afforded and possibly excessive persuasion if not pressure may have been used. Baldwin (1973) in a survey of Glasgow shops found that those catering for the poor pushed sales hard, with repayments quoted in weekly terms and neither total cash nor credit price were stressed. Ison (1979) was particularly critical of the selling practices of the Gas Board. He commented that after the discovery of North Sea gas, 'Their desire to expand markets became so compulsive that other values fell victim in its path', and 'They adopted marketing standards lower than those prevailing in the private sector.' Door-to-door salesmen were recruited, they were paid on commission, and Gas Board literature indicated the need 'to take advantage of impulse buying'.

In her study of prisoners and their families, Morris (1965) did not find that high pressure salesmanship was a serious problem. At most 2% of the prisoners' wives she interviewed complained of it. But she went on to say that it did not mean no pressure was exerted, merely that it was not necessary. 'The conditions for exploitation already exist . . . a desire to keep up with the Joneses or to impress the neighbours and a strong temptation to buy when some one calls at the door and offers something one wants on what appears to be very easy terms.'

Door-to-door selling has been condemned by many writers including the Maloney (Board of Trade, 1962) and Crowther (Department of Trade and Industry, 1971a) Committees. The Maloney Committee found that 'The activities of these men provoked greater wrath and indignation than on any other subject.' The Director General of Fair Trading (Office of Fair Trading, 1979a) referred to dubious canvassing and hard selling in relation to the door-to-door selling of such commodities as central heating and double glazing. It described some salesmen as not revealing the true purpose of the visit until they had crossed the threshold, while others press agreements on vulnerable sections of the public.

Ison's carefully controlled survey data provided support for the view that those who buy from door-to-door salesmen suffer a greater proportion of unfortunate experiences. The worst salesmen, from a consumer welfare point of view, were those without retail premises selling only one type of item. The best of the home salesmen were the regular ones selling different types of goods. But overall the frequency rate and seriousness of reported objections were roughly double for sales at home than for those in shops or through mail order. Looked at in conjunction with Ison's finding that where home conditions were 'good' the proportion of sales taking place at home was 4%, and where conditions were 'poor', the figure was 22%, this suggests that 'poor' families may be significantly disadvantaged by their disproportionate use of door-to-door salesmen.

Tallymen, the traditional salesmen to the poor, get varied mention in the literature. Ison found that advisory agencies did not indicate any substantial volume of complaints about them, but three social workers and one CAB organiser complained that they talk people into things they can't afford, which leads to debt.

The Government's response to widespread criticism of the activities of door-to-door salesmen was to introduce a cooling-off period in the Hire Purchase Act 1965, later amended in the Consumer Credit Act 1974. The underlying principle was that home-buyers of goods above a certain value should have a certain number of days in which to reconsider. However Ison felt that the cooling-off period was of limited value in giving protection against abuse. In particular he noted that the buyer is often not aware of his rights, and Ison listed eleven ways in which the unscrupulous seller can deny them.

Malpractice and Misrepresentation

Marketing is legitimate; sales pressure doubtfully so; malpractice, by definition, is not; and each shades into its neighbour almost imperceptibly. Within the field of malpractice, the nature and incidence of illegitimate trading practices are inevitably difficult to discover and assess, and there have been no attempts to examine them as a cause of debt or other financial difficulty.

Undoubtedly there is malpractice at the margin, however wide or narrow that might be. In the credit and hire industry, the Director General of Fair Trading (Office of Fair Trading, 1976) referred to those 'manifestly unfit' to be in it, and expressed his determination to weed them out. The undesirable practices he drew attention to included charging interest on money not advanced, overcharging on rates of interest, using unfair and misleading terms and conditions, imposing unfair terms for early settlement, cancellation of credit agreements, and misleading advertisements of credit facilities (Office of Fair Trading, 1981a). From 1976, when credit-licensing began, to end 1981, 115,570 standard licences were issued and 179 were refused or revoked (Office of Fair Trading, 1982a).

Caplovitz (1963) and Ison (1979) both gave detailed accounts of various common undesirable selling practices used in America and this country. The techniques used in the two countries were ingenious and broadly similar, including 'bait' advertising and misrepresentation of prices. Caplovitz (1963) reported that one-third of the poor and unsophisticated people in his sample felt that they were misinformed or deceived at the time of transaction.

Ison (1979) gave a vivid description of the tactics used in home-selling of encyclopaedias. One customer, or 'mooch' as he was called, was skilfully handled. He agreed to pay 10p a day for 10 years and then, since he 'wouldn't want to be bothered by these trifling amounts over the years', he ended up paying £365 over three years. Ison also quoted a vacuum cleaner salesman who said that it was fairly common to sell a cleaner not as good as that taken in part exchange.

However these are individual examples which may be exceptional. In his random sample of the whole population, Ison found only 8% who felt there might have been misrepresentation, and he thought that possibly even this figure was too high. But a far higher proportion, 18%, had major or substantial complaints about selling methods. Ison suggested that some selling methods, accepted as legal, are nevertheless thought to be distasteful.

A very small proportion, only 2.3% of Ison's sample, felt that they were misled or misinformed about price alone. But 25% understood that the price was less than the usual one. Ison commented that 'the ordinary shopper faces an almost constant bombardment of claims', suggesting that goods are worth more. The Price Marking (Bargain Offers) Order 1979 was intended to stop unjustified claims. It made illegal any claim that goods are priced lower than their worth, all comparisons with unspecified prices elsewhere, and any claim that a range of goods is offered at 'up to a certain amount off'. The order, which required nine-and-a-half pages of closely typed explanatory notes from the Department of Trade, was widely criticised as 'obscure and full of loopholes' (*The Times*, 23 March 1981). Some companies were reported as skirting the letter of the law by making claims such as '50% off the after sale price'. In many other cases, it was suggested that the law was just ignored (*The Times*, 31 December 1980, 21 January 1981; *Guardian*, 26 March 1980). The Office of Fair Trading (1981c) published a six-month review of the operation of the Order which concluded that although it had resulted in fewer misleading 'worth' and 'value' claims, it contained substantial ambiguities, and that it would be feasible to make amendments to simplify interpretation. The Minister for Consumer Affairs subsequently announced his intention to prepare new simpler legislation which would confine the order to comparative price or value claims (Hansard, 29 July 1982, vol. 28, cols. 628–9W).

Value for money: bad buys and poverty-induced costs

The poor are as affected by variable value for money as they are by changing income. Yet surprisingly little attention has been paid to value compared with that paid to income.

The trickle of books specifically on value for poor people started with Caplovitz's book *The Poor Pay More* (1963), followed by Piachaud's pamphlet *Do the Poor Pay More?* (1974), and later by the NCC book *Why the Poor Pay More* (1977).

Caplovitz's book, to which reference has already been made, is primarily about consumption and marketing practice. However, it established that in some circumstances these can lead to reduced value for money. Piachaud widened the scope of the subject and discussed other factors that may cause the poor to pay more.

The NCC book was an ambitious attempt to develop the concept into one of consumer detriment. Williams, in the introductory chapter, explained that it arises where 'poor people get less or worse quality goods and services, pound for pound spent than richer ones'. Williams emphasised that detriment is a separate dimension from that of income but both are relevant to inequality. The term 'detriment' was interpreted fairly freely so as to include, as well as the straightforward cases of poor value, circumstances where 'value' for the individual is affected by part of the cost being paid by external sources, as is the case with car expenses for example.

'The poor pay more' is a simple phrase which covers many circumstances. Paying more may take the form of reduced value or additional cost and it may arise from consumer circumstances or the market situation.

Consumer Circumstances

Consumer circumstances affecting value for money are varied and complex. In a strictly purist sense, consumers possess complete freedom and buy what they want. Hence value, in terms of their own judgement of it, is a somewhat elusive concept. More usefully, it can be argued that the poor as consumers have freedom, but pressures act upon them which affect their consumption pattern. The Consumers' Association magazine *Which*? makes frequent use of the notation 'best buy'. Using the inverse, the poor suffer unduly from 'bad buys' for two major sets of reasons: inadequate income and capital and lack of knowledge. Included in the former category is the loss of flexibility which results from having to balance a tight budget every week.

Low Levels of Income and Capital

A low level of resources is a major cause of people getting reduced value for money. Of the four reasons Williams (1977) gave for consumer detriment, three related to low income and little capital. The poor cannot afford to buy in large quantities; they cannot afford cars and so cannot travel to the cheaper shops; and being paid weekly discourages the kind of capital spending which can save money in the long run.

Aird (1977) stressed the 'enormous' value for money variations there are for practically every product. He pointed out that there was no evidence that poor people have some natural 'nose' for good buys rather than bad ones, and he added that what sketchy evidence there is suggests the opposite. For example, NCC tests in 1975 on clothes bought from tallymen – a source of goods mainly used by poor people – showed that although they cost more than similar clothes from ordinary shops, they were poorly made up, used unsuitable material, and were out of fashion. The poor value obtained is partly disguised by payment being made in small weekly amounts.

In some circumstances, getting a 'bad buy' is more visible but a low level of resources makes it unavoidable. Fuel is a good example. Because of their low income, the poor are less likely to have central heating and well-insulated houses, although this may be less true of those living in local authority housing.

Electric fires are more likely to be bought than gas fires which are more expensive to buy and install but cheaper to run. Low incomes tend to lead to less fuel being used and so to higher tariffs. Aird (1977) compared a poor family using electric fires with a richer one in an insulated house with central heating and on a cheap gas tariff. To keep their house warm, the poor family would spend £44; the same amount of warmth would cost the rich family £6. Aird acknowledged that this was an extreme example, and using figures from the NCC fuel survey (1976c), based on all fuels, he calculated that, on average, poor families paid 36% extra for their warmth. He did not analyse the contribution made to this by the various factors – type of fuel, unit cost of fuel and insulation. But his figures suggested that the poorer families used a larger proportion of solid fuel which for them was particularly expensive and a smaller proportion of gas which at the time was the cheapest fuel.

Marsden (1969) provided a further illustration of the diverse ways in which circumstances can reduce value. He found that eight of the 116 lone parents that he studied were using small expensive bags of fuel. Their income was so low that they could afford only one or two normal sized bags, and the coal man would not deliver such small numbers. The mothers had to buy bags of a size that they could carry, and these were of high unit cost.

Poor families tend not have the liquidity and flexibility that savings and a good credit status provide. As a result they may have difficulty in achieving the regular and frequent balance of income and expenditure which is required of them, and this can lead to additional costs. Marsden and Duff (1975), in their study of unemployed families, noted the selling of £20 club tickets for £16 in cash. The money was needed for the immediate payment of bills and as a result the family lost 20% of the face value of the ticket as well as having to pay the credit charge imposed by the club. A similar situation was described by Land (1969). A low income mother of a large family had to sell her sewing machine. She was quoted as saying, 'have to pay more for clothes now but . . . we needed food'. Land commented, 'Economising and saving were luxuries she could no longer afford.'

Coates and Silburn (1970), in their study of housing conditions in a very poor area of Nottingham, gave several examples of the wasteful nature of poverty-induced costs arising from housing conditions. Water cost more to heat where there was no proper hot water system. Damp caused high fuel bills; if clothes were not well-aired they got mildew. Decorating was more frequent because of damp, and money for protective action against it could not be afforded. Coates and Silburn commented on the costs arising from these deprived conditions. 'The expense of the necessary heating and drying is not only considerable but is ultimately hopeless . . . not a tax . . . which ultimately augments a person's living standards, but like protection money, it merely staves off for a little longer, an absolute loss.'

Consumer Ignorance
Ignorance is often given as a reason for poor value being obtained for money. As the earlier discussion of credit has shown, it can undoubtedly lead to a more costly choice although, in the credit market, ignorance operates in a subtle manner.

Lack of knowledge is no less important in the wider consumer market place. Aird (1977) stressed its crucial role: 'Perhaps the greatest personal obstacle preventing a poor shopper getting good value for money is simply lack of information.' He quoted NOP polls of 1975 and 1976 on 'Consumerism' and 'Shopping Problems' in support of his view. They suggested that customers rely mainly on shops for information and, in large shops, assistants take money and 'don't seem to be able to advise on anything'. Aird added that a NCC survey found that rich people were up to four times more likely than the poor to know of specialist or generalist consumer councils, and one in four or five richer people said they read the Consumers' Association magazine *Which?* as a source of shopping advice while poorer people tend to rely on advertisements instead. Aird gave no figures for the use of consumer councils, but it is known to be generally low. His comments seem to suggest that although there are differences between rich and poor, the vast majority of the population, rich and poor alike, when they require consumer advice, rely on shop assistants rather than experts. If so, it is not surprising that ignorance is a cause of poor buys.

Caplovitz (1974) in his study of debtors in three American cities, found that the well off were just as vulnerable to deception as the poor, except for the important qualification that the characteristics of people channel them to particular types of sellers. He felt that there should be more emphasis on changes relating to the seller rather than to the debtor. Caplovitz noted also that working class people took their problems to professionals less often than did people in other strata. He went on to comment that, 'It seems ironic that merchants in low income areas – exploiters if you will – are more prepared to organise their services to fit the special requirements of the consumer than are the public agencies to deal with their troubles.'

Illiteracy referred to by the Birmingham Settlement Money Advice Centre author interview, 1979) as being a factor in debt problems, must obviously limit understanding of money matters. Its role has been little discussed, and it is not possible, at present, to assess its importance.

The Office of Fair Trading is the Government body with the responsibility of spreading information about consumer problems and related law. Although conscious of the need to reach those most in need of help, the Office of Fair Trading in its First Report (1975) considered it to be a 'long-term challenge' and an 'immense' task. The Second Report (1976) commented on the difficulty for all but the most sophisticated of understanding consumer law. It noted that even many shopkeepers are ignorant of the meaning of the term 'merchantable quality'.

Market Influence

The workings of the market readily cause variations in value or additional costs. One obvious, but rather neglected, cause of bad value is defectiveness of goods. The Office of Fair Trading (1981a) received notice of 531,470 consumer complaints in 1980, but the number does not indicate the size of the problem because many people are reluctant to complain. A high proportion (38%) of those who bought on hire purchase in the OFT/NOP survey complained or wanted to do so because the goods were defective. Ison (1979) found a smaller percentage (18%) complaining of the condition of the goods but his survey included all forms of purchase. The figures above relate to the population as a whole, but it is reasonable to assume that poor people, because they buy cheaper goods, are more likely to find them defective.

A more subtle influence of the market is the effect of where people shop or their 'shopping scope' as Caplovitz termed it. His early work (1963) indicated that shopping scope affected the value obtained for money, although it was not as important as the variation arising from the use of credit. The people Caplovitz studied were poor, and a high proportion were coloured. It is not surprising therefore that he found that shopping scope was affected by the degree of sophistication in the ways of urban society, including knowledge of English.

The Crowther Committee (Department of Trade and Industry, 1971a) noted the pressures to shop in the local market. Its report referred to the semi-captive market possessed by local traders because of people's inability to get credit elsewhere, their shyness, and the cost and inconvenience of moving outside. Baldwin (1973) gave a simple and succinct description of a pressure which restrains poor people from shopping in middle class shops which give better value for money. The shops were 'snooty', and were thus alien to the poor.

The relevance of shopping scope to value for money was developed by Piachaud (1974). He examined various shopping studies, and concluded that, although the evidence was slight, a picture emerged of people in lower social groups living in low income areas, using small local shops. These provided a personal, indeed social, service that could not be measured in terms of price. But the price of goods was higher. In extreme circumstances where there was a combination of adverse factors such as the consumers being unable to buy cheaper 'own brand' goods from supermarkets and buying only more expensive small size packs, Piachaud estimated that the additional cost could be as much as 40% above the average. In general he found that the total cost of selected items was, on average, 8.3% dearer in small shops than in supermarkets. Calculating on a different basis and expressing it in terms of detriment, Aird (1977) derived an average figure of 5–6% for food.

An extreme example of the effect that shopping scope can have on living costs is illustrated by the circumstances of the inhabitants of the island of Colonsay in the Inner Hebrides, who claimed additional supplementary benefit on the grounds of exceptional circumstances arising from a higher cost of living on the island compared with the mainland. Food cost 20% more and electricity four times as much. In 1981, the islanders' case went to the House of Lords who ruled against them. The higher cost of living was not disputed, but it was not considered to be an exceptional circumstance in the terms of the Supplementary Benefit Act.

The relationship between shopping scope and value for money is not a simple one. Supermarkets in working class areas are often keenly competitive. Compared with middle class areas, the emphasis tends to be more on price than on service, and goods are often left in cardboard boxes rather than displayed. Market stalls tend to have the lowest prices of all, mainly because of high turnover and low overheads. But mobility is usually needed to get the best value. Those unable to travel because of cost, time or infirmity, and thus dependent on corner shops will almost certainly pay more. For some, the corner shop has the advantage of providing credit for small everyday purchases which is not available at the larger shops. But to secure the credit, the customer has to pay the higher corner shop prices.

The Market Response to Savings and Insurance Needs
In general, poor people have few savings, but value for money is as important in relation to savings as it is to consumption. Masey (1977) reviewed the options available. She pointed out that the poor have particular savings requirements which are not of interest to commercial organisations. They are able to save only small sums usually at irregular intervals, and withdrawals may be necessary at short notice. Masey suggested that these requirements can only be met by a government-supported scheme. Inflation led to a negative return for most of the decade that preceded the time of Masey's writing. National Savings, popular with poor people, had almost halved in real value. The only savings guaranteed not to do so had been index-linked SAYE schemes and retirement bonds for the elderly. Despite index-linking SAYE schemes are unsuitable for poor people because such schemes demand regular savings which are locked away for long periods. In September 1981, index-linked National Savings similar to retirement bonds were made available to everyone irrespective of age, subject only to a maximum holding of £3000, increased to £5000 in October 1981. The limit is unlikely to trouble poor people, but the scheme is not as simple to use nor as familiar as the post office savings book. The extent to which poor people will use index-linked bonds as a secure and inflation-proofed home for any savings they may have remains to be seen. Parker (1980) commented that for clients of the Birmingham Settlement Money Advice Centre exhortations to save had a 'hollow ring'. In addition, a decline in the rate of inflation, as happened in 1982, makes index-linking less necessary.

Insurance is another area where poor people tend to get reduced value. The prevalance of small insurance policies amongst low income groups has been noted by many writers, and the lapsing of policies leading to loss of money is referred to by Marsden (1969), Land (1969) and Baldwin (1973). Masey (1977) described the two systems of life insurance, ordinary insurance and industrial life. The latter is sold only on a door-to-door basis and gives a low return for the money spent in premiums. Expenses are high, ranging from 32 to 52 pence in the £, compared with 18 pence for ordinary insurance. The percentage of policies that lapse, giving nothing back to the policyholder, is also high, ranging from 8 to 47% for different companies in 1975. The intractable difficulty is that poor people need or prefer door-to-door collection, and this inevitably raises costs, leading to poor return on the premiums paid. Masey called for more widely available comparative information, greater use of conversion of the policies to ordinary ones, and more experiment in paying methods. Although much of the apparent poor value of the policies arises from the cost of the additional service of door-to-door collection, the range of Masey's proposals suggests that it would be possible to improve, even if only slightly, the poor return on the policies. In 1980, those with capital greater than £2000 became ineligible for SB, and the paid-up value of any insurance policies was included in capital. Paid-up value, i.e. the value when there is early termination, is usually very low. This is helpful if it leads to eligibility for SB, but damaging to those ineligible who may be forced to cash in their policies. These people will get a poor return on the premiums they have paid. The change in SB policy strengthens the need for a fresh assessment of insurance schemes used by poor people.

Differential price increases
A different type of poverty-induced cost is a differential price increase. The real cost of living for a family depends on the prices of the goods and services that the family consumes, and not on the official retail price index which reflects the average cost of living for the population. Food, housing and fuel have weights of 22.8, 17.8 and 14.3 per 100 respectively, in the official index. Poor people tend to spend a higher percentage of their income on these necessities. If the price rises for one or more of them are significantly higher than price rises in general, there will be an adverse differential price rise for poor people.

There is no dispute that there is usually an adverse differential, but there is controversy about its size. A special price index for pensioners has been calculated since the mid-1960s, but there is not an official one for low income groups. Pond (1977) outlined the history of the controversy, and argued that the official retail price index 'substantially underestimates' the rate of inflation that low income groups experience.

Pond analysed the low income prices indices that had been produced by Tipping (1970), Piachaud (1976) and Muellbauer (1974), noting that they all agreed that lower income groups suffer more from inflation than the rest of the population. But the extent of the difference depends on the years chosen for analysis and the sophistication of the method used. The Low Pay Unit (1977) reported to the RCDIW that their specially constructed price indices rose by 77.8% for low income households and 73.2% for high income ones during the period March 1974 to March 1977 (Pond, 1977).

Muellbauer (1978) divided the 30 years between 1946 and 1976 into five-year periods, and claimed that the evidence showed that in four out of six periods there was 'substantial bias' against the poor in the retail price index. This differential inflation more than wiped out the modest equalising trend in money incomes which had occurred between 1957 and 1974.

A major criticism made by Muellbauer (1978) was that the weighting of the retail price index corresponded to the expenditure pattern of a family approximately two-thirds of the way up the income distribution because weights are based on the average expenditure on an item expressed as a percentage of total expenditure, and this method of weighting gives the expenditure of the rich a greater importance. In an article in the Department of Employment *Gazette* (1979) it was argued that a 'democratic' index would differ only 'a little' from the RPI, but no estimate of the size of the difference was given. The same article responded directly to the criticism made by the Low Pay Unit. It concluded that 'the difference in the expense of low income households is small and . . . not sufficient to justify the calculation of a separate monthly official index. To support its conclusion, the article gave the following details of changes in the RPI and the two-person pensioner index:

	RPI	Two-person pensioner
January 1974	100	100
December 1978	206.7	207.4

The figures for a low income index would lie between the two. However, the *Gazette* did not give figures for the years used by the Low Pay Unit.

In addition, Pond argued that the difference between the two indices 'almost certainly understates the true bias of inflation', because the poorest may have to pay higher unit prices for basic goods and the weighting for the pensioner index does not truly represent the pattern of expenditure of the poorest.

The controversy is fundamentally about the methodology of constructing price indices. It is important because unless there is an accurate estimate of the burden of inflation on poor people, it will not be compensated for in wage negotiations, nor by appropriate changes in the levels of social security.

The literature on the money environment indicates some areas where low income families may be at a disadvantage because of circumstance, attitude or ignorance. The credit market is the area which has been most investigated. Constraints on the granting of too much credit are slight while inducements to use it are strong and sometimes undesirably so. Poor people tend to pay higher charges for credit which are not always justified and are in part the result of an unquestioning acceptance of credit systems whose use has become embedded in a life-style.

Unquestioning acceptance and lack of knowledge and sophistication make poor people vulnerable to marketing pressure and dubious selling methods. British evidence is slight but it leaves little doubt that advantage is taken of some people.

'Value for money' is by no means a simple issue in the money environment. Restricted shopping scope, inadequate knowledge and lack of initiative may all inhibit wise buying, while low levels of income and capital can induce a variety of additional costs.

Overall, academic interest in the social implications of an adverse money environment has not been strong but it is growing. The disadvantages suffered by poor people can be indicated but the detail of many topics relevant to the depriving effect of an adverse money environment has still to be explored.

7 Money Management

The adequacy of income in relation to wants is central to a family's welfare. Matching the wants permitted by the income with purchases over time is a secondary but still important matter. It can be a demanding process requiring skill in money management. The more effectively it is done, the greater is the subjective value of the money available to a family. In relation to money problems, money management is a modifying force comparable with the money environment.

Money management usually becomes a matter of interest to those outside the family only when there are social problems requiring outside help. When help is needed, it is often presumed that there has been a failure to manage financially. Inability to budget may or may not be the cause of such difficulties but it is one to which there is frequent and prominent reference. For example, the joint report of the SBC and Local Authority Social Services Departments (1976) observed, 'Some requests for help may represent an inability to budget within the limits of his available financial resources.' In 1980, Circular S/5 to be used by SB officials was reported (*Guardian*, 9 October 1982) to contain the words, 'A repeated need for such ENPs probably indicates an inability to cope with essential living expenses which in turn suggests persistent financial mismanagement . . .' The latter comment approaches the extreme position of those who blame faulty budgeting for every failure to manage, while the former is more centrally placed between that extreme and the other one of attributing failure entirely to inadequacy of resources.

Budgeting and coping
'Money management' is a general term being used to imply some conscious effort to ensure that money is spent roughly according to family preferences and that predictable financial crises do not arise. Budgeting is a more precise word implying some form of allocating process to ensure that a family retains the liquidity required for day-to-day living, and that income matches with expenditure over a longer period. Efficient budgeting will take account of changes in relative

65 poor families in contact with the Family Service Units (FSU) commented that, 'When families have too little money, every bill paid means a shortage of funds elsewhere. It is the accumulation of necessary expenditure on a low income which causes families such financial difficulties.'

Goldring (1973), writing about the work of the FSU with problem families, described various approaches to coping: 'many have found their own ways of coming to terms with their situation, by cheerfully ignoring it, by manipulating available services, by going to bed or by living in a fantasy world'. One example is that of the families helped by the Brotherhood of St. Lawrence in Melbourne, Australia, who coped by developing expertise to convince social workers that they were deserving and needed charity. Salmon (1974) referred to it as a humiliating experience but the only method which continually provided them with financial aid.

Those who cope rather than manage their money are obviously likely to get into debt. But when this happens, people again cope by avoiding confrontation and hence a crisis over their debts. In his study of fuel debts in Manchester, Hesketh (1978) found that administrative decisions triggered crises, and the timing of the trigger related more to the attitudes of those in authority than to the level of debt. Families coped by robbing Peter to pay Paul and by taking advantage of time lags in procedures to postpone the onset of crises. Marsden (1975) wrote similarly about unemployed families. 'Budgeting had come to involve the calculation of which debts could be missed this week, and court orders became part of the way of life.' The skill which some families displayed in judging which debt must be given priority was noted by Hesketh (1978).

Land (1969) found that amongst the large families she studied, one of the worst aspects of poverty was the lack of reserves. They had nothing for emergencies, or for crises. The poorer families felt they were perpetually on the edge of a crisis. Some had one every week, resulting in regular borrowing from neighbours, relatives, money lenders and pawn shops. Blamire of the Birmingham Settlement Money Advice Centre has also spoken (author interview, 1979) of the lack of a 'cushion' amongst those who came for help from the centre.

For many low income families, money management appears to range from coping in almost any way possible, to more calculated forms of budgeting, with credit playing an important role. Whether the particular method affects the standard of living is mainly unobserved or unrecorded. Exceptionally, Marsden (1969) noted 'it was very difficult to see whether the mother's particular method of housekeeping made much difference to the family's standard of living. The ability to buy coal in bulk rather than in small bags, payment for clothing in cash rather than by checks . . . were time and again found to be not marks of superior thrift so much as indications of greater income or outside help or smaller needs.'

The non-copers
At one extreme of money management is the meticulous allocation of pennies to various commitments. At the other is a wayward disorganised casualness. Those with adequate incomes can surmount the financial hazards which accompany this style of living, but where income is low, families are likely to be non-copers – although they are not always easily distinguishable from those that just cope. Some of the non-copers have become known as problem families.

Philp and Timms (1957), in their review of the literature on problem families, concluded that the term is ill-defined, and is probably best left that way. Problem families are largely a self-selected group because usually they are only identified when they seek help.

Although the difficulties of problem families do not relate only to money, one of their accepted characteristics is financial mismanagement and debt. An early and vivid account of the way of life in 62 families was given by Stephens (1946). He wrote of the disorder in their lives, of rent almost always in arrears, of deferred debts being regarded as the last charge on income, and of mothers paying out allowances as soon as they received them against a multitude of loans and shopkeepers' bills which occurred again almost immediately. Many years later Burghes (1980), writing about families requiring help from the FSU, noted the 'shuffling of debts and the repayment of only those immediately pressing'.

Ashton (1956) described problem families as being 'lawless in the economic sense . . . [they have] an irrational disregard of ordinary common-sense management of income'. However Philp and Timms (1957) disputed the causal effect of bad money management. They suggested that attempts to assess problem families are heavily influenced by a general notion that primary poverty is abolished, and hence poverty must be due to mismanagement. They went on to say that estimates of the effect of the presence of primary poverty vary, but there is a more general agreement 'that it would take more intelligence and more stability than that possessed by most problem families to budget on the income provided and to balance successfully long term and immediate needs'. Problem families tend to have a larger number of children than the average family and, as this review has already indicated, this fact alone would tend to make them vulnerable to money problems. But there are no detailed studies of their budgets to show the nature of financial pressures upon them.

Philp and Timms (1957) and Blacker (1952) described the chequered history of the concept of a problem family group. Booth's surveys (1886–1901) originated the idea of a 'submerged tenth'. The Mental Deficiency (Wood) Committee (1929) introduced the term 'Social Problem Group' and the Departmental Committee on Sterilisation (Brock) Committee agreed that 'low mentality and poor environment form a vicious cycle'. A letter in *New Statesman* on 5 May 1945 called for a survey of problems including a study of three generations. Various reports and investigations followed, usually with children as the starting-point. The most important, edited by Blacker (1952), *Problem Families: Five Enquiries*, surveyed families from five areas. The selection of the families was influenced by the interest in them of the local Medical Officer of Health, and the interviews were done by local authority staff. This survey was strongly criticised, primarily because it defined the families in terms of symptoms, not essential conditions or causes (Hinchcliffe, 1953). Partly because of the criticism Blacker's study marked the end of a period of research into problem families, although workers in Sheffield continued to observe the situation of some local problem families and their off-spring (e.g. Tonge, James and Hillam, 1975; Tonge, Lunn, Greathead and McLaren, 1979).

Descriptions of the way of life of problem families are discouraging. Tonge, James and Hillam (1975) uncovered a 'mosaic of maladjustment' in their study of the psychiatric pathology involved. Another psychiatrist, Irvine (1954), commented on the 'lack of foresight', 'no sense of the value of money', 'no sense of time', and 'no sense of property'. She suggested that the symptoms indicated an extreme immaturity.

Sufficient evidence exists to confirm that many problem families live in a state of financial chaos, frequently accompanied by a general lack of organisation. But there is no accepted view of their numbers, the reasons for their life-style, or the long-term implications. Philp and Timms (1957) drew attention to the paucity of detailed studies of causes of problem families, and complained that those published are totally inadequate. 'They give no idea of family relationships and the dynamics of family life.' It is worth noting that members of problem families may not feel that the consequences are necessarily all adverse. Tonge *et al*. (1979) found that the married sons and daughters, and in particular the daughters, were appreciably more cheerful than the married children of a comparison group.

The feeling of hopelessness, almost a state of disorientation which overwhelms some families, appears in other literature besides that on problem families. Blamire and Izzard (1978) of the Birmingham Settlement Money Advice Centre, in their booklet on debt counselling, referred to the ostrich-like behaviour of some of those they help. These people try to ignore the problem, hoping and deluding themselves that it will go away. Blamire had also spoken (author interview, 1979) of the unrealistic view some people have of debts over £50. The addition of noughts tends to make the debt meaningless. He added that some of his clients were totally haphazard. Some gave priority to rent, others didn't. Some functioned by pretending not to be in, others worked on the robbing Peter to pay Paul system. Every case was unique and few patterns were discernible.

A similar sense of unreality was observed by Heywood and Allen (1971) in an early study of the use of Section 1 payments. They referred to a report on homeless families which noted that many of the families (under threat of eviction) seem 'only dimly aware of the reality of the threat of eviction or else are taking no steps to avert it'. Those imprisoned for debt are another group described in this way. The Payne Committee on the Enforcement of Judgement Debts (Lord High Chanceller's office, 1969) referred to prison governors having an almost unanimous view that the majority of civil debtors in prison are 'social inadequates, people incapable of managing their affairs and overwhelmed by the burden of debt'. The Committee concluded that the vast majority are inadequate, unfortunate, feckless or irresponsible persons; but they are for the most part not dishonest.

The evidence suggests that a very small minority of families, who are not typical poor people, have virtually no system of money management, not even coping. This may happen for a number of reasons such as intent, inability or no knowledge of what is required for a simple budgetary system. It could also be for external reasons such as circumstances so adverse or so variable as to make even minimal money management appear futile. Evason (1980), in her discussion of the debt problem of low income families in Northern Ireland, suggested that where the normal expectation of paying one's way is 'unrealistic', and households are faced with 'unrealistic' demands, one predictable and unsurprising reaction is to 'give up attempts to manage altogether. . . .'

The budget cycle

For low income families the rhythm of expenditure is often closely tied to the rhythm of the receipt of income: the lower the income, the closer the tie, and the greater the difficulties that arise if demands for money do not accord with the income cycle.

Jahoda, Lazarsfeld and Zeisel (1933) described how the timing of unemployment payments dominated the life of a small unemployed community. 'The entire economic life moves in this fortnightly cycle.' The debts were paid off as far as possible the day the unemployment relief was paid. The family meals improved. The children took a better lunch to school the day after. As the days passed the meals deteriorated and debts rose until the next pay-day when the cycle recommenced.

In Britain 40 years later, the cycle is still important for some families although the duration is different. The habit of buying on credit and paying weekly has already been discussed. Parker (1980) drew attention to its strength amongst some of the lower class families who asked the Birmingham Settlement Money Advice Centre for help, when she observed that, for these people, overall cost of purchases was not as important as whether the instalment could be fitted into the weekly budget and goods not bought on the weekly were not bought at all (NCC, 1980). Land (1969) described how some of the large families she studied were caught on daily or weekly cycles. They bought most of their food daily but even so they were short on Thursday. The family allowance was vital for these families, both for the amount and because it was paid on Tuesday, thus providing some money for the mid-week days before wages were paid at the weekend. Brown (1964), in a study of ways of helping homeless people in Manchester, noted that some wage-earners tried to solve their problems by buying cheap properties. 'But such families are accustomed to a weekly budget and tend to have no resources to meet the sudden large demands for repairs or rates.'

Goldring (1973), writing about problem families helped by the Family Services Unit, acknowledged the importance of the cycle when he wrote, 'A case worker who collects rent every week on the day the family receives its pay packet or social security payment performs a vital service which can make the difference between a family managing and not managing.' Goldring also noted the almost predictable response of some families to the arrival of quarterly bills. 'By their habits of mind and because of the practical realities of their situation they [FSU families] cannot think in terms of saving money they have not got for a contingency three months in the future.' 'No provision is made for electricity and the bill for a sum of money outside their usual expenses comes as a great shock.' This attitude inevitably leads to debt.

Acknowledgement of the financial cycle may be important not only for the avoidance of debt but for the greater welfare of families. Marsden (1969) noticed that the sense of deprivation amongst lone mothers on social security was heightened because they did not get their incomes at the same time as most families. They were out of time with the life of the community and with their own former pattern of spending.

Control and distribution of money within the family

Distribution of money within the family is relevant to deprivation, because the welfare of children is as much, if not more, affected by the level of housekeeping money as by the size of the family income. Surveys have shown that the two do not always correlate. Young (1977) in an article entitled 'Housekeeping money' quoted two NCC surveys of June 1975 and May 1977 which showed that although overall money given to the wives by their husbands during each of the years preceding the surveys, had gone up by more than the husband's net earnings – 26% and 16% compared with 13% and 7% increases in net earnings – 31% of the wives said they had had no more in the last year, and the poorest wives suffered most. This was not entirely avoidable because many of the poor husbands had had no pay increases. When they did, they passed a generous proportion on. The wives who had most reason to complain were those of one-fifth of the husbands who had pay increases and passed none of it on to their wives.

Young raised the question of whether family income is a 'faulty compass' for social security and the study of poverty. He made the logically attractive but administratively difficult suggestion that the qualifying income used for remission of charges of school meals should be 'not that of the husband but that of the wife including any money she gets from him'. The implication is that wives are not given their appropriate share of family income but no satisfactory definition of this has been attempted.

There is little reliable evidence about inter-family distribution of income despite its importance. The OPCS (1981) gave the reason for this when it commented that the household is the smallest feasible unit for the collection of useful figures. 'To attempt to measure expenditure for part of a household would involve sorting out a complex pattern of intra-household transactions, many of which can be ill-defined by household members.'

Research in this area presents other obvious difficulties. Merely considering the proportion of family income that the wife receives for housekeeping money is useless without information about the expenditure for which she is responsible. Questions on the topic can be sensitive, particularly if the inter-family distribution differs significantly from the norm for the local community. The crucial replies may be evaded or distorted. A further problem is that maldistribution serious enough to cause real hardship is likely to be relatively rare in a random sample and reliable conclusions could not be drawn about its nature and incidence unless the sample size was large.

One of the few representative surveys has been a small Australian one by Edwards (1981) based on a quota sample of 50 families. Both husband and wife were interviewed and Edwards felt that the expense was justified by the extra information that two interviews provided about the financial decision-making process in the family. Although the sample was small, the study provided interesting pointers for further research. Edwards concluded that 'if the level of personal spending money is taken to be a major factor in the distribution of income within the family . . . there was an inadequate transfer of income from husbands as main income recipients to their wives'. The interpretation of personal spending was inconclusive and the data were far from complete. Nevertheless the study showed a strong tendency for the husband's spending to be considered by both parties to be 'committed expenditure' in the same category as urgent bills. In eight of the families where the wife spent on herself only when desperate, five of the husbands had set amounts of spending money and the other three took it as they wanted. Amongst these families, one husband had personal spending money consisting of over 30% of take-home pay, another had 10%, and three had over 5%. Overall, the husband's spending money did not vary with his or the family's income level as much as Edwards had expected. In many cases, personal spending was equated with the money to be used at the pub once a week.

Most British comment on maldistribution refers to people with special problems, but it generally supports the findings of the more representative Australian study. For example, the Birmingham Settlement Money Advice Centre considered the husband's contribution to be inadequate in as many as 50% of the families it helped (author interview, 1979).

Philp and Timms (1957), writing about problem families, indicated the type of situation that can arise when money is not fairly shared. 'Debts are very frequent with bizarre patterns of borrowing in some neighbourhoods. The mother has no resort to these chancy ways . . . because the father fails to give her a fair share of the income or fails through sickness and instability to work regularly . . . he often keeps what seems to outside observers a disproportionate amount of income.' Philp and Timms viewed this tolerantly, suggesting that it could be seen as part of the husband's social role – a view unlikely to be universally shared.

A more forthright remark was made in response to the question put by Spencer and Crookston (1978) to SB officers: 'Who most needs social work help?' One of them replied, 'Families where the husband is unemployed and where he boozes the money and doesn't give it to the wife. There are an awful lot of families where the wife is virtually having to live off the family allowance.'

It is not known whether such situations are frequent or rare. Marsden and Duff (1975) noted that in one of the 12 unemployed families they studied, hardship was caused by the father's inflexible demands for money for himself. But it was more common for men not to eat properly because they worried that the children might not be getting enough.

Marsden (1969), in his study of 116 lone mothers and their children living on SB, found that one in six of one group of mothers said they were no worse off than they had been when married, and one in three said they were better off on SB. In other words, overall only half the women got more from their husbands when they were married than they got from SB. However, the husband's income during the life of the marriage was not given, so the extent of 'unfair' sharing can only be guessed at. The fact that the married women in Marsden's study had left their husbands indicates there was an unsatisfactory relationship which may have affected – or been affected by – the unfair sharing of money between the partners. Although almost certainly untypical, the circumstances of some of the women showed the extent to which 'unfair' sharing can be taken. During her marriage, one divorced woman was reported as having to live for three days on nettles from the garden, and at other times on what she could collect by returning her husband's empty beer bottles. Another one went from pub to pub to get money from her husband for food.

A.M. Gray's (1974) investigation into the housekeeping arrangements of 97 manual workers in Edinburgh is one of the few research studies into budgeting. She found that the most typical housekeeping arrangement was that where the husband retained some money for himself and gave the wife an allowance to meet most or sometimes all of the housekeeping expenses. The 'whole wage system' where the wife was given the wage, returning pocket money to the husband, was rare, as was the pooling of all money with no firm allocation of budgeting responsibilities. She distinguished between two types of system. In one, the husband was responsible for at least one major housekeeping item and in the other the wife was given all the housekeeping money and was completely responsible. The husband's involvement led to him being more willing to do voluntary overtime, and the additional earnings were more likely to go into the housekeeping purse. Gray felt that the rent arrears of 23 families could be attributed to bad management, with six of them illustrating in an extreme form the husband's non-involvement in budgeting. She suggested that the greater involvement of the husband in some budgeting might be a solution to budgetary problems. However, Salmon (1974), writing about the experimental income supplement scheme run by the Brotherhood of St. Lawrence in Melbourne, Australia, reported that the families being helped in Melbourne generally managed more successfully if the income was handled by the women, although he found that most of the wives in two-parent families had no certainty that they would keep the money their husbands had given them. The conflict between the conclusions of Gray and Salmon may arise from the fact that Gray's families had working heads able to increase the family income if they chose, whereas many of the Australians were on fixed benefit. Land (1969) noticed that as income declined, and particularly as the source moved from wages to social security, the primary responsibility for managing it moved from the husband to the wife.

In her Australian study, Edwards (1981) distinguished between four types of financial management: wife management, husband management, joint management, and independent management. The most popular type occurring in about half of the 50 families was management by the wife. This included cases were the husband's unopened pay packet was handed over and where a deduction for personal spending was first made. Eleven families kept their finances independent, while there were seven families in each of the other two categories. Regrettably Edwards did not give information on how the type of management varied with income level and with the wife's earnings. However she made a sharp distinction between management and financial control. In just over half the cases there was joint control, in a further 40% of cases husbands had 'much more say' than wives, and only three wives had overall control. In general the wives tended to manage but not control. The effect of level of income on inter-family distribution is referred to by Pahl (1979), who looked at the patterns of money management in the marriages of 25 battered wives, 14 of whom received either no money or an 'unreasonably low' amount from their husbands. She found that the 'whole wage' system was more common when incomes were low. In these situations Pahl suggested that managing the budget was a chore rather than a source of power within the marriage. The 'allowance' system was the most widespread and most complicated, and the allowance tended to relate not to the husbands' wages but to some community norm, which supported Edward's similar finding. A 'pooling' system characterised couples, both of whom worked, although sometimes the woman's earnings went mainly to pay for items of collective family expenditure. Pahl related the distribution of income within the household to poverty and social policy. She argued that decisions about sharing income are related to deeply rooted cultural values about 'the nature of the sex roles and the sexual division of labour', and that poverty is concealed 'by assuming that all the income . . . is shared among all members of the family', although she acknowledged that relatively little is known about the extent of hidden poverty amongst the dependants of heads of household.

G. Parker (1980) found that, in a sample of clients of the Birmingham Settlement Money Advice Centre who had debt difficulties, almost half of the husbands in two-partner households took no part in the financial arrangements other than handing over the wages or the housekeeping allowance. Even when there were serious debt problems husbands gave their wives 'totally inadequate' allowances. Parker suggested that use of a system inappropriate to household income many lead to financial problems. She felt that a whole wage system would be more suitable for those households that had a low total income.

To a very large extent, the manner in which husbands and wives manage their money remains a personal and undisclosed matter. But there are indications that, at all levels of income, the husband's share of available spending money takes priority over the wife's, and the amount the husband personally spends can be influenced more by local custom than by whether it can reasonably be afforded. Money problems arise either when the family income is so low that the customary amount can not possibly be afforded or when the husband takes a totally disproportionate share. If, because of his lack of involvement in the family's financial affairs, the husband is unaware of the problem that his level of spending brings, the solution of involving him, is obvious. If, however, it is a question not of unawareness but of determination to maintain a life-style, the problems that arise are of a different nature, and they have no easy or obvious solutions.

The housekeeping contribution made by children who work and live at home was criticised by Young (1977). In an NCC survey discussed by Young 60% of sons and 64% of daughters made no increase at all in their contribution in 1976/7. Young described them as a privileged class, living at home at small expense, and having large amounts of money left over for discretionary spending and treating their mothers shabbily. The Birmingham Settlement Money Advice Centre has been equally critical of the housekeeping contribution made by working children. In conversation (author interview, 1979) it was suggested that some parents may be going into debt because they are subsidising their children by amounts of up to £10 a week. Philp (1963) and Land (1969) both observed the same phenomenon. Less than half the home-based working children in the FSU families studied by Philp made contributions which were both adequate and regular, while Land commented in her survey that the children's contribution to the income of the large families was small – rarely more than £3 a week.

In his discussion of the effect of income maintenance payments on poverty in Britain, Beckerman (1979) commented, 'One of the biggest gaps in our knowledge of poverty is our complete ignorance about the degree of income-sharing in multiple-unit households.'

The evidence, although largely anecdotal, supports Beckerman's view. Without doubt there is maldistribution of income within the family, but little is known about incidence and severity nor about the effect on the style of living of women and their children. But where low income and maldistribution within the family coincide, the wife and any children face severe problems, for they have not even the safety net of SB.

The literature on money management relates more to the problems that arise as a partial consequence of its failure than to the nature of money management itself. Very little is known of the style or effectiveness of common budgeting practices. The role of faulty money management in contributing to social problems is difficult to assess because of the paucity of the evidence. There is a danger that it may become a scapegoat substitute for other causes of social problems. But that does not mean that the importance of money management should be denied. The views of the Birmingham Settlement Money Advice Centre and the work on problem families make it clear that serious money management difficulties can arise and they are probably more common amongst low income families who are happiest with a weekly budgeting cycle. This type of problem has been generally neglected except by a few pioneering groups.

8 Debt Difficulties

The repercussions of money problems are likely to be as subtle and varied as the causes of them. But a direct and obvious consequence is debt, using the word in its colloquial sense. More precisely, debt is money that is owed, and it is not necessarily a problem. As the counterbalance to credit, it is an essential and generally desirable part of sophisticated economies. Debt becomes a problem when scheduled payments are evaded or can't be met. In the first case only the creditor has a legitimate problem. In the second, both creditor and debtor have one, and the problem of the debtor is likely to be the greater.

Debt is a controversial topic about which views have tended to polarise. In his sociological study of debt collection, Rock (1973) contrasted the two extreme positions. Those who support the social control ethic see defaulters as culpable people who should be exposed to deterrent and punitive methods of control, while those accepting the social work ethic, based on hard determinism, do not accept that there can be purposeful free-willed dishonesty. For them, debt is a sign of poor adjustment and inadequacy which calls for social action in the form of treatment. Rock suggested that lawyers and legislators straddle both positions, contending that there are both culpable and inadequate debtors.

The extent of debt repayment difficulties

The number of people who have debt repayment difficulties is unknown. Published figures relate only to debt default cases where a legal remedy is sought, but as G. Parker (1981) pointed out in an unpublished paper prepared for a Welsh Consumer Council seminar on money management and debt, 'It may well be that fewer creditors now bother to pursue their claims through the courts, preferring to rely on less formal methods of pursuit or cutting their losses by selling debts to debt collection agencies.'

Overall the numbers in trouble may be considerable. For example in 1980 there were 1,584,000 actions entered for the recovery of money in the county courts of England and Wales; 131,000 related to hire purchase and credit sales and 64,000 to loans from money lenders, banks, and finance houses (Lord High Chancellor's Office, 1981). In Scottish courts there were 111,867 debt related actions in 1978 (Scottish Law Commission, 1980c).

A survey of Scottish debtors (Scottish Law Commission, 1981b) showed a high incidence of public authority debt with 37% of those who had court actions taken against them owing money to the local authority, and 14%, to the gas and electricity boards. There is no reason to suppose that the picture for England and Wales would be significantly different. Rent arrears and fuel debts are serious problems which are dealt with separately in this review.

The point at which use of credit leads to difficulties varies with individual circumstance. The NCC (1980) suggested that credit commitment could be described as 'heavy' when the instalments were over one-tenth of income. On this criterion the NCC survey found about 10% in each income group with 'heavy' credit commitments. Since a smaller proportion of those in the lowest income groups used credit, there was an above average incidence of heavy users amongst them.

Credit surveys give different estimates of the incidence of difficulties. The NOP research of 1969 commissioned by the Crowther Committee on Consumer Credit (Department of Trade and Industry, 1971b) gave the highest British estimate. Of those surveyed 10% had difficulties in making repayments, 3% defaulted to the extent of failing to make several successive payments and 1% had legal action taken against them by a creditor. NOP carried out a later consumer credit survey in 1977 for the Office of Fair Trading (1979b). Of all respondents 5% had difficulty in keeping up with credit repayments. Most of these were in the lower income groups. Of HP users 15% were 'troubled'. In his survey, Ison (1979) found that over 4% of the buyers of consumer goods had, at some time, had one overdue payment. The lowest estimate came from the NCC (1980) which reported that 1% of those who had recently bought on credit had difficulties with repayments. The difference in the findings make it impossible to derive more than an indication of the broad dimensions of the problem. Part of the variation is due to different interpretations of 'difficulty' in repaying. The NCC noted that the 1% figure it gave tallied with that given by lenders as the approximate percentage of credit extended which led to bad debt, whereas the Crowther Committee clearly gave the term 'difficulty' a wider interpretation.

Cranston (1978) commented that more acquisitive societies may have higher rates of default and he noted that one survey in the United States found that 39% of all debtors were in 'some trouble' because of their credit commitments and about 11% were in 'deep trouble'.

Evidence from the creditors' side is as imprecise as that obtained from surveys of debtors. Rock (1973) found it very difficult to get information. Wide-ranging verbal estimates suggested that between 50 and 90% of creditors' accounts went into default at some time. The

Scottish creditors in Doig and Millar's (Scottish Law Commission, 1981c) survey gave lower figures, ranging from one in four to one in ten for the proportion of accounts that required pursuit. Overall, pursuit appears to enable creditors to safeguard their money fairly well. The United Association for Protection of Trade Ltd reported to the Crowther Committee (Department of Trade and Industry, 1971a) that bad debts were about 0.5% of credit extended. As already noted the figure given by lenders to the NCC (1980) was 1%. Rock (1973), after discussion with some creditors, felt that about 1% of accounts were irrecoverable. In their survey Doig and Millar (Scottish Law Commission, 1981) reported that creditors regarded some default as an inevitable result of being in business, but only a very small percentage (less than 1%) of credit that went into default was not recovered. As a proportion of all credit granted, the figure would be even lower.

Doig and Millar pointed out that the perspective of creditors and debtors is very different. 'To the debtor subject to diligence [legal proceedings] the procedures have an impact on all aspects of his life, not just the "business side"; they form a major, often all consuming, part of his concerns for a time, not a relatively minor part all the time.' To understand the impact of debt on debtors, their circumstances and the underlying and precipitating reasons for debt have to be considered.

For many years, the only major detailed study of debtors was an American one by Caplovitz (1974). He interviewed 1331 default debtors sampled from court records in three American cities. His research is of interest because of its analysis and the large size of the sample. But his findings have to be interpreted cautiously because they relate to a different society (65% of the sample were coloured Americans) and the response rate was only 61% – mainly because people could not be traced.

British evidence came mainly from poverty studies and surveys related to consumer credit. More recently a mass of information has emerged from the series of research reports published in 1980 and 1981 by the Scottish Law Commission. Included was a large OPCS survey of defenders in debt actions in Scotland carried out by Gregory and Monk (Scottish Law Commission, 1981b). In this survey 1223 debtors were interviewed, with a response rate of 58%. Adler and Wozniak's (Scottish Law Commission, 1981a) research into the origins and consequences of default was also part of the Law Commission programme. Selection of their sample of 100 debtors was complicated because adequate representation was wanted for the various stages of the legal procedure. The overall response rate was low (44%). But once contact was made, it was high for those who were available and eligible. In England, Berthoud's large scale investigation (approximately 2000 interviews) into the fuel boards' code of practice has produced much valuable detailed information about the circumstances of fuel debtors.

Underlying causes of debt default

Not surprisingly debt problems are very common amongst those with low or declining income. For example over half of the 1479 unemployed men in Daniel's representative survey (1974) said they were not able to meet some commitment. They had greatest difficulty with loans taken on when they were at work and such items as motor tax insurance, rent, mortgage, gas, electricity and phone bills. Daniel observed that the extent of borrowing during unemployment would mean a serious burden of indebtedness when the men were back in work. He did not speculate about the possible consequences of debt if a man did not resume work. Debt difficulties were noted by Clark (1978) in her survey of 0.6% of the unemployed on SB. Of the sample 25% had debts from borrowing and 25% had rent, rates and mortgage arrears, 18% had fallen behind with HP or other regular payments and 17% had fuel bills they couldn't pay. Some of the sample had multiple debts and in all, 44% had debts at the time of the interview.

Although the incidence of debt amongst some low income workers – those of FIS – appears to be less than amongst the unemployed, it is far from negligible. Knight and Nixon (1975) reported 21% of FIS claimants they surveyed had debts compared with 44% of the unemployed (Clark, 1978). Knight and Nixon noted that when net resources were already insufficient, the extra outgoings to clear a debt, however small, made the financial circumstances even more precarious.

The follow-up study of FIS recipients by Knight (1976) found that 9% had liabilities such as large unpaid bills, HP and tax arrears and payment on maintenance and court orders. Perhaps significantly some of these families had other problems besides low income, such as recent sickness or unemployment or a domestic crisis.

Of those on SB, surveyed by Marshall (1972), up to a third had debt other than rent arrears. More of the two-parent families were in debt than the lone mothers even though in some respects, such as the possession of household equipment, two-parent families tended to be better off. Marshall suggested that families affected by sickness or unemployment may think of SB as a temporary state and may have (realistic or unrealistic) hopes of an early return to work. They were less concerned about debt because they were more confident of being able to pay it off at a later stage. Alternative explanations are that the lone mothers, who had been on SB for longer, had developed a greater skill at managing on a low income or that they benefited from having sole control of the family income.

G. Parker (1981) of the Birmingham Settlement Money Advice Centre noted that the people who came to the centre for help, were more likely to want it for debt problems if they were young, had low incomes and children, or were unemployed. At higher income levels there was no association between having children and debt problems. Pensioners tended to come with problems of a different nature.

Gregory and Monk's (Scottish Law Commission, 1981b) comprehensive survey of Scottish debtors had similar findings. A very small percentage were pensioners. Almost half were less than 35 years old and nearly all (95%) were currently or had been married. A disproportionate percentage (20%) lived in large households containing six or more people compared with a figure of 6% for Scotland as a whole. Of the debtors' households 75% had dependent children. The comparable national figure was 41%.

A high proportion of the Scottish debtors in Gregory and Monk's survey were in the three lowest social classes, and many of them had low incomes; 20% were unemployed (compared with the national figure of 5%) and a further 31% were not working because they were pensioners, housewives, or others not seeking work. In 41% of the cases neither the debtor nor the spouse (if any) were working. Gregory and Monk stressed the importance of this finding since spouses 'are the most likely sources of financial help, or at least those turned to earliest for financial help'.

From an analysis of their data, Gregory and Monk produced a typology of debtors. They were typically male, married, with dependent children, and were in manual occupations.

Adler and Wozniak (Scottish Law Commission, 1981a) also found disproportionately low incomes amongst the debtors they surveyed; 43% had incomes below 120% of SB at the time they incurred their debt, and 60% were below this level when the summons was issued. The corresponding figure for the population as a whole was 23%. However, the sampling frame used was likely to have led to some bias towards those with lower resources.

Debtors are not always poor, but all the studies related to debt show that the income levels of debtors are disproportionately low. The NOP survey for the Crowther Committee on Consumer Credit (Department of Trade and Industry 1971b) found three times as many debtors in social classes D and E as in A and B. However a causal relationship between low income and debt is often not accepted because debt is a subject about which there are opposing and sometimes emotive views. In her study of poverty in Belfast Evason (1980) criticised the critics. Refuting what she considered to be the false viewpoint that debt in the form of arrears normally arises from the misallocation of resources by those with adequate incomes, she argued that there is a consistent relationship between debt and income, particularly when allowance is made for family type. Although she acknowledged that many households living below the poverty line of 140% of SB were not in debt whilst some, who were, had incomes above the line, she pointed out that those not in arrears were overwhelmingly households containing no dependent children. Arrears also related to the proportion of income spent on food, fuel and housing. The majority of those with arrears spent more than 50% of their incomes on these commodities, whereas for those without arrears, the opposite was true.

At a Welsh Consumer Council Seminar (1981) on 'Money Management and Debt Problems', Blamire claimed that debt problems rarely arose from absolute poverty. He attributed them more to the 'creation of unfillable levels of expectation', especially amongst the less well off. He and others attending the seminar argued that the media, and in particular television, was responsible. It promoted a relatively affluent life-style as a norm rather than an exception.

Berthoud's (1981) detailed analysis also showed that debt – in this case, fuel debt – is associated with low income and family commitments. Arguing that, on their own, they do not adequately explain debt, Berthoud ventured into the difficult area of which personal characteristics might be associated with fuel debt. He suggested that three areas of behaviour should be considered. One was the feeling of fatalism, the assumption that nothing effective could be done. The second was the level of ability to manage effectively on whatever income one might have, and the third was the extent of willingness to pay. Berthoud acknowledged the difficulty of identifying the third when motives cannot be assessed, and it is impossible to distinguish between fatalistic activity and a conscious attempt to evade payment. Berthoud also discussed the interplay between resources and attitudes. Low income and a reluctance to pay can separately lead to the non-payment of a fuel bill. But when they are combined, the likelihood of non-payment is of course much greater. In this situation, it can be argued that either one is the precipitating factor.

Comment in the NCC report (1980) is relevant to Berthoud's second area of behaviour – the ability to manage. As already noted, the Report emphasised the tendency of particularly vulnerable groups to perceive expenditure almost entirely in weekly terms, and it went on to say that 'squeezing the largest possible instalment into the confines of a weekly budget . . . leaves the deep pitfall that people then have no leeway to cope with unexpected or higher than usual expenses which crop up later'. Also important is the easy but potentially dangerous slide from manageable credit purchases into a vicious circle of cash loans and increasing indebtedness – all with the same cash caller.

Rock (1973) reported other views of underlying causes of debt which illustrate the range of opinions about debtors. He observed that those who carry out the business of debt collecting and credit sanctioning classify debtors as professional, feckless and unfortunate. The unfortunate require almost no enforcement effort; the feckless, a more restrained one; and the professional, a considerable effort. Rock showed his scepticism of the collector's classification when he observed that they may 'become committed to it [. . . feel they] have an insight . . . an ability to probe behind the debtor's cunning mask'. From his investigation of the debt recovery process Rock concluded that 'most defaulters are normal customers, whose payments have temporarily lapsed. They usually resume if tactfully dealt with.' He summed them up as 'erratic payers', and felt that default which receives a deviant label is often due to 'sheer inaction of the debtor'.

Activities of the creditor which underly debt default include the encouragement of overextension of credit and the charging of excessively high interest rates. These practices are part of the money environment already discussed in Chapter 6.

Precipitating causes of debt default

A Drop in Income
Evidence from surveys suggests that the most important reason for default is a reversal in the debtor's flow of income. It was a primary cause in 43% of Caplovitz's (1974) cases and a contributory factor in a further 5%. In Adler and Wozniak's (Scottish Law Commission, 1981a) study, 37% gave it as a primary cause, and 16% as a secondary one. In both surveys, employment factors were the main reason for the changed income. A very high percentage, 62%, in Gregory and Monk's (Scottish Law Commission, 1981b) study attributed their debt to reduced or lost income, and again lost earnings were the major factor. It was less dominant in the NOP survey for the Crowther Committee (Department of Trade and Industry, 1971b), but here also change in income, because of illness (20%) and employment (15%), was given as the most frequent reason for default.

Commitments Too Great: voluntary and involuntary
Voluntary overcommitment is an area of debt where supported

evidence is slight and prejudice easily creeps in. Survey data relies heavily on the subjective views of the debtor and some distortion is to be expected if the debt has been caused solely or mainly by the individual's lack of realism. However the bias may be balanced by the debtor being subjected to excessive marketing pressures, previously discussed, of which he may be largely unaware.

Overcommitment seems to have a small but significant role in debt default. Caplovitz (1974) found in his survey that voluntary over-commitment of income was the second most important reason for default; and it was a major or contributory factor in 25% of the cases. Corresponding figures for Adler and Wozniak's (Scottish Law Commission, 1981a) and the NOP (Department of Trade and Industry, 1971b) samples were 10 and 6%. Gregory and Monk (Scottish Law Commission, 1981b) analysed their data differently, but they found that although only 6% of debtors doubted their ability to pay when they took on the commitment, 57% were struggling to make repayments before they finally defaulted and 4% made no or only one payment. However the Birmingham Settlement Money Advice Centre did not consider that imprudent or even reckless credit use produced serious debt on its own. A sudden reversal in the family fortunes was also required. The reversal did not have to be large, the budgets were in such delicate balance (G. Parker, 1980).

Voluntary overcommitment may be related to an individual's character and temperament. Caplovitz commented, 'Undoubtedly many overextended debtors are unable to discipline themselves to keep their debts within the range of their income.' Philp (1963) found that 37% of families helped by the FSU had major debts and some of the many reasons he gave for such debts indicate a lack of discipline similar to that referred to by Caplovitz. Included amongst them were the inability to say 'no' to tallymen and an impulsive need for gratification in both husbands and wives. Items for which families such as these were most likely to incur debt had the following characteristics: satisfaction and payment separated in time, consequences of non-payment usually delayed, money owed to impersonal authorities.

The Crowther Report (Department of Trade and Industry, 1971a) admitted that, 'most do not overcommit themselves', but it felt it necessary to emphasis the improvidence of 'many, particularly in the low income group'. 'Such people will, for example, spend a slice of their income not on articles they really need but on other less important items; and they will spend regardless of whether they are getting value for money.' The ease with which such situations can arise is given credence by the NCC's (1980) descriptions of weekly patterns of payments, the ongoing and close relationships with weekly credit callers, reliance on familiar practices, and fear of unknown ones. But the term 'improvidence' does less than justice to the complexity of the situation.

Figures for overcommitment arising for reasons outside the debtor's control are likely to be more reliable than for those for voluntary overcommittment because it is a less sensitive issue. However the figures are not usefully compared because Caplovitz's American ones reflect unexpected medical bills, which are not relevant to Britain. But on one important aspect of involuntary overcommitment, marital problems, there is some agreement. In Caplovitz's survey 6% offered these as a prime cause while NOP (Department of Trade and Industry, 1971b) and Adler and Wozniak (Scottish Law Commission, 1981a) both had comparable figures of 5%.

Debtor Irresponsibility
Debtor irresponsibility or intent to avoid payment is inevitably an elusive issue for survey investigation. It would be unwise to place too much reliance on answers from debtors themselves and low response rates in surveys undoubtedly cause bias in this area. Berthoud (1981) found that an unexpectedly high proportion – over a quarter – of his sample of disconnected fuel consumers were not contactable at addresses which were on the fuel boards records only a month previously. It was not clear whether the customer had moved because of disconnection or 'to skip payment'. In Berthoud's opinion, the fuel boards take the view that most of those disconnected are not in hardship but are trying to avoid payment for the fuel they have consumed. Berthoud commented that his survey contradicted the first half of this hypothesis but that did not in itself contradict the second.

Caplovitz (1974) judged that amongst those he surveyed only 5% were defaulting primarily or partly because of irresponsibility or bad faith. The 5% was a heterogeneous group including, as well as those who never intended to pay, those who said they forgot, were temporarily out of town, or no longer felt obligated because the goods were stolen or destroyed. Adler and Wozniak (Scottish Law Commission, 1981a) reported that 13% of their sample were defaulting because of 'irresponsibility', but they did not discuss what this involved. The NOP (Department of Trade and Industry, 1971b) survey more cautiously did not include this type of question. But 37% told the NOP that they had unknown or forgotten reasons for their default. Gregory and Monk (Scottish Law Commission, 1981b) did not pose the question of debtor irresponsibility directly, although they reported that 1% of debtors 'paid late on principle'. Possibly there was an element of debtor irresponsibility amongst the 13% who did not realise that payment was due and the 4% who thought it had already been made, but the authors of the report did not suggest that this might be the case.

The Role of Creditors

In Gregory and Monk's (Scottish Law Commission, 1981b) survey 10% said they defaulted because they refused to pay, and the vast majority (90%) in this category did so because of a dispute with the creditors. Defective goods and subsequent dispute led to 5% of the sample defaulting in the NOP survey (Department of Trade and Industry, 1971b). In Caplovitz's study 21% blamed creditors for their default. The same figure was given by Adler and Wozniak. As they pointed out, the similarity in response of the samples is striking and surprising, 'when one considers that they took place in different jurisdictions at different periods of time.' Caplovitz classified 14% of the responses under the heading 'fraud and deceptions'. The complaints Adler and Wozniak received were classified under more moderate headings, such as misrepresentation, excessive pressure, and misunderstanding with creditors.

Debt recovery

The effect of debt recovery on families has to be considered against the background of the causes of debt. There are likely to be two main types of effect. Irrespective of whether or not a legal remedy is sought or other pressure exerted, the debt is usually cleared by the defaulting debtor agreeing to repayment by instalments. The required cutting back of expenditure by a person or family having obvious difficulty in managing is not easily nor painlessly achieved. The hardship that arises from difficulty in managing is discussed in Chapter 10. The second and more visible effect of debt recovery is the impact of the legislative procedure. Very little is known about the situation in England and Wales, but recent research by the Scottish Law Commission has provided much information about the Scottish position.

The legal procedures (known as diligence) in Scotland were criticised by Adler and Wozniak (Scottish Law Commission, 1981a) for still being essentially those that were developed to deal with debt problems in the nineteenth century, and for taking no account of individual circumstances nor of the factors giving rise to debt. The two major systems of enforcement are warrant sales procedures and 'arrestment of wages, salaries and other assets'. The salient points of the first process are that if payment is not made after there has been a formal demand (a charge) from the courts, the debtor's goods are poinded, i.e. inventoried and valued. If there is still no payment, an advertisement is placed in local newspapers giving the time, place (usually the debtor's home) and nature of the sale. Finally the sale is executed.

If fully implemented, the process is of marginal direct benefit to the creditor. In a survey by Connor (Scottish Law Commission, 1980b) in 1978, 94 personal warrant sales realised only 40% of the principal sum (i.e. the original debt), plus expenses due. The amounts realised at the sales are small and the expenses are relatively high, amounting on average to 35% of the principal sums. In 30% of cases, expenses were higher than the principal sum. The benefit to the creditor is further reduced because often there are no bids for items in the sales, and the goods are then assigned to the creditors at the low poinded value. No money is exchanged. In 58 out of the 94 cases investigated by Connor, all the goods were adjudged to the creditor. Adler and Wozniak (Scottish Law Commission, 1981a) found that in eight of the nine cases in their survey where this happened, the creditors did not remove the goods. If their findings are representative, the direct financial benefit of completing the diligence process is almost neglible.

Adler and Wozniak's survey of 100 debtors, interviewed at various stages of the diligence procedure, showed that the apparent ritual imposes a heavy burden on the debtor. For the majority the worst aspect was the humiliation and horror they felt about the public advertisement of their private difficulties. Although in practice, neighbours did not generally react adversely to the advertisements, debtors still felt ashamed and stigmatised.

In addition to personal distress, the financial disadvantage of warrant sales to debtors was severe. They lost ownership of many of their possessions (since 1973 a few necessities may not be poinded if they are reasonably necessary for the avoidance of undue hardship) and gained little or nothing. In 97% of the cases, Connor found that debtors still owed money after the sale, and in 40% of the cases, the money owed was more than the original principal sum. This happened primarily because of the low values placed on the goods at poinding, which, in most cases, were all that was obtained. Allegations that poinding undervalued goods by a considerable amount have been made by many people, including MPs Dennis Canavan and James Dempsey (Hansard, 13 May 1981, vol. 4, col. 764–5). Adler and Wozniak (Scottish Law Commission, 1981a) noted that nearly new articles were given 'incredibly low valuations' and that items of similar quality were often valued very differently. The fact that the goods were not generally removed by the creditors after the sale was not the bonus for the debtors which it might appear. Creditors exerted further pressure by threatening removal if payments were not made.

One aspect of the warrant sale procedure that has aroused concern is that sheriff's officers unlike bailiffs, the English equivalent, are not full-time court employees. In Parliament Dennis Canavan MP suggested that there are connections between them and unscrupulous secondhand dealers and auctioneers (Hansard, 22 January 1980, vol. 977, col. 217).

The debts, for which the warrant sale procedure was used, were generally small: 53% were for less than £100, and the largest in Connor's survey was for £944. As already noted those creditors who completed the complex procedure gained little benefit. Not surprisingly it was the policy of some not to pursue the process to the point of sale (Scottish Law Commission, 1980a).

In one important respect, however, the procedure is very effective. At each of the various stages of the process, more and more debts are repaid. Doig (Scottish Law Commission, 1980a) estimated for the Scottish Law Commission that the incidence in 1978 of the various stages of the procedure was as follows: 46,000 charges served, 20,000 poindings carried out, 6200 sales instructed, 3000 sales advertised, and 300 sales executed. Doig and Millar (Scottish Law Commission, 1981c) pointed out that many creditors use diligence more as a threat to get a response from the debtor rather than as a direct method of obtaining payment. For this reason they stressed that the low level of recovery obtained from warrant sales is a misleading measure of its effectiveness and its role as a spur to settlement has also to be considered. The figures for the various stages of the process drop sharply and the Solicitor General for Scotland, Mr Nicholas Fairbairn, felt that this filter effect 'was important' and 'put the matter in proportion' (Hansard, 2 June 1981, vol. 5, col. 905). The alternative view was put by Dennis Canavan who argued that, 'The whole coercive system is a form of public humiliation and punishment rather than a constructive effort to get a debt repaid' (Hansard, 3 June 1981, vol. 5, col. 928).

The other legal procedure used in Scotland to effect debt repayment is arrestment. Adler and Wozniak (Scottish Law Commission, 1981a) surveyed 25 debtors whose wages were arrested, and found that the material hardship was greater than for those who had undergone warrant sales. On average, just under £29 (range being from £10 to £62) was withheld from the wages, and the men were left with take-home pay of just over £32 (range being from £18 to £60). Of the 22 households for which there was complete information 14 had incomes less than SB levels, and of these, nine had incomes less than 80% of SB and four were less than 50% of SB. Connor (Scottish Law Commission, 1980d), in her review of the employers' involvement in arrestment of wages, noted that there were 9000 arrestments of wages and salaries executed in Scotland in 1978, so that if Adler and Wozniak's figures were typical, many families were living on incomes well below SB levels as a result of arrestment.

Not all creditors go to law when there is default. Many choose to use debt collectors, but the number who do so is unknown. Rock (1973) in his investigation of debt from the creditor's point of view, described debt collecting as an 'invisible' but 'massive enterprise regulated by minute calculation of cost'.

Doig and Millar (Scottish Law Commission, 1981c) interviewed five debt collection agencies as part of their survey of creditors. Agencies or solicitors were used by 76% of the creditors to pursue debts after the failure of the creditors' own informal methods. The practice of the debt collectors varied, but it usually involved sending letters of an increasingly threatening nature. Failure to get a response led to court action but usually only after a 'pre-sue' visit to assess whether court action was worthwhile.

A clue to the style of operation of some debt collectors was provided by the strong warning issued by the Director of Fair Trading, Mr Gordon Borrie, in February 1981 about the use of strong-arm tactics and other unfair methods. Mr Borrie added that he was afraid that the complaints received were the tip of the iceberg, with many people being too frightened or embarrassed to complain. He singled out the use of 'blue frighteners', letters similar in appearance to court summonses, and the sending of vans emblazoned with the slogan 'Debt Collections'.

Debt spirals
A serious aspect of debt is its potential for spiralling. Those under severe pressure to repay a debt when they have no resources to do so can become trapped, with the only way out being further borrowing. Blamire (author interview, 1979) described how the financial balance for many of the people helped by the Money Advice Centre was so fine that they lived on a seesaw with no room for manoeuvre; or, if there was one, it was expensive and that tended to start a spiral of borrowing. Many of the FSU families surveyed by Burghes (1980) were caught in the spiral. Of the families interviewed, 56 were in debt, and 17 had had to borrow from another source to meet repayments on existing debts. Four of these families complained about the charges on the second loan.

Information about debt spiralling is slight, probably because those under the greatest pressure would not be considered creditworthy by reputable lending companies and they turn to illegal money lenders. Some of their crude forceful activities have already been discussed.

Most of the references to illegal money lending comes from Scotland. Sutherland (1980) wrote of those with fuel debts being forced to turn to illegal borrowing, and Adler and Wozniak (Scottish Law Commission 1981a) noted that in their survey of debtors some had taken out loans, 'often using their child benefit book as security', a clear indication that the loans were of an illegal nature.

The evidence reviewed suggests that debt default is most common in low income families, and it is often precipitated by adverse changes in income. Overcommitment is an accepted factor but one of uncertain importance. The behaviour of creditors may be relevant in about 20% of cases, while other factors such as debtor irresponsibility and marital problems are thought to be significant but less important. Debt can have an obvious and direct cause, but it can also result from the coincidence of several adverse circumstances. However, debt default is difficult to investigate. The low response rates in all the surveys and the fact that Caplovitz's survey related to America mean that despite the integrity and care of the researchers, the figures given in the surveys should be thought of as very useful indications rather than precise data.

Debt recovery is an important subject because of the numbers involved and the harsh effects of the recovery process on some of them. It is an obscure area, that has in the past, been bedevilled with prejudice and lack of knowledge. The fundamental and very difficult problem is to devise procedures which will inhibit dishonest default but not have, as a corollary, the coercion of defaulters who are genuinely unfortunate and hapless.

9 Major Forms of Debt

Rent arrears

Rent arrears are a visible and well known form of debt. This is mainly because most rented accommodation now belongs to local authorities. Their public nature therefore ensures that statistics are available, and it stimulates interest in the size, nature and handling of the arrears problem. Arrears are measured as a proportion of the annual debit, i.e. the total of rents due. Radford (1980), reporting on the Institute of Housing survey, noted that after adjusting for technicalities, the average level of local authorities arrears in 1978 was 1.4%. The figure varied with the type of authority and in areas where there was acute social stress it rose as high as 5%. Nationally there had been an upward drift in the size of arrears since 1975, but only at the gradual rate of 0.08%. The overall distribution of arrears amongst authorities tended to be relatively stable over time.

In the early 1980s, the upward drift in arrears became stronger. In March 1982 the London Tenants' Organisation claimed that overall arrears owed by London's council tenants had risen in 1981 by more than half and within the authorities, by between 32 and 110% (*The Times* 30 March 1982).

Some default is to be expected with all forms of credit or payment arrangements, and commercial factors usually determine the level that is acceptable. Since local authorities' tenancies tend to be granted because of circumstances which imply some degree of money shortage, a relatively high level of default is to be expected. The social responsibilities of local authorities will influence the level that is felt to be acceptable, but there are no agreed criteria determining it. The cost effectiveness of recovery measures is one relevant factor. Alpren (1977) argued that the cost of collecting arrears may be greater than the cost of carrying them, but the cost effectiveness of recovery procedures is not easily assessed since there is some evidence that high rent arrears generate even higher ones. But the indirect costs of the recovery process can be high for, as the National Consumer Council (1976a) noted, evicted families may have to be rehoused or children taken into care. It is however possible for local authorities to disclaim responsibility for those made homeless because of a failure to pay rent by defining them as 'intentionally homeless' under the Housing (Homeless Persons) Act 1977. Nevertheless the welfare responsibilities of the authority have to be balanced against its housing management responsibilities.

Ungerson and Baldock (1978) suggested that rent arrears constituted a 'form of social welfare; an unevenly distributed financial supplement to the existing income maintenance scheme for families'. But they recognised that, as almost all arrears are eventually paid off, the supplement took the form of an interest free loan and was very small. A more conscious and controllable welfare scheme related to rent arrears is a rent guarantee scheme whereby the social services department pay the rent for a specific period or underwrite occasional arrears. Gray's (1973) study of the Portsmouth scheme suggested that on average rent supervision could go on for nearly eight years before the costs would exceed the costs of eviction in the first place. But rent guarantee schemes have not become common, partly because the 1977 Act transferred responsibility for homelessness from Social Services to the Housing Department, thereby reducing the involvement of Social Services. In addition rent guarantee schemes do not easily gain public support because they affect the attitudes of tenants and their neighbours. Local authorities have to be seen to be being fair to all their tenants and to their ratepayers, and arrears tend to be viewed in what Ungerson and Baldock described as a 'somewhat charged context'.

Tenants also cannot lightly disregard arrears. In material terms they may, at worst, lead to the loss of a home or possessions, and, at best, to a black mark being recorded against them by the local authority which may have a detrimental effect on requests such as those for transfer (NCC, 1976a). Being in arrears is undoubtedly an unpleasant and disturbing business generating stress within the family that is likely to be exacerbated by efforts to pay off the debt (Alpren, 1977). Harvey (1979) described some families as being at the edge of despair. However, as she noted, her sample was not representative, and other comments in her study make it appear likely that there were additional reasons for the despair.

The total of rent arrears is understandably of interest to local authorities and central government. Aspects of arrears such as composition, duration, and causes also matter because these influence the effectiveness of recovery procedures. These aspects are relevant also to money problems and deprivation.

Being in arrears appears to be a common occurrence. Walker (1978) found that of 217 tenants in a West Midlands area that were monitored for three years, 23% were in arrears at any moment of time, while 43% had been in arrears on occasion during the period, and 8% were continuously in arrears. Radford (1980) summarised the position with his comment that decreasing percentages of tenants owed increasing amounts of rent. He reported that, in a typical local authority, 8% of tenants owed at least four weeks' rent, but the percentage fell to $2\frac{1}{2}$% for those owing eight weeks. For the average authority, just over a third of its total arrears were due to small debts (less than three weeks' rent) and just under a third, due to large ones (over twelve weeks' rent). Larger authorities usually have more big debts, and smaller authorities, more small ones.

Survey knowledge of the circumstances of those with rent arrears grew gradually in the 1960s and 1970s and more rapidly in the late 1970s and early 1980s. However the evidence obtained needs to be treated with some caution as all the studies were small, some were based on unrepresentative samples and in only one (Ungerson and Baldock, 1978) was there a control group. As with so many aspects of debt, rent arrears has not been a subject easily surveyed. Of the tenants initially contacted for Ungerson and Baldock's survey 47% refused to take part, although surprisingly those not in arrears were more likely to refuse. The NCC (1976a) and Alpren (1977) both noted the difficulty they had in getting samples to interview, while Harvey's aim was to help those in difficulty as well as studying their particular circumstances.

The Department of Environment's prospective larger scale study with a control group should lead to conclusions based on firmer grounds. However their pilot study indicated that there is no reason for supposing that the conclusions will differ materially from those of earlier studies.

Discussion of rent arrears has been approached in a variety of ways, usefully categorised by Ungerson and Baldock into five different ones: managerial, individualistic, structural, poverty and crisis. Research studies usually consider a range of the approaches, but with a final emphasis usually on one or two.

The Department of Environment pilot study (Duncan and Kirby, 1981) looked at several aspects of arrears although ultimately the emphasis was managerial. They drew attention to the circumstances surrounding tenants in serious arrears which were so complex that it 'was rarely possible to pinpoint a single causal factor', and they concluded that 'arrears had most frequently arisen as a result of a complex interplay of various related factors'.

An earlier survey of arrears in a London borough carried out by the London Borough of Hammersmith (1975) had a similar finding, and it noted that some of the factors involved were measurable while others were more difficult to quantify. Over the years the emphasis placed on the various factors has changed. Less importance has become attached to the individualistic approach and more, to structural and crisis explanations.

As would be expected, shortage of money, in one form or another, is the dominant cause of rent arrears. But the shortage can arise and be felt in different ways. Families with rent arrears are generally found to have incomes below average levels. Duncan and Kirby (1981) reported that on average the income level of their Enfield sample was considerably lower than the average for Greater London. Ungerson and Baldock (1978) in their study of rent arrears in Ashford, Kent, calculated that although average gross income was not lower for those in arrears compared with those who were not, it was when it was measured per head. In Harvey's (1979) unrepresentative sample of people with rent arrears in Camden, only 11% were not dependent on benefits in some form. Earlier studies by Nairn and Tait (1963) and Harbert (1965) of rent arrears in Aberdeen and Southampton respectively, also stressed the importance of low income.

In some cases, arrears have been attributed to a drop in income caused by, say, sickness or unemployment coupled with a slowness to adapt. Unemployment has often been frequently stressed as a factor in rent arrears. In Alpren's (1977) sample of those in arrears in a South London borough, the majority were unemployed when they got into arrears, and 25% blamed unemployment for their problem, as did 28% in Ungerson and Baldock's (1978) survey. Duncan and Kirby (1981) found that even though two-thirds of their sample were employed, they were six times as likely to be unemployed as individuals in the borough as a whole.

Adjustment to low income can be particularly difficult for some groups. A study in Brent (Tenants Rights Information and Research Unit, 1982) focused on the difficulty newly redundant older workers who had had relatively good wages for years experienced in reducing commitments.

A Department of Environment Occasional Paper (1978) suggested that low income was increasingly being seen as a continuous factor rather than being felt to be important only at a time of changing circumstance. Subsequently Ungerson and Baldock (1978) argued that although crises, such as unemployment and sickness, leading to low income were very commonly given (by 75% of their sample) as critical reasons for arrears, they did not believe these to be the true cause. They argued that short-term crises were symptoms of the long-term financial circumstances.

The demands on income, as well as its level, obviously affect rent-paying ability. In early studies, family size was clearly discernible as important, with between 70 and 76% of those surveyed in Southampton and Aberdeen having three or more children (Nairn and Tait, 1963; Harbert, 1965). In most later studies, large families were still disproportionately represented (Duncan and Kirby, 1981; Alpren, 1977), but the importance of family size had diminished with the introduction of rent and rate rebates, and by the increasing incidence of one-parent families amongst those in arrears. An analysis of Lambeth's Housing Management Sub-Committee, reported by TRIRU (Tenants Rights Information and Research Unit, 1982) in Brent found that 40% of households with children in arrears were one-parent families.

Many types of pressures act on incomes squeezing them and reducing rent-paying ability. The Brent Tenants Rights Information and Research Unit (TRIRU) (1982) drew attention to a range of trends which had combined to bring about a sharp fall in the standard of living of council tenants in the few years immediately preceding their report. They noted that the percentage of Brent tenants who owed more than four weeks' rent had increased tenfold in just over a decade (from 2.4% in 1970 to 24.1% in 1981), while during the years 1978–81 inclusive the incidence of large debts had grown considerably (from 67.7% of the total to 77.5%). The report blamed the scale of the increase in large debts on economic circumstances, including changes in the prices of basic essentials, in particular that of fuel, changes in taxation and national insurance, increasing unemployment, short-time working and cuts in overtime, and the declining values of some social security benefits. Similarly Ungerson and Baldock (1978) stressed the importance of the financial and economic circumstances of tenants as causes of arrears.

The dynamics of rent arrears relate mainly to economic factors. The Department of Environment Occasional Paper (1978) pointed out that economic aspects have received limited attention, and it is difficult to establish how the relationship between them affects individuals' rent-paying abilities.

Where there is low income, rent-paying ability is affected by the fact that a family's incomings and outgoings tend to be in a state of delicate balance with few if any savings to give cash liquidity or ease temporary difficulties (Duncan and Kirby, 1981; Harvey, 1979). These circumstances are conducive to the non-payment of rent, because it is generally a relatively large amount to find, and it is a payment that is fairly easy to avoid, even if temporarily. Non-payment is therefore an easy and effective way of getting ready money. Gingerbread (1978), the organisation representing one-parent families, described it as 'the poor man's overdraft' in their evidence to RCDIW. This use of rent money has been noted by many others including the Birmingham Settlement Money Advice Centre (author interview, 1979), Knight (1976) in his follow-up survey of FIS families, the NCC (1976a) and Ungerson and Baldock (1978).

Going into debt in one area to avoid it in another may be no more than a question of expediency. But sometimes it may result from a more deliberate decision about priorities. The NCC (1976a) felt that the tenants they interviewed gave their home a very high priority but they were also aware that the path to eviction was a long one. By contrast, as the Brent TRIRU (1982) pointed out, the London Electricity Board (and other fuel boards) readily disconnect.

It is therefore not surprising that studies of rent arrears have reported a high incidence of spontaneous comment on the high cost of heating (Harvey, 1979) and in many cases priority was acknowledged to have been given to the payment of fuel bills rather than the rent (Ungerson and Baldock, 1978; Alpren, 1977). The Brent TRIRU (1982) reported that social workers and advice agencies were almost universally advising low income households to pay their fuel bills first. As a result, rising fuel prices have had repercussions on local authority rent arrears figures.

Attitudes undoubtedly have some influence on rent arrears. The elderly form one low income group which has been consistently reported as avoiding arrears and also fuel debt. This has generally been felt to be a reflection of their attitude to debt although the relative stability of pensioners' resources and requirements may also play a part (Duncan and Kirby, 1981).

Whatever may be the feelings of the elderly, there is evidence that others feel some tolerance towards debt. Alpren (1977) found that lack of pressure to pay from the local authority affected tenants' readiness to do so. Indifference on one side bred it on the other. Nevertheless, some tenants feel anxious about being visibly in debt. Alpren noted in his survey that rent payments were never less than for one week's rent even though part payment would have helped to contain arrears. He explained this by suggesting that people preferred to defer payment rather than pay a proportion because they were ashamed to show visibly in the Housing Office that the rent money had been 'broken into'. Pressure from neighbours was discussed by the NCC (1976a) who argued that the social code on the estate mattered a great deal. If all bad payers were put together, the estate became a 'ghetto' which further encouraged arrears.

The suggestion that rent arrears may be due to refusal or unwillingness to pay, as distinct from inability, is inevitably an issue in the literature on rent arrears. The Department of Environment's Occasional Paper (1978), commenting on earlier discussions, referred to 'incorrect attitudes' and noted that although there was no evidence for it, officials considered it important. The Brent TRIRU (1982) strongly refuted this approach and denied that 'sheer bloody minded-ness' was a factor in rent arrears. Other studies have also discounted the notion although less vigorously. Alpren (1977) found little evidence of 'irresponsibility' and felt that only 1 tenant out of 42 was 'withholding' rent. Harvey (1979) reported little evidence of refusal to pay. Ungerson and Baldock (1978) took a balanced view and acknow-ledged that there would always be 'outstandingly bloody-minded and opportunist' tenants, but the 'memorable minority' should not be allowed to colour understanding of the overall pattern.

Weakness in budgeting is another theme in the literature which is often linked with wilful evasion. In some cases it has been associated with HP commitments which were felt to be disproportionately high, thereby implying extravagance (Nairn and Tait, 1963; Harbert, 1965). In later studies, use of HP was investigated but not criticised. In the samples studied by Ungerson and Baldock and by Duncan and Kirby, over half used HP or similar credit schemes. Duncan and Kirby noted that the majority of purchases were of household goods or clothing for children and that despite high interest payments, HP type purposes are frequently characterised by low, if long-term, weekly repayments. Harvey (1979) found only 12 out of 46 in her sample were using HP, but for them it did have 'dire' effects. One of the other tenants commented that HP was a luxury which could no longer be afforded by those with low incomes now that heating costs were so high.

Theories linking rent arrears with evasion of payment or extrav-agance in budgeting can theoretically be partially tested by examining the style of living of those concerned and several researchers have attempted this. In no case has evidence of extravagant living been found. Duncan and Kirby found that the ownership of consumer goods was often below average for tenants in arrears, and they were much less likely to have washing machines, telephones or cars, while Ungerson and Baldock concluded that there was 'absolutely no evidence' that rent arrears were being used to fund luxuries.

However, as already noted, there is some unwillingness among tenants to take part in rent arrears surveys; and it is a realistic assumption that if some wilfully use rent money for other purposes, they would be likely to be among the non-participants. Other ways of probing the validity of such theories are required.

The Brent TRIRU noted that acceptance of these theories underpins the belief that tough policies will largely clear up the rent arrears problem, for the belief rests on the assumption that tenants have the resources to pay but will not do so. However Radford (1980) reported that the results he obtained from his analysis of the effects of management practice in the Institute of Housing's national survey, made theories linking tough management style with arrears 'untenable'. Whether the practice differs from the theory will eventually be shown by the experience of Birmingham, which in 1982 started to use debt collectors to reduce rent arrears. At an early stage, the Housing Chairman, Mrs Edwina Currie, was reported as saying 'It's a harsh and wicked policy but distress warrants work a treat. They don't half make people cough up' (*Guardian*, 27 August 1982).

The only management practice that Radford found to be associated with lower arrears levels was the use of a weekly payments cycle. This is a predictable finding suggesting that some with rent arrears have low weekly incomes and few reserves, and so have difficulty in anticipating and preparing for future commitments. Another indication of these characteristics is multiple debt, and this has been found to be fairly common amongst those in arrears (25% in Duncan and Kirby's sample).

Multiple debt can arise for many reasons, and the budgeting failure which it implies requires interpretation. There is certainly evidence of attempts to balance the budget. Duncan and Kirby (1981) noted that all but two in their sample mentioned strategies they used to help 'make ends meet', and the researchers got the impression that people were being quite resourceful in their attempts at budgeting.

Harvey's (1979) Camden survey presented a vivid picture of some tenants' inability to budget or cope with their many problems, which is, in part, predictable as her sample was chosen from referrals to an advice centre. Some in the sample were so unable to manage their affairs because of acute anxiety or mental disorder that Harvey was led to comment that 'local authorities could be readier to acknowledge that some cases of this kind simply have to be "carried". The alternative is that children will suffer or tenants become totally homeless or both.'

Harbert's (1965) early study commented that those in serious arrears were 'weak and immature personalities who burden themselves out of proportion to their strengths'. This type of individualistic approach has been repudiated by later studies (Brent TRIRU, 1982). As with wilful evasion, there is an obvious risk that any emphasis on budgetary problems will divert attention from the more general causes of rent arrears. Nevertheless if there are individual families unable to cope, they require recognition and assistance.

Many surveys have indicated that arrears problems would be lessened if tenants were given more help. The help can be of two kinds. One, based primarily on the local authority interest, is early and personal contact with the housing department so as to facilitate the control and paying off of arrears while they are still relatively small. The other, based on the individual interest, is the comprehensive provision of advice in welfare rights, so as to ensure that the general financial position of the family is as satisfactory as possible. Both Ungerson and Baldock and the Brent TRIRU argued that use should be made of the housing department's familiarity with a family's circumstances that develops when there is an arrears problem. This provides a valuable starting point for an extension of welfare rights advice. The need for more help and advice was argued strongly by Harvey who claimed that the major cause of rent arrears in her survey, although it was not one mentioned by the tenants, was their unawareness of their financial rights. Only a few were not penalised by their ignorance.

Harvey drew attention to the 'remarkable' extent to which rent arrears could be traced to what she claimed were faults within the SB system, including mistakes, misuse of discretionary power, mislaying of papers and dilatory dealings. The SB scheme makes special provision for rent, but no one in Harvey's sample knew how much was being allowed for it nor had they any idea of how the scheme worked, and in many instances, Harvey argued, it worked to the disadvantage of the unsophisticated claimant. However, the SBC have not been complacent, and it was its awareness that claimants were baffled by the complexity of the provision for help with housing costs which led it to become an early and strong advocate of a unified housing benefit, to which reference has already been made.

The introduction of a unified housing benefit may reduce the number of administrative problems of the type which so concerned Harvey. Where the tenant is entitled to the payment of full rent and rates there is an obvious simplification, and no risk of arrears, if the local authority and DHSS make a paper transaction not involving the tenant, although this procedure will take away from the tenant his freedom to 'borrow' from the rent money. Where there is more doubt over the size of the entitlement, there seems to be no reason why local authority officials should make fewer mistakes than the number alleged by Harvey to have been made by those in the DHSS, except in so far as comparisons between two different schemes will no longer be necessary. A major disadvantage of the new scheme for some tenants will be that the local authority will not be obliged to deal with claims in 14 days as was the case with the DHSS. The money problems of tenants with very low incomes could be intensified while they wait to hear the amount of rent and rates they have to pay, and they could become serious for private tenants who face a greater risk of eviction in the event of arrears.

Although information is growing about the circumstances and characteristics of those with rent arrears, there is as yet no answer to the question posed by the Department of Environment Occasional Paper (1978) of why, given similar incomes and family circumstances, some tenants fall into arrears and others do not. So far it has been tackled only by Ungerson and Baldock, whose research study is the only one to date (1982) with a control group. They noted that although low per capita income made rent arrears more likely, only one in seven of families with such incomes were in arrears. They explained the absence of arrears for the vast majority by suggesting that their survey was a snapshot picture and by hypothesising that those with the appropriate characteristics were likely at some time to encounter a financial crisis and fall behind at least for a few weeks. Ungerson and Baldock concluded that the short-term rent crises were symptoms of long-term financial circumstances, and lack of savings in particular made people susceptible to crisis.

As with debt in general, the literature on rent arrears reflects a division of opinion. At one extreme are those who attribute rent arrears primarily to personal characteristics such as wilfullness, extravagance, inability or failure to budget or claim rights with competence; and at the other extreme are those who discount these factors, alleging that the major cause is the socioeconomic structure of society which leaves some with resources so inadequate that rent arrears are inevitable.

Fuel debt

In common with many social problems, paying for fuel creates difficulties for only a minority of the population: 92% of electricity and 94% of gas bills are paid well before demand or final notices are issued (Berthoud, 1981). But the evidence suggests that the minority includes many disadvantaged and vulnerable people.

The most visible aspects of the fuel debt problem is disconnection with the obvious hardship it imposes; and it is this issue which has been the most hotly debated. Berthoud (1981) in his review of the Electricity and Gas Industries Code of Practice (based on over 2000 interviews and other data) described disconnection as 'very rare' with a frequency of 71 per 10,000 for electricity and 30 per 10,000 for gas in the year April 1980 to March 1981. However, in terms of people, this represented 135,521 electricity and 38,429 gas customers, and since only a small minority (16%) were lone adults, and nearly three-quarters of those disconnected had children, the number of people living in a household disconnected from a fuel supply during the year 1980/1 was likely to have been over half a million, although precise figures are not available. A quarter of those losing electricity were reconnected the same day and three-quarters within a month, whereas with gas only 18% were reconnected within the month.

Berthoud described those for whom disconnection procedures were initiated or carried out as mostly suffering 'one form or another of social disadvantage'. Only a third of those disconnected were in stable full-time work; over a quarter were unemployed; others were inter-mittently unemployed, sick/disabled, or were full-time housewives (mostly lone parents). Nearly half had incomes below the lowest SB level and nearly three-quarters were below 130% of it. The net standing of living of disconnected households was about half that of non-debtor households.

Berthoud noted the relatively small number of pensioners who were disconnected even though many had low incomes. He suggested this was because of their determination to avoid debt. However he also noted that social security provides a higher income per head for pensioners than for other low income families.

Four-fifths of the SB claimants, who were disconnected and for whom information was available, were getting the lower rate, while all pensioners are entitled to the higher rate. A further reason given by Berthoud for the relative avoidance of disconnection by the elderly in comparison with other families was 'that the presence of children in a household has an effect which is not adequately allowed for in standard comparative measures of low income'. Since most standard compar-ative measures of low income are based on SB allowances, Berthoud's comment implies that SB child allowances do not meet the full cost of children. About three-fifths of those disconnected had children under the age of 11, compared with a quarter of normal customers.

Disconnections do not indicate the full extent of the fuel bill prob-lem. A guide to the scale of the pressure, although not the intensity, that fuel bills put on families' budgets is Berthoud's figure of $3\frac{1}{4}$% of electricity and $1\frac{3}{4}$% of gas consumers who could pay overdue bills only by making arrangements to do so by instalments. These figures are four times greater than the 0.71% and 0.30% of electricity and gas customers who are disconnected.

The hardship arising from disconnection is likely to encourage families to try hard to avoid it. Its unwelcome nature is shown by the high proportion – 38% for electricity and 49% for gas – who borrow in order to get supplies reconnected within a couple of days (Berthoud,

1981). The 1977 Report of the British Association of Settlements Right to Fuel Campaign described how this can have a spiralling effect with finance houses cashing in on desperation and advertising unsecured loans at exorbitant rates of interest for paying fuel bills. 'Such loans simply had poor consumers even deeper into debt.'

Causes of Fuel Debt

National data, discussed earlier, indicate why some families have high fuel expenditure relative to income. Reports of small surveys of families with fuel debt point to the importance of the fuel budget share in individual cases. For the 29 households with fuel debts surveyed by the Merseyside Right to Fuel Action Group (1980), the budget share rose from 16 to 25% during the years 1976 to 1979. North Lewisham Law Centre (Bennett, 1981) reported a 22% budget share for the 38 consumers with fuel bill difficulties who approached them. Some of these people lived in all-electric tower blocks. These figures compare with an average of 5.5% for all families (McClements, 1978).

Berthoud's (1981) large survey supports the smaller ones with its finding that the size of the bill in relation to household income appears to be of critical importance. Of the households disconnected 83% had bills equivalent to four or more weeks 'income per head', compared with only 3% of those who paid before 'disconnection listing'. By contrast, Berthoud found no strong link between debt problems and fuel expenditure.

Many debts leading to disconnection were large because they included arrears. 10% of electricity and 4% of gas disconnections were because of debts for amounts greater than £200, or almost five times the size of the average bill. In London, in the period under review, a quarter of a million bills were issued for amounts of £250 or more. Bearing in mind the low income level of many debtors, it is not surprising that Berthoud described the largest debts as 'literally insoluble'.

Gray et al. (1977), in a Fabian Society pamphlet suggested that it is unexpected difficulties or even tragedy which makes it impossible to meet fuel bills. The Merseyside Child Poverty Action Group (1977) took a different view, suggesting that for many, fuel debts were caused by poverty, although it was undeniable that for some they were part of a larger problem of being unable to cope, and of personal malfunctioning within the family.

Over a long period, expectations of how warm a house should be and of how much of it should be heated are likely to have risen with the general rising in living standards. But the sharp increases in the price of fuels during the second half of the 1970s is almost certainly the factor which precipitated the fuel bill problem. Table 9.1 shows the pattern of price change that took place over the decade.

Table 9.1   Annual percentage increase in price of domestic fuels and the general index or retail prices

Period	Coal	Gas	Electricity	Heating oils	RPI
1970	6.1	2.2	1.4	11.2	6.4
1971	10.1	8.4	12.7	2.2	9.4
1972	9.0	4.0	4.6	6.5	7.1
1973	2.8	1.6	7.0	33.1	9.2
1974	25.8	6.7	31.9	48.6	16.1
1975	27.0	35.2	41.1	24.0	24.2
1976	21.3	11.2	18.6	28.5	16.5
1977	15.1	9.7	10.9	3.3	15.8
1978	12.5	0.2	7.7	0.0	8.3
1979	22.1	8.0	19.2	53.2	13.4
1980	30.4	27.7	29.8	17.8	18.0

Source: Hansard, November 30 1979, vol. 974, cols. 839,840 written; March 2 1981, vol. 1000, col. 16 written; Economic trends

In five of the seven years between 1974 and 1980, the price of electricity and coal rose by over 18%; in one year electricity rose by over 40%; in two of the years the rise in gas prices was very high; and in five of the years both coal and electricity rose by more than the retail price index. In these circumstances it is only to be expected that low income families would have difficulties in paying fuel bills.

Billing procedures are of secondary importance, but they affect the ease of payment and can significantly influence the avoidance of debt. The standard arrangement in the fuel industry is quarterly billing in arrears. In his survey, Berthoud (1981) found that easy payment budget schemes are available but not common, being used by $5\frac{1}{2}$% of electricity and $10\frac{1}{2}$% of gas consumers and probably rarely by potential debtors. They preferred prepayment meters which were slightly more common with $6\frac{1}{2}$% of electric and $14\frac{1}{2}$% of gas consumers having them (Berthoud, 1981). The pattern of payment with its emphasis on quarterly billing makes budgeting an important element in fuel bill problems.

Budgeting problems are predictable when people on weekly benefit or with low weekly incomes are presented with fuel bills for the past three months' consumption. Saving is a difficult exercise for families struggling to find money even for necessities, and voluntary savings schemes are not an adequate substitute for monthly billing. The SBC's policy of paying benefits, including heating allowance at the same rate throughout the year, is another factor which can make life difficult when the heavy winter fuel bills arrive (NCC, 1976c).

The fuel boards have not made extensive efforts to make payment easier for their consumers. In particular, prepayment meters, an obvious help to families with low weekly incomes who can't cope with three-monthly credit bills, have not, in the past, been readily available. Berthoud (1981) found that, between 1977 and 1980, use of meters declined even though between 40 and 50% of customers who had been disconnected or who had incomes below SB level showed a clear preference for them.

Up to 1980, the fuel industries offered prepayment meters to customers only in particular circumstances which included being in debt and in hardship. Partly as a result of Berthoud's (1980) interim report it was made clear that prepayment meters would be readily available provided their installation was safe and practical. (Hansard, 8 December 1980, vol. 995, col. 926 oral, 435 written).The SBC (1980) welcomed the change of policy by the Board, but it criticised the tariff changes of April 1980 which penalised those using prepayment meters.

In his final report Berthoud (1981) strongly advocated the increased use of prepayment meters, suggesting that they should become compulsory, where safe and practical, for debtors who could not keep to a repayment arrangement, which Berthoud recommended should be offered to all debtors. Berthoud argued that disconnection should only take place where meters could not safely be installed. He gave several reasons for the more extensive use of meters. The evidence showed that in periods when meters had been most frequently installed, there had been the greatest fall in disconnection rates. Meters provided customers with at least some fuel whereas disconnection permitted none. Their use was in accordance with the long-established principle that suppliers of goods and services on credit should allow no further credit sales if previous bills are not paid, but the refusal of cash sales was another matter. For Berthoud these advantages outweighed the fuel boards' dislike of meters on the grounds of cost and fear of fraud.

'No Disconnections'

The fuel boards' right to disconnect has dominated discussion of fuel debts since 1975 when the British Association of Settlements (BAS) report *A Right to Fuel* (1975) called for its limitation. The case has been argued forcibly by the BAS and the pressure group it spawned, the National Right to Fuel Campaign.

The BAS (1975) argued that fuel debts should be treated in the same way as other debts and the fuel boards should go to court to pursue them. If disconnection was not such an easy option it would be in the interest of the boards to take effective measures to ensure that existing debt was not increased. The NCC (1976c) also called for no disconnections, estimating that removal of the fuel boards' power to do so would add only 1% to fuel bills, a figure which the boards disputed.

The BAS National Right to Fuel Campaign in its 1977 report was particularly critical of the boards' view that brinkmanship was a characteristic of bad payers. It pointed out that the NCC survey suggested that about half of those disconnected had low incomes, and the fact that many bills were paid after disconnection indicated not brinkmanship but the lengths to which people go to get the supply back. The Oakes Committee (Department of Energy, 1976b), set up by the Department of Energy to look at the methods of making fuel payment, recommended that the power to disconnect should be ended. However the Secretary of State made it clear in the House of Commons, 10 June 1976, that publication of the Report did not imply that the then Labour Government endorsed its recommendations. The 1979 Conservative Government took the same view of the fuel boards' right to disconnect. On 14 July 1981, John Cartwright, MP introduced a private member's bill on the control of disconnections which would require fuel boards to get court permission before disconnection and would restrict the circumstances in which permission could be given. The Bill did not receive Government support, and it made no progress in the House of Commons. In the same year, Mr Cartwright specifically requested the Government to take steps to make disconnection illegal without a court order. The answer was 'no' (Hansard, 11 March 1981, vol. 1000, col. 343).

The arguments and campaigns did not succeed in getting a policy of no disconnections but they led to a code of practice being introduced in 1976. This encouraged those in difficulty to seek help, and particular 'hardship' cases were referred to the DHSS or social services departments before any disconnection took place. The Code had some initial success in reducing disconnections but they rose again and were particularly high in London. The London Electricity Board was strongly criticised by Levin (1980) of the London Electricity Consultative Committee in a report later published by The Child Poverty Action Group. He accused the Board of 'sharp practice' and 'simply not honouring the Code of Practice'. The complexity of the issue is illustrated by the comment of the Midlands Electricity Consultation Council (1979) who monitored 2653 cases covered by the code of practice over 30 weeks. It was disturbed to find that, 'Since the supply was not in danger of disconnection, consumers were lulled into a false sense of security, and when ultimately faced with disconnections, the debt had increased to unprecedented proportions.'

Berthoud's proposal for compulsory meters where safe and practical would make disconnection normally unnecessary, and, in effect, it bridged the gulf between the critics and supporters of the 'no disconnections' policy. But it was rejected by the fuel boards who made only a limited response. In a revised code of practice they proposed that they should in future take the initiative in offering a repayment agreement before disconnection, and repeated their willingness to install prepayment meters where safe and practical. They also said that all requests for meters would be recorded, technical alternatives to traditional slot meters would be investigated, and there would be offers of arrangements for repayment of large accumulated debts over a reasonable period (Hansard, 29 March 1982, vol. 21, col. 25W). But the boards were not willing to forgo their right to disconnect.

Overall Berthoud (1981) found that the fuel industry had not systematically taken hardship into account in its operation of the code of practice. Nor did he feel they would effectively do so in the future, and he argued that they should be relieved of their welfare role. The National Right to Fuel Campaign, commenting on Berthoud's final report, called the code of practice an 'elaborate confidence trick', and called for an amnesty for those with huge debts (*Guardian*, 15 October 1981). Berthoud (1981) stressed the importance of not permitting such debts to accrue in the future and he recommended consideration of a 'once only' paying off of a part of the very largest debts as the only solution to the current practical problem.

The code of practice delays disconnections; it gives information about easy payments systems; it encourages consultation and referral; it helps some people get benefits to which they are entitled but might not claim. Less usefully, but probably inevitably, it provides social services departments with extra work, estimated to be costing £13m in 1980 (Association of Directors of Social Services, *Community Care*, 23 July 1980). Overall it can only be a solvent and not a cure. The fuel bill problem is primarily a money one and the code of itself provides no money.

The fuel boards have consistently argued that they do not see it as their responsibility to defray unpaid bills, even where there is hardship, for this would mean the cost falling on the boards' other customers. If this view is accepted, the responsibility for providing money for hardship cases with fuel bill problems inevitably falls on national and local government.

The Government's Response

Governmental response to the fuel bill problem has been pragmatic rather than having a defined policy aim. Supplementary benefit discretionary payments have long been the major source of help to poor people in paying for heating but by definition they are restricted to those eligible for SB. The numbers of those on SB receiving a regular heating allowance rose from 194,000 in November 1971 to 1,100,000 in May 1976, and to 1,400,000 in May 1977. As fuel debts increased, the SBC became increasingly unwilling to make exceptional needs payments (ENPs) for fuel bills, since claimants are expected to pay for fuel from their standard allowance. By 1980 the SBC would no longer pay off fuel debts after claimants had been on direct payments scheme for two years, as had previously been the case, and single payments were made only in very special circumstances.

Some SB claimants choose to have payments for fuel made directly to the fuel boards. This may be to pay off past debt, to avoid it in the future, or a mixture of both. Pressure group organisations frequently complain about the high percentage of income that fuel boards demand for such payments, e.g. BAS National Right to Fuel Campaign (1977), National Council for One Parent Families (1979). Berthoud (1981) found that the average figure for fuel direct deductions in his sample was £6.80 for electricity and £5.60 for gas (in 1979/80): 19% were paying £10 or more for electricity and 2% were doing so for gas. Regardless of average figures, allegations have been made about excessive amounts in individual cases. For example, it was claimed that a Scottish woman was asked to pay £17.50 a week out of an income of £17.88 (Scottish Fuel Poverty Action Group, *Community Care*, 31 January 1980).

Variation of tariff or tariff tilting is one way of helping poor consumers. Tariffs which have a fixed initial charge result in consumers of small amounts of fuel paying higher average costs. A Department of Energy (1976a) report concluded that tariff adjustment was an extremely complicated way of dealing with the hardship of a minority of consumers. The report met vigorous criticism from Trinder and Clark (1976) in a BAS Right to Fuel Campaign Report. They argued that the Government report used data for a period before fuel prices had begun to rise, and it did not discuss fuel expenditure as a percentage of income.

In a later paper the Department of Energy (1980) again maintained that tariff tilting would not help poor consumers. This time they were challenged by Bradshaw and Hutton (1981) of the Social Policy Research Unit at the University of York. In a 1981 working paper they considered the effects on poor people of four different progressive tariff tilts. Each produced a greater proportional drop in electricity expenditure for low income households than for others. Although the gains were relatively modest, they compared favourably with the heating help provided in other ways. Inevitably a minority of poor customers, those who are also relatively large users of electricity, would lose, and for this reason Bradshaw and Hutton acknowledge that tariff tilting is a blunt instrument for (income) redistribution. Nevertheless they argued the case for rescuing it 'from the scrap heap of policy options'. In their footnotes, Bradshaw and Hutton questioned the extent to which pricing should be based solely on efficiency criteria, the degree to which today's prices should take account of tomorrow's likely energy costs, and whether energy, like housing, is too important a commodity in household budgets to be left to the free play of market forces.

The most direct form of help to ease the pressure of fuel bills is the provision of cash. In terms of amount, the cash provided by social service departments of local government, through their use of Section 1 of the Children and Young Persons Act 1963 is of minor importance. The study by Hill and Laing (1978b) of the use made of this section by six local authorities showed that in 1976/7, £4.3m was distributed to families and, on average, 17% was for fuel bills, although the percentage varied from 12 to 29% between authorities. Despite the relatively small sums involved, the flexibility of help provided by Section 1 payments make them uniquely valuable in some circumstances.

The first government cash payment, prompted by the fuel bill problem, was the payment of 25% of the electricity bill for one quarter in the winter of 1976/7 to those on SB or receiving FIS. The following year, the scheme was modified to give a £5 lump sum and a rebate of 25% on the amount by which a quarter's bill exceeded £20. The cost in both years was approximately £25m. These schemes were criticised for their restricted eligibility (SBC, 1977a), and the then Labour Government responded in the winter of 1978/9 by extending the payments to those who received rent or rate rebates.

The Conservative Government of 1979 chose to give fewer people more help, initially at a reduced overall cost. The previous scheme was abandoned and a new one introduced. The basic heating allowance of 95 pence per week was automatically given to all SB pensioners aged over 75, and to all SB families with children under 5. Additionally an extra £1 a week was given to FIS families (Hansard, 22 October 1979, vol. 972, cols. 35–7). Since two-thirds of supplementary pensioner householders were already getting the heating allowance, the major gain was for some families with children. On 27 March 1980, it was announced that coverage of the scheme was to be extended, with the basic heating allowance going automatically to those over 70. The level of the SB heating allowances was raised, the basic rate going up nearly 50%, and the number of allowances was reduced from 3 to 2. FIS families were given a further £1 a week. By 1981 the Government was spending £250m on helping $2\frac{1}{4}$ million people to pay for their heating. (Hansard, 11 March 1981, vol. 1000, col. 892 oral). But nearly all of this was expenditure on normal SB heating allowances. A Parliamentary reply (Hansard, 21 May 1981, vol. 5, cols. 152–153W) stated that at current prices, additional help with heating costs for the years 1979/80, 1980/1, 1981/2, was, or was expected to be, £5.5m, £21.75m, and £39m respectively.

For the individual householder, home insulation and particularly loft insulation, is important. It can greatly reduce the money spent on heating or increase the warmth of the house, albeit at some capital cost. The Government's home insulation scheme for which £12.5m was allocated for 1980/1 appears to have energy conservation rather than social policy as its major aim. Although old age pensioners have to pay for only 10% of the cost of loft insulation, the Government paying the rest, other low income groups are given no preference. Like other applicants they have to find a third of the cost themselves. Insulating a loft is likely to cost from £80 upwards. Low income families with fuel bill problems may well be unable to afford to gain very much from this Government provision, and since it has been little publicised, many may be unaware of its existence.

Paying for fuel is likely to continue to be relevant to money problems for some years ahead. For those on low incomes, fuel is an essential commodity becoming increasingly expensive in real terms. The effective cost varies considerably with circumstance, and the highest cost per unit tends to fall on the poorest. Payment methods have adapted only slightly to match the budgetary practices of poor consumers. Disconnection has been an effective debt collection weapon, but it has given the fuel boards an immunity from normal commercial pressures and has probably slowed the development of effective easy payment methods for those that need them. The SBC was particularly conscious of the need for a long-term solution to help all low income groups with heating bills. However, its proposal for a 'comprehensive scheme' (SBC, 1978a) did not receive immediate support from either of the main political parties. In its final report published in 1980, the SBC again pressed for a comprehensive fuel allowance scheme. It described the Government's policy as the 'strategy of the blunderbuss' and pressed for money to go to those who need it most, the criteria to include both the difficulty people have in meeting fuel costs and the cost of heating their homes.

Government intervention with regard to fuel costs is of relatively recent origin. The complexity of the factors contributing to fuel bill problems suggest that the nature of intervention will be modified over time. The extent to which low income families will benefit depends on whether social or economic policy considerations dominate.

10 Repercussions of Money Problems

Money has a pervasive influence, and shortage of it is likely to be similarly all-embracing, affecting relationships and personalities as well as the material aspects of life. The repercussions of money problems are very relevant to deprivation although not all are easily investigated.

This chapter looks at a range of repercussions. The most direct and obvious is the effect on a family's style of living. Less tangible is the connection between money problems and relationships. There can also be what is best described as a personal impact. For example, money problems can subtly change expectations or induce feelings of stress and apathy. This latter group of feelings can readily lead to ill health. Finally the last section of this chapter looks at fertility which has a tenuous but important link with money problems. Some of these repercussions are of an imprecise and general nature, lacking clear concepts and objective measures. Conclusions have therefore to be of a tentative nature. Nevertheless examination and discussion is valuable for it can illuminate and give pointers for further investigation.

Style of living

Style of living is a convenient umbrella term but the mass of tangible objects and intangible feelings that contribute to it are not easily summarised. Here only a few of the major component elements are discussed, but they outline the life-style of poor people.

In most cases it is not possible to make any quantitative assessment of the deficiencies in the style of living of those with money problems. The studies of low income living do not generally give figures of cut-backs or reduced expenditure on food and clothing; and where figures are given, they are rarely accompanied by comparative figures for those better off. As a result, there has to be reliance on the subjective comment of those surveyed. Nevertheless the detail and the similarity of view emerging from a wide range of surveys gives an unquestionable credibility to the overall picture.

Difficulty in Managing

Difficulty in managing is a problem that is particularly difficult to formalise or measure, but undoubtedly it is a pressing reality for many people. For over 30 years, the market research organisation Gallup has been asking people what worries them. In 1951 and 1966, 'making ends meet' was the problem which more people worried about than any other (40% in 1951 and 20% in 1966). By 1982, it was in third place, having been overtaken by health worries and concern that there might be another war, but the percentage figure (33⅓%) was even higher than in 1966 (*New Society*, 15 July 1982). In view of Gallup's findings, it is surprising that the topic was not included in the Quality of Life Surveys, carried out by the SSRC Survey Unit in the 1970s. The most closely related indicators used then were money and prices, and living standards. These were considered important by 18 and 17% respectively of those surveyed (Hall, 1976).

It is, of course, the poorest of the poor who have the most difficulty in managing and suffer the greatest hardship. Of all the major groups it is the long-term unemployed on the bottom rate of SB who have the lowest incomes, and they are likely to feel the problems arising from shortage of money in their most acute form. Piachaud (1981b) used FES data on the expenditure of low income of non-retired single people to show how an unemployed man would be likely to spend the £21.30 a week he would receive from supplementary benefit in 1981. Piachaud gave revealing details of what this might mean: consumption at a level of, for example, 4 kw of electricity for heating per day, 1 wash at the launderette, 1 visit to the cinema every six weeks, 3 pints of beer, and 50 cigarettes per week. Piachaud concluded that the level of material living available to unemployed people was 'basic and bleak'.

To manage, the unemployed have often to choose between goods usually considered to be essential. For example, food may be bought at the expense of clothes or furnishing (Marsden and Duff, 1975). Clark (1978) attempted to look behind SB levels to see how the poorest unemployed families were coping in absolute terms as well as in relation to their own standards when in work, and to those of the rest of the community. In her national sample of men on SB, she found, not surprisingly, that the main method of coping was to cut down on usual purchases. The greatest strain was in the first month and again after six to twelve months when the long-term effects of low income were beginning to be felt. Families with children were much affected: 50% cut down on food and clothing and 18% on heating. The importance of these commodities to the families was shown by their being the most common items for which savings were spent or money borrowed. Of unemployed men with three or more children 89% felt they had unmet needs and nearly three-quarters said they had difficulty in managing financially.

Many low income families with working heads of households are also under financial pressure. Knight and Nixon (1975) found that 30% of the 800 FIS families they interviewed had had to cut back during the preceding four weeks for major reasons such as reduced earnings and the receipt of a large bill and for minor ones like a child's return to school, clothes, holidays, extra food, repairs, admission to hospital and funeral expenses. Concern over money was widespread and 40% felt they had to do something to make ends meet. The action most often taken was to reduce food expenditure. The basic items, food and clothing, were the ones these families found most difficult to afford, with fuel and rent of some but lesser importance.

Many Scottish debtors subject to the arrestment of wages have been reported as being left with incomes so low that extreme difficulty in managing is inevitable (over 60% have incomes below SB level and some are much below). Of the 25 debtors surveyed by Adler and Wozniak (Scottish Law Commission, 1981a), who had an average of £29 a week withheld, 9 'reported bluntly that they were quite unable to manage', 4 had to make substantial sacrifices, 5 had to borrow from friends and relations, and only 7, less than one-third, could manage on the income they had left. As already noted, arrestment of wages and salaries is fairly common in Scotland, there being 9000 cases in 1978 (Scottish Law Commission, 1980d).

A small study by Evason (1973) of 71 households on a housing estate in Northern Ireland illustrated the greater pressures and more acute choices which larger families compared with smaller ones face. The affairs of the poorest large families were described as chaotic. Their resources ran out more quickly than in smaller families. Despite cutting back and doing without in many areas, mothers had regularly to borrow to make ends meet. Those a little better off spent only on 'basic necessities', but generally they kept out of debt. Only when income was over 120% of SB was the acuteness of choice diminished, and even then four large households at this income level managed only by borrowing or spending noticeably less on food. Once again food and children's clothing, particularly coats, were mentioned by the families as causing particular concern.

A later study of poverty by Evason (1980) in four areas of Belfast attempted to quantify the relationship between a feeling of shortage and level of income. Of those with incomes below 120% of SB 22% felt short of 'everything', compared with only 6% of those with incomes over 140% of SB. Of the lower income group 31% felt short of 'nothing', compared with 56% of the better off group. Evason also asked the households how they would deal with an unexpectedly large bill. About half said they would try to pay it off weekly, and the proportion varied only slightly with income. Nearly a tenth of those interviewed felt there was just no way they would be able to cope.

Food and Clothing

Cutting back on food is a predictable reaction of families with money problems. Food expenditure is one of the few relatively large expenditures over which a family has immediate control. But the pressures determining food consumption are varied and often subtle. For example, although Marsden (1969) found that one in ten of the 116 lone mothers he interviewed had 'eaten literally no solid food on the day before the interview', and 'between a quarter and a third were missing out meals every day or were regularly eating very little', he commented that 'these patterns of eating were moulded by past hardships and the influence of relationships within the family as much as by the present budget'. He noted, amongst the lone mothers, a 'stress reaction to living on a low income, which was shared to some degree by many [other] women who had been on assistance for a long time'. Some ate less so that their children could eat more. In other cases, women had little incentive to cook. In one of the areas where the mothers lived there was an attitude that fresh meat was 'an extravagance in itself, the right of male manual workers only'. Marsden commented, 'These cultural restrictions on diet tended to cut down feelings of deprivation with regard to food.'

Other studies show that food is important for reasons other than its nutritional value. It was described as being 'our only luxury' by one of the 86 large families surveyed by Land, while others felt it was a conscious expression of indulgence. Butter had a particular psychological significance, as did Sunday lunch. Most of the families made a major effort to provide a joint even though much more of a cheaper form of meat could be bought for the money. But overall, Land found evidence of reduced consumption of most foods except the cheaper ones. Nearly half the families drank less milk than average. They seldom had fruit, but they ate more potatoes. In 22 of the families, only the father had a cooked evening meal.

Cutting back on food as a way of making ends meet is so frequently referred to in surveys of those with low incomes that it is unfortunate that the severity of the cut-backs cannot be properly judged because the necessary detail accompanied by comparative figures for consumption of similar families with higher or average incomes is not provided.

Clothing has caused difficulties for most low income groups for both utilitarian and social reasons. Land (1969) found that shoes were a constant worry to poorer large families, with children missing school because they had none. She observed that the mothers found discussion of their own clothes a particularly sensitive issue. Seventeen out of the 86 she interviewed had bought them secondhand or from jumble sales. The evidence of Gingerbread (1978), an organisation of lone parents, to the RCDIW described the depression felt by some younger mothers because they could no longer afford to keep themselves looking fairly fashionable, and the parents of older children said that they were concerned at the obvious distress felt by the children who could not dress as fashionably as their school friends at the weekends. A detailed OPCS survey by Hunt (1973) of samples of fatherless, motherless and two-parent families living in five areas of the country concluded that even the worst off of the two-parent families were better clothed than the average fatherless families.

Evason (1980) found, that, amongst the 71 families she surveyed in Belfast, clothing was the commodity they felt most short of, with as many as 66% of the lowest income group saying they lacked some children's clothing. In the survey by Burghes (1980) of 65 FSU families living on SB, half the parents had not had any new clothes in the previous year. Nine had not bought any for over five years or could not remember when they last did so, it was so long ago.

Clark (1978) found in her large national survey that many of the unemployed on SB had difficulty in paying for clothing out of a weekly allowance, although the level of initial stocks affected the position. Half of the sample had less clothing than suggested in the SB guide. Family men were more likely to be below the SB level and the longer they had been on benefit, the fewer clothes they possessed.

The Home Environment

The depressing environment which goes with a low standard of living is noted in several studies. Many of the large families in inner cities surveyed by Wilson and Herbert (1978) commented adversely on the absence of household amenities such as baths, lavatories and hot water, and on dampness and the state of decay of the houses. In his study of lone parents, Marsden (1969) stressed that a decent home could only be built up at the expense of an adequate diet and clothing. Ferri and Robinson (1976), also writing about lone parents, commented that long-term reliance on subsistence income inhibited the building up of resources to replace major items of furniture and household equipment.

Hunt's (1973) detailed OPCS survey showed that ownership of household equipment was at a lower level for lone parents compared with two-parent families for every item enquired about. Marshall (1972) found in her national survey, that the differences between groups of fatherless families regarding ownership of household equipment was greater than the differences between one and two-parent families. Unmarried mothers and separated wives were the worst off. Widows fared best which is an expected finding since equipment tends to be accumulated over time, and widows are likely to have an obvious time advantage over other lone mothers, as well as a probable financial one.

Money as a Resolver of Problems

Money problems result in more than a relative lack of material goods. They also prevent poor families from buying time or energy to ease difficult situations. Less than a third of the lone parents surveyed by Ferri and Robinson (1976) had the use of a car, which the writers felt would be a valuable asset for overburdened lone parents. Land (1969) indicated that many of the problems of large families could have been removed or reduced if the solvent of money had been available. She noted how money could remove much of the drudgery from house-work, enabling weekly buying, ordering, or the purchase of a car. As it was, some poor families did a daily shop, with bulky food, sometimes carrying coal and paraffin up to flats. Although all the families had five or more children, 55% had no washing machine.

Relationships

Patterns of friendship are complex and money problems cannot be expected to affect them in a simple way. There has been very little research into the extent to which lack of money can inhibit friendship and restrict relationships. Causal links have not been established, and in view of the infinite variation in human nature, it could be difficult to do so. Nevertheless there are many indications of an interaction between money problems and relationships.

Social Activities and Friendships

Various studies have noted the reduced level of social activity of groups that have standards of living below the average. A national survey by Daniel (1974) of registered unemployed found that over half had given up various activities, and these 'going out activities' were sorely missed. Hill and Stevenson (1976) found that very few of the unemployed they surveyed were interested in leisure activities per se as distinct from the social relationship associated with them. No doubt this is true of many people in society, but it means that the cut-back in leisure activities often noted amongst the poorest groups in society also harms their relationships. Of relevance is Clark's (1978) comment that reduced spending on social activities had a significant effect on the life-style of the unemployed on SB, with implications for their relationships with family and friends. However, Clark's figures are difficult to interpret for there is no information on how much money is spent on the pursuits, the priority attached to them, nor the amount by which they were cut down.

The subtlety of the connection between low income and relationships is indicated by the Report of the North Tyneside CDP's (1978) study of local unemployment. In general it found that people were subdued by the 'experience of unemployment' and it 'undermined the social side of going out'. But possibly this reaction is as much due to feelings of stigma as of poverty for one man is quoted as saying, 'When you do go out you cannot socialise. You're frightened to talk in case you're criticised.'

In their evidence to the RCDIW (1978), Gingerbread made more direct reference to the isolating effect of money problems. Lone mothers were 'put off' inviting people to their homes because they were so shabby and drab, and tight budgets led to a gradual decline in socialising, with families being ultimately isolated. The isolating effect was similarly noted by Ferri and Robinson (1976) who commented that 'poverty forced . . . [some lone parents] back upon themselves and thus reinforced the sense of isolation'. The part played by factors other than poverty was noted by Marsden (1969), who felt it was mainly social difficulties which led to the one in five of the 116 lone parents he studied having 'no outside friends whatsoever'. He suggested that some of these more isolated parents were becoming an 'under class', slipping into a 'well' as they lost hold in the local community.

Many of the 65 FSU families surveyed by Burghes (1980) spoke of the 'misery of being trapped in their homes' as a result of dependency on SB. Their depth of feeling was indicated by replies to a question asking what they would most like to do if they had the money. Nearly three-quarters chose an outing or holiday for the whole family.

The social isolation of problem families has been noted by several writers including Philp and Timms (1957) and Philp (1963). Many families have been observed to have difficulties with neighbours and to have few if any social relationships. Perhaps most strikingly, two-thirds of those studied by Philp were either excluded from the family network or were severely limited in the help they received, which contrasts with the close family ties found in other studies of working class life. Stephens (1946) referred to ostracism as a constant difficulty, and Philp (1963) suggested that 'overwhelming emotional impulses' make it difficult for the parent in problem families to have satisfying relationships with other people. He went on to argue that many of them had been children in a period of general unemployment, when there was poverty and little material comfort. As children they experienced these environmental difficulties in the context of personal relationships. For example, unemployment meant a father's skill was not required and this could lead to 'conflicting evaluation' of parents and their role in society.

Family Relationships

For many people, the most important relationships are those within the immediate family. The frictional irritants arising from money problems were observed by Marsden (1969). He commented that the lone mother's dependent position and low income 'brought constraints even in the normal exchange of small gifts between relations'. The possibility of irritants escalating into something more serious is suggested by Marsden's comment that 'differences in living standards meant social awkwardness could more readily harden into permanent estrangement'. One example he quoted was the tension which can arise from the visibly different standards of living of working children living in a family dependent on social security. In addition Marsden commented, 'The whole delicate balance of duties, obligations, expectations and rewards normal to and derived from a more affluent society was seriously disturbed in a family undergoing hardship, and it was not too much to say that the shortage of money was contributing to the early break-up of the family.' The North Tyneside CDP (1978) reported that the majority of the unemployed in its survey felt that their family relationships were affected by unemployment. The report noted that rows were reported with 'depressing regularity', although the less the responsibility for other family members born by the unemployed person, the less the strain.

Rainwater (1974) attempted to analyse why low income couples in America were twice as likely to experience divorce as middle income couples. He suggested that not having enough money to support a family properly led to both partners being vulnerable to accusations from the other. The husband could be accused of making inadequate provision and the wife of not being 'sufficiently energetic making do'. However reasons for marital breakdown are complex, as Hollingshead (1954) indicated when he attributed the high rate (50–60%) of break-up amongst lower class American families to both economic insecurity and the values that develop in such groups.

Marital difficulties are often linked with debt although they may sometimes be a symptom and not a cause. 74% of Caplovitz's American sample of debtors were married at the time of the default. Of these, 9% were subsequently divorced or separated, 'in their view, because of the debt problem'. Caplovitz added a footnote referring to a question in a NORC national survey in 1967 which asked whether the respondent knew of anyone whose marriage had split up because of debt problems – 23% answered in the affirmative. A high proportion, 43%, of the married respondents in Caplovitz's sample reported that the debt had had 'some negative impact on their marriage'. In Scotland, as many as two-thirds of the debtors surveyed by Adler and Wozniak (Scottish Law Commission, 1981a) reported that diligence had led to serious marital arguments, and the researchers felt that 'in some cases, this clearly contributed to the break-up of the debtor's marriage'. A very high proportion (84%) of those who had had their wages arrested experienced marital problems, which Adler and Wozniak believed was not fortuitous but was in part because of the large loss of income from the arrestment.

Support for the view that debt affects marital relationships come from other sources. The Birmingham Settlement Money Advice Centre reported that debt leads to family tension and breakdown (Houghton, 1973). Ison (1979) noted that the 1976/7 Annual Report of the National Association of Citizens Advice Bureau said that, 'Many bureaux report marriage difficulties are stemming from money troubles in general and debt in particular.'

Personal impact
The personal impact of money problems is particularly difficult to evaluate because of the entanglement with other factors and the part inevitably played by subjective judgements. But its obvious importance to the individual and its relevance to deprivation means that it cannot be ignored.

Expectations
Poverty may lead to the hardships described earlier, but it may also condition them. As Ferri (1976) pointed out, feelings of hardship and deprivation are related to attitudes, expectations and previous experiences; and none of these are unaffected by poverty. Clark (1978) noted the gradual adjustment of the long-term unemployed to living on SB and the development of a certain resignation to 'going without'. Ferri and Robinson (1976) expressed surprise that a lone father felt that his accommodation, a three-bedroomed house for ten children, was satisfactory. Similar uncritical acceptance was noted by Marshall (1972). Of 83 families living on SB and with no inside lavatory, one-fifth were very satisfied with their accommodation, and only a quarter thought it was unsatisfactory because of inadequate facilities.

But not all poor families have low expectations. As already noted, many of the inner city large families studied by Wilson and Herbert (1978) commented adversely on their lack of household amenities. Nevertheless there seems to be a relationship between expectations, class, and income. Bradshaw (1974) reported that the Rowntree Trust Family Fund found that aspirations varied with class. Grants to families with handicapped children, in response to requests for help, were £50 higher in social class I and II than in IV and V.

An alternative interpretation to that of low expectations is provided by Marsden's (1969) comment that various pressures tended to discourage lone mothers from revealing deprivation. He found that substantial numbers were very reluctant to say anything that might indicate dissatisfaction, for that 'was tantamount to asking for charity'.

Stress, Strain and Apathy

The experience of poverty may, for some, lower the level of expectation, and dull the senses. But for many the sense of what Hoggart (1957) described as 'tightness and contriving' remains. As already noted worry over money is frequently reported in relevant surveys. It would be surprising if the poorest were not worried about money, but the intensity of the worry seems to stretch from some natural concern to very severe stress. However few studies have focused directly the stress arising from poverty, and there have been no attempts at objective assessment. The comments below are some subjective views of those involved in surveys. They are not necessarily representative but they provide an indication of the stressful effect of prolonged and acute money problems.

Marsden (1969) reported that one-third of 116 lone mothers he surveyed said they felt 'hard up all the time', 'terribly poor', or 'not living, just existing'. The main worry of a nationwide sample of 348 mothers on SB was found by Marshall (1972) to be 'lack of money'. Burghes (1980) used more colourful language when writing about some 65 FSU families living on SB. She referred to 'the misery of always worrying about money', 'the dread of a week's money running out', the difficulty of meeting basic necessities, the feelings of helplessness and humiliation.

Ferri and Robinson (1976) described lone parenthood as bringing many mothers and fathers 'prolonged and unrelieved anxiety about money. . . . state benefits provided a minimum standard and guaranteed a life of continual pinching and scraping'. A vivid description of a life-style adopted to avoid the payment of bills was given by one unemployed man interviewed by Marsden and Duff (1975). 'You sit here and you've no money, and a knock comes at the door and you all have to fly in the airing cupboard, all of us and the bairns.'

A supporting view of the stress that can arise from money problems was given by Blamire and Izzard (1978) of the Birmingham Settlement Money Advice Centre. Describing money as an 'extremely emotive subject', they added that, 'The strain involved in receiving final demands, solicitors' letters and court orders by every post and continually answering the door to satisfy all the demands can hardly be overestimated.'

Wilson and Herbert (1978) laid considerable emphasis on the stress which they felt was being suffered by the 185 large inner city families they were studying. These were selected from those with five or more children, who were known to Social Services Departments, so there may have been problems additional to financial ones which could have contributed to the stress. Nevertheless poverty dominated the lives of the families. Wilson and Herbert wrote of stress as 'all pervading in the sense that there is a chronic condition of being in want of something that is needed or desired – quite often this is an essential article . . . sometimes a craving . . . that can assume an overpowering force. The mothers were asked if they ever felt at the end of their tether. In almost two-thirds of the replies, they described particular situations in which they felt 'deep despair', and in many of them shortage of money was a factor. Wilson and Herbert reported situations such as 'the toilet out of action for six weeks', 'water dripping all the time on the floor'. Examples of the many quotes they gave are, 'Trying to manage made me a nervous wreck', 'I took two overdoses, both times the electricity had gone off. . . .' Wilson and Herbert felt the stress had a depressive effect on many mothers, with '. . . loss of self-respect . . . feelings of persecution . . . loss of motivation, suicidal action. . . .' The depression of some of these mothers may have been exacerbated by exhaustion. Only a quarter of them said they had sufficient energy to be alert to their children's needs by teatime.

The circumstances of these families suggest that lack of money was unlikely to be the sole cause for the depressed and exhausted state of the mothers. Research such as that by Brown and Harris (1978) has shown that depression has no simple relationship with class (and thus with likely income level). They suggested that factors such as inadequate relationships, the wife not having a job, and the presence of three or more children at home can explain what appear to be class-related differences in the incidence of depression. Nevertheless the comments of the women in Wilson and Herbert's study make it clear that, in some circumstances, acute pressure on stressed women would be greatly lessened if money were available and channelled to eliminate major material irritants, such as toilets out of action and water perpetually dripping on the floor.

All the families surveyed by Wilson and Herbert had at some time 'expressed' feelings of 'hopelessness and powerlessness'. These feelings have often been noted in people living on low incomes for long periods. The early study of unemployment in an Austrian village by Jahoda and his colleagues (1933) concluded that prolonged unemployment leads to a state of apathy in which even the few opportunities left are not utilised. The 'blunting monotony' of unemployment was observed. The people became accustomed to owning less, doing less and expecting less. Leisure was a tragic gift and any effort to use the superfluous time sensibly appeared superfluous. 'The feeling of irrevocability and hopelessness was more paralysing than economic deprivation itself. . . .' A much later British study by North Tyneside CDP (1978) indicated that the local unemployed people underwent experiences similar to those of the Austrians four decades earlier. Initial optimism gave way to pessimism, depression, and inactivity. These were followed by resignation and fatalistic acceptance. However the CDP found that this type of problem ended with the onset of a new job, whereas the financial recovery of the family took longer.

There can be no certainty about the extent to which the depression and despair, highlighted in so many studies, arise from the money problems that go with unemployment. They may be intensified by the boredom, frustration, and stigma of having no work. It seems likely that each corollary of unemployment has some effect, but the total impact will depend on the personality, temperament, and circumstance of the person concerned.

Health

Stress, listlessness and exhaustion drift easily into mental and physical ill health and the latter are frequently reported in poverty surveys. For example in Marshall's national survey of families on SB, 40 to 50% said they had current health problems. A higher incidence of ill health has been reported in other families with multiple problems. Philp (1963) found that three-quarters of the fathers and two-thirds of the mothers in his survey of families being helped by the FSU had some form of physical illness, and as many as 84% of the fathers and 90% of the mothers showed evidence of mental disorder or personality difficulties. Marsden (1969) found that over a quarter of the lone mothers he surveyed had had nervous breakdowns, and one in ten had attempted suicide. Causes of such problems are rarely easy to establish, but Marsden was in no doubt that 'a minority of the breakdowns could be clearly connected with the added difficulties of a low income'.

Ferri and Robinson (1976) suggested that nervous strain and the unrelieved responsibility of coping single-handed were responsible for the high proportion (53% of fathers and 72% of mothers) in their sample of poorer one-parent families who said their health had been affected by the family breakdown.

The relationship between class and ill health is complicated, and has a large literature. This review aims to touch only on a few aspects which are of particular relevance to the effects of money problems on health, although these are difficult to distinguish from the effects of class. The DHSS publication *Inequalities in Health* (1980b) commonly known as the Black Report, attracted wide attention despite its early limited circulation. Its recommendations were not endorsed by the Government on grounds of expense, but its thorough review of the literature was commended. The Report concluded that there were marked inequalities in health between social classes in Britain. It found that at birth and in the first month of life, the mortality of babies was twice as high for the lowest socioeconomic class as for the highest – a finding later confirmed and expanded upon by the House of Commons Social Services Committee in its report *Perinatal and Neonatal Mortality* (1980). For most causes of death in all age groups, there was a class gradient.

Rates of self-reported 'long-standing' illness (as defined in the GHS) rose with falling socioeconomic status and tended to be twice as high for unskilled manual males and $2\frac{1}{2}$ times as high for unskilled manual females as for males and females respectively in the professional classes. For severe or 'limiting' long-standing illness, the unskilled groups were found to be at a still greater disadvantage. The Report paid particular attention to inequality in health service availability and use. It felt that the 'greatest and most worrying' inequality was the differential use of the preventive services. The Report attributed this to 'a complex resultant of underprovision, of costs (financial, psychological), of attendance and perhaps of a life-style which profoundly inhibits any attempt at rational action in the interests of future well being'.

Many theoretical explanations for health inequality were considered in the Report, including cultural and behavioural ones. But it was argued that 'cultural variation in cognition and behaviour is merely a superficial overlay for differing group capacities of self-control or mastery which are themselves a reflection of material security and advantage'. Although they acknowledged that amongst all the evidence, there was much that was more convincingly explained in terms of culture, social selection, etc., the authors of the Report believed that the best answers lay in some form or forms of materialist approach.

The Report noted that few health data are related to income and wealth, so that only inferences could be made about poverty and health. Despite this, it concluded that, 'The evidence relating financial poverty (causally) to ill health is convincing, though only indirect.' Attention was drawn to the need to widen the concept of income, to include benefits in kind, and to consider all the dimensions of socio-economic position that might exert an active causal influence on health status.

The Black Report, although enthusiastically welcomed by some commentators, was criticised by others. For example Dr Digby Anderson, director of the Social Affairs Unit wrote that he was unable to take its conclusions seriously (*Health and Services Journal*, 26 November 1981). In a parliamentary debate, the Under Secretary of State for Health and Social Security, Sir George Young, argued that there were factors other than economic ones in health. However in a critique of the Report, A. Gray (1981) welcomed the willingness of its authors to 'step out of the bounds of the traditional medical models of ill health and consider socioeconomic factors'. He concluded that despite some ambiguities and an inability to produce causal evidence at some times, it did not follow that they were 'heading in the wrong direction. . . .'

The nature of the direction in which the Report was heading was well illustrated by the Report's discussion of accidents which are a major cause of the higher death rate of lower class children, particularly for those aged 1–4. 'While the death of an individual child appears as a random misfortune, the overall distribution clearly indicates the social nature of the phenomena', and the Report concluded that lower class households 'simply lack the means to provide their children with as high a level of protection as that which is found in the average middle class home'. In addition, it noted research by Brown and Harris (1978) which found that the higher incidence of stressful life events, and the lack of means to resolve recurrent domestic setbacks indirectly lead to a greater prevalence of accidents in working class homes.

The medical profession is becoming increasingly conscious of the relationship between illness and what they term 'life events'. Frequent use is made of the Social Readjustment Rating Scale which relates the life changes that a person undergoes to the likelihood of their becoming ill. The scale gives a rating to various events, e.g. the death of a spouse is 100, and divorce and marital separations are 73 and 65 respectively. 'Fired at work' is 47 and change in financial state, 38. It was estimated by Dr Kent Smith in America that 37% of patients with scale readings of 150 to 199 had associated illness within two years, and when the scores went over 300, the percentage rose to 79%, and the higher the score, the more serious the illness (*Pulse*, 4 August 1979).

The event that has provoked most controversy in relation to its effect on health is unemployment. Fagin (1981) provided a useful summary of the research that has been taking place since the 1930s. He noted that the seminal study of Eisenberg and Lazarsfeld (1938) which showed that joblessness is accompanied by periods of 'emotional instability', mild or moderate depression and alcoholism has been confirmed by all researchers who have studied unemployment. The detailed statistical analysis of the American, M.H. Brenner (1973, 1979), who correlated health and economic indices in America and Britain, has been more controversial. Brenner examined many aspects of ill health, and concluded that admissions to mental hospitals and the suicide rate were closely linked to the level of unemployment, and unemployment affected mortality rates after an appropriate time lag. He suggested that the downward trend in the death rate is a consequence of long-term economic growth. But the downward trend is slowed by both unemployment and rapid economic growth. Economic instability and insecurity tend to make people lead more unhealthy lives; and lost friendships and income reduced by unemployment affect health.

Three British economists, Gravelle, Hutchinson and Stern (1981) claimed that Brenner's model was a poor predictor and that the time period chosen affected the result. They found that although the unemployed often have more than their fair share of ill health, it was difficult to distinguish cause from effect. However, although the three economists were critical of Brenner's calculations for Britain, they did not argue that unemployment had no adverse effects on health, only that there were no data which could be used to estimate their magnitude, timing or form.

Ramsden and Smee (1981) analysed evidence from the DHSS cohort study, a nationally representative sample of men registered as unemployed in the autumn of 1978. They too did not dispute the association of unemployment with ill health, but they joined Gravelle *et al.* in disputing the causal relationship, arguing that the worse the sickness record, the lower the likelihood of finding a job; hence the long-term unemployed were likely for this reason alone to have a worse health record than the unemployed in general.

The same cohort study was used by Fagin (1981) to provide a sample of unemployed men with dependent children who had been unemployed for at least 16 weeks, and who had been employed throughout the previous year. The assumption was that in these circumstances, health problems had not led to the unemployment. The response rate was low (45.5%) and the final sample was small (22 interviews) but the case study touches on several interesting aspects of the health problems of the families of unemployed people. Fagin, like others, felt that stress was the mechanism by which unemployment could lead to illness. But there was no common pattern of reaction. Some unemployed men with previous histories of ill health had relapses or aggravation of previous illness after becoming unemployed, while others improved. Generally the loss of a job resulted in psychological changes, such as those already discussed. In some cases there were also physical symptoms. When this happened, the tension felt because of having no job as a result of unemployment was relieved. The health of wives and children was often affected. In the case of the children it was generally an adverse reaction, but for the wives, the reorientation of roles within the family had a mixed effect.

The literature shows that some men undoubtedly go through a predictable pattern of psychological response involving a loss of self esteem, and this is likely to be greater for those who obtained benefits from their jobs which were other than financial ones. As already noted, stress is often singled out as the mechanism by which unemployment may lead to illness. There has been no analysis of the contribution that shortage of money makes to stress and it is referred to only in general terms. For example, Fagin commented that, amongst other things, stress may be related to 'poverty, worrying about making ends meet . . . and accepting lower standards'.

Colledge (North Tyneside Community Health Council, 1981), in a study of health and unemployment in the poorer areas of Newcastle on Tyne, argued that stress linking unemployment and ill health arose from financial difficulties as well as from the disruption of the daily pattern, and the challenge to the ingrained work ethic.

An association between ill health and unemployment is generally accepted, but whether or not there is a causal relationship is hotly disputed. For example Colledge claimed that there is a strong proven link between unemployment and social class and between social class and ill health. At a meeting in September 1981, most European health ministers were sufficiently convinced about the relationship to call upon their governments to take 'appropriate measures' to combat unemployment because of the health risks involved. The British Parliamentary Under-Secretary attending the meeting, Mr Geoffrey Finsberg, opposed the resolution, arguing that the link was not scientifically proven (*The Times*, 25 July 1981). His comment was criticised by Peter Draper, the director of the Unit for the Study of Health Policy at Guy's Hospital Medical School in London. Describing the remark as wishful thinking, he argued that it demonstrated 'a failure to master the findings of research which go back over half a century' (*The Guardian*, 16 November 1981).

Fertility

The link between fertility and poverty is indicated by a remark made by Cutwright (1971) about the American situation. 'If the lower class families had only the number of children they wanted, poverty would be cut nearly in half.' No defensible social policy could attempt to limit poverty by enforced family limitation but Cutwright's statement raises the question of whether unwanted pregnancies increase poverty in Britain. To what extent are children in poor families unwanted? Does poverty lead to unwanted children as well as unwanted children leading to poverty? The meaning of 'unwanted' has also to be considered. Does it mean 'unintended', 'regretted', or something between the two?

Obviously not all large families are unintended or regretted. Some, perhaps many, are wanted and Philp's work (1963) with FSU families suggests that this may have applied to these families despite their severe problems. He commented that, 'In general, the worth for the mother seemed to be closely associated with motherhood' and that, 'Family limitation is unlikely to be accepted . . . until they (the mothers) come to feel that they have more value in other areas of their lives, but in general they do not seem to feel this.'

A similar view was expressed by Rainwater and Weinstein (1960) in a study of the psycho-social factors involved in family planning in the American working class. 'Motherhood is much more completely her reason for being than it is for the middle class woman who is taught the value of outside interest for establishing her validity as a person.' Despite this Rainwater and Weinstein were clear that not all children are wanted, for they described family planning as a 'confusing' problem for many working class people. It is 'another facet of a world seen as chaotic, difficult to understand and very difficult to master in a personally effective way'. In a later book Rainwater (1974) suggested that a lower class milieu affects family formation quite dramatically: 'expecting no better prospects is a dynamic factor in producing early marriage and early pregnancies'.

All the large families surveyed by Land (1969) had five or more children. They were not asked whether the children were unintended. The issue was approached more obliquely. Only 9 out of 86 thought more than four was ideal and none of the poorest hoped their own children would have large families. Although the companionship of large families was valued two-thirds of the mothers and fathers thought the children suffered some disadvantage, and the most important reason the parents gave for this was material deprivation. Land found some association between number of children and level of income. The poorest families were less successful with contraception and having failed they were less likely to try again. The successful users, on average, were the better off couples and only one came from the bottom income group. Land felt that ignorance, embarrassment, and a feeling that contraception was unnatural appeared to be the biggest barrier to the successful use of contraception. In conclusion, she was ambivalent, finding it hard to say whether the majority had deliberately chosen to have a large family. 'Many lacked the necessary information as well as the confidence to plan their families.'

The early studies by Philp (1963) and Rainwater and Weinstein (1960) suggest that some or perhaps many of the poor who had large families may have wanted them. However there is an undoubted incidence of unintended pregnancies in Britain. Cartwright (1978) found that 47% of births to mothers with husbands in unskilled jobs were unintended compared with 26% for all mothers. In Class V 18% regretted the unintended births, whereas 13% of all classes did so. The percentage of fourth pregnancies that were unintended was even higher, ranging from 52 to 67% according to the age of the mother. Of mothers under the age of 20 54% of pregnancies were unintended. No great variation was found in the use of contraceptives between the classes although class V had a higher use of the less reliable methods. The proportion of those with two children who hoped they would have another did not vary with social class in 1975, although two years previously the top and bottom classes had wanted the most children. In practice, mothers married to husbands in classes IV and V had the most. In an earlier study Cartwright (1970) had found that 28% of working class mothers felt birth control was 'unnatural' in comparison with 8% of middle class mothers.

The reasons for variations in fertility, both over time and between classes, are neither simple nor fully understood, judging by the frequency with which predictions of the number of births are proved wrong. Some writers such as Askham (1975) consider that the situation regarding working class births is particularly complex. Askham hypothesised that 'the greater the impact of situational factors such as economic and social deprivation, insecurity and powerlessness, the greater the need for adaptation in terms of norms and behaviour patterns involving no planning ahead and being unable to control one's environment'. To test her hypothesis, Askham surveyed four groups of Aberdeen families: with two children and with four children, in social class III and social class V. She felt that 16 out of the 90 cases interviewed were atypical for a variety of reasons. She concluded that,

'On the whole however it is felt that differential family size between social class III and IV can be explained in terms of orientations developed as a means of adaptation to, or recognition of, situational factors.' She added the more familiar comments that the only certain solution to the problem of lower working class couples having more children than they want is an improvement in their economic and social situation, although she acknowledged that changes such as greater ease of access to efficient means of contraception would also be helpful.

Askham's views and those of earlier writers suggest that in some circumstances poverty may combine with certain characteristics to increase the size of families, and this in turn enhances poverty. Hence the cycle of poverty, which may also be a cycle of deprivation, continues. In reality many influences act upon families in ways that are difficult to distinguish. An unpublished study by Tonge, Lunn, Greathead and McLaren (1979) suggested that the cycle of deprivation is far less marked than in the past. They surveyed married adults who had once been children in problem families previously surveyed by Tonge James and Hillam (1975). Adjusting for age and sex, it was found that the number of children in the second generation had declined by about half. The reason was the much greater use of contraception. The report suggested that this 'fortunate change' had occurred because contraception had become easy, cheap and socially acceptable. Additionally, for people 'who wish to savour the other pleasures of life as advertised on the media', children had become too expensive and demanding to rear in large numbers. Attention was also drawn to divorce becoming more common because of its greater social acceptance. This was reducing the number of unsatisfactory marriages which 'struggled on with one child arriving per year for ten to twelve years'.

This section of the review has considered some of the repercussions of poverty. In some instances the literature is slight, and in others it is diffuse. No attempt has been made to give a comprehensive review of the extensive literature on poverty, but by selecting from it, some indication has been given of the effect of the pressures that money problems bring. Much of the comment is inevitably subjective and it is difficult to disentangle the effect of money problems from other factors such as upbringing or temperament. However, an impressionistic picture emerges of families struggling to manage, living in a tense and stressful atmosphere, with emotional, physical and marital breakdown a common occurrence.

11 Summary

The purpose of this review has been to examine the nature, causes and possible depriving effects of money problems. As previously indicated, the term money problems is used to mean an imbalance of resources and requirements which leads to crises, debt or the restriction of living standards to a level that is low in comparison with others in society. A low level of income inevitably predisposes to money problems; the overall level of resources and requirements which contribute to or cause these problems is affected by an extensive range of factors; and both the money environment and the ways people handle their money exercise strong modifying influences.

Vulnerability to money problems
Money problems are exacerbated or reduced by a wide range of factors so that not all those with low incomes relative to requirements are necessarily in difficulty. But low income creates vulnerability. Vulnerable families are particularly likely to be those with children, for the pressure on requirements arising from children is rarely matched by the increase in resources. However the literature shows that assessing the additional cost of children, or the equivalence scale as it is known, is surprisingly complex and controversial. One approach has been to assess the extra money needed for parents to have the same standard of living as they would have had if they had remained childless. But an acceptable measure of standard of living and, in particular, one that allows for the fact that preferences change with parenthood, has yet to be devised. Additionally it can be argued that having a child – unless he or she was unwanted – contributes to the standard of living in the same way as the possession of other goods and valuables.

The alternative method of assessing the cost of children requires some normative input relating to 'needs', which are then costed using budgetary studies. The normative aspects of this method invariably provoke argument, but this approach has the advantage of presenting expenditure figures for children on different explicit assumptions, and these provide a useful basis for further discussion.

Despite the conceptual difficulties, the use of some form of equivalent income – with acknowledgement that it is approximate – is essential for any meaningful comparison of living standards between households. Without it the significant effect that children have on living standards is obscured.

The level of SB allowances for children is important because as well as providing additional resources for many children in low income families, it is part of the commonly used measuring rod of the adequacy of family income. It has not been derived directly from equivalence scales, although no doubt the SBC took note of work that has been done in the field. Several writers have criticised the allowances as inadequate, and the SBC themselves consider that for families with children, SB income is barely adequate to meet their needs at a level consistent with normal participation.

There is no sharp income dividing line separating those who are vulnerable to money problems from those who are not. But some indication can be given of the number of those more likely to be vulnerable. Of nearly 13m children in the population in 1979, approximately 2.4m lived in families with incomes less than 140% of SB level. Nearly 900,000 are in families receiving SB and just over a quarter of a million lived below SB level.

Of those receiving SB, the unemployed have the lowest long-term incomes relative to requirements, because however long they are on SB, they stay on the short-term rate of benefit. As a result they are particularly prone to hardship. Getting the long-term rate for the unemployed was the top priority of the SBC during the last year of its existence, but it was unsuccessful.

The hardship of the long-term unemployed is likely to be greater, but the number of children involved (170,000 in November 1978) is much less than in the case of one-parent families (approximately $1\frac{1}{2}$ million). These families are nearly six times more likely to have low incomes than couples with two children or less, and compared with families with three or more children, the likelihood of low income is one and three-quarter times as great. Earned income, particularly for lone mothers, tends to be small and state benefits – except for widows – are means-tested. The common treatment of lone parents as a homogeneous group is misleading. At one extreme are the few with professional salaries or generous maintenance payments. At the other are a larger number of younger unmarried mothers and deserted wives with little or no resources and a low earnings potential. Within the group, both resources and requiremens vary. The comment of the RCDIW that for lone parents income is not necessarily a good measure of standard of living suggests that their true position is obscured by inadequate knowledge of the costs that lone parenthood brings.

Of the approximate 2.4m children living below 140% of SB level in 1979, over a million had working parents. These families are more likely to be poor rather than very poor, but their overall numbers are such that half of the very poorest children, those in families living below SB level, have working parents. Their living standards are important both because of the number of people involved, and the comparative effect their standards have on levels of social security benefits. Means-tested provision for low income families has increased in recent years, with the introduction of FIS for working parents being of particular importance. But the take-up of FIS has been surprisingly low (50%). Means-tested benefits and transfers only partially compensate for the extra costs of children as measured by the level of SB child allowances. As family size increases, the discrepancy becomes increasingly important. The main reason for the greater poverty of large families with working heads is not their slightly lower level of money income but the additional requirements arising from the larger family size. It is not surprising therefore that families with three or more children were 36% of all low income families although they were only 20% of those receiving child benefit.

Resources and requirements

The lower the family income relative to requirements, the less is the financial flexibility and the greater the difficulty in managing. For poor families even minor changes in resources and requirements may precipitate or prevent money problems, and the effects may be disproportionate to the amount of money involved. Whether or not the wife works is the most important factor preventing a family from living at poverty levels. Noted in many surveys, it is emphasised in some as being the crucial determinant of poverty. A factor about which there is less certainty but much conjecture is 'fiddling'. Interest in the so-called 'black economy' is growing, but the extent to which it raises the incomes of those thought to be poor is unknown. Irregularity of income combined with a low income can lead to financial crises. The flow of income of the 'persistent poor' in industrial countries has been described as 'chaotic'. Compared with other countries, the UK social security system responds relatively promptly and regularly to need. For those in work the position is more obscure. There is no information about the circumstances of the 20% in the Department of Employment's New Earnings Survey who are not traced, but who it is thought work intermittently.

Savings and assets of various kinds obviously diminish or prevent money problems but, as expected, they are rarely possessed by the most vulnerable families. Townsend (1979) found that for the population as a whole the level of assets (if houses are excluded) is low. It is particularly low for families with children and the poorest of these tend to have debts, not assets. Low income makes saving difficult, but there is some evidence that accumulation of money is not a traditional part of working class culture. Money is scarce and even saving for specific things imposes a discipline which some find difficult to accept. The presence of relatives and friends willing to help in times of crisis is a different kind of asset, but one of obvious value. Those without are particularly disadvantaged.

The potency of social pressure on requirement is evident throughout the literature and is particularly stressed by Townsend. But there has been no comprehensive reseach into the motivation underlying patterns of expenditure and virtually nothing is known of the influence of upbringing, the family, the neighbourhood, the peer group or television as stimulators of what people want. Pressures of a different nature arise from personal characteristics. The desire for an occasional extravagance appears to be widely felt, and is of particular importance to those living on low incomes for long periods. It is possible that this general tendency may be exaggerated in some people leading to a compulsion to spend. Compulsive habits such as drinking and smoking are familiar, and the health aspects are well researched, but little is known of the financial burdens they impose on low income families.

On the requirements side, housing and fuel are two major items of expenditure liable to cause money problems. For many years Governments have given wide ranging help with housing costs. Money problems in this area, although not eliminated, appeared to be reasonably contained. But in the early 1980s, rent arrears escalated. The introduction of unified housing benefit should ease the rent arrears problem although only perhaps at the cost of intensifying them in other areas. General assistance for low income families in affording and paying for fuel is of fairly recent origin, occurring mainly since the sharp price rises of 1974. Since then fuel debt and disconnections have risen to record levels, and there are something like half a million people living in families whose fuel was cut off at some time during the year.

Official help with fuel bills has been erratic as Governments have changed, with much variation in the criteria for help. Despite financial assistance, codes of practice, and attempts to provide acceptable easy payments schemes, a general comprehensive solution has yet to be found for the problems of poor people with heavy bills which they cannot afford to pay. Fuel debt stands out as a major unresolved social problem of the early 1980s.

The money environment

The money environment is the term being used to describe the financial structure and commercial practices and pressures facing consumers. Several differences are noted between the environment of the poor and that of others although there has been little detailed analysis.

Credit is a part of the money environment which is notable for the conflicting attitudes toward it. Although widely used, it is often done so only with reluctance. It is criticised both for being extended too freely and refused too readily. Some believe it to be an instrument for raising living standards, while others condemn it as an encouragement to trading malpractice. The evidence indicates that no viewpoint is fully proven, and all contain some truth. One important argument is about whether credit boundaries should be determined solely by commercial considerations regardless of the social consequences for those who become easily over indebted. Again the literature provides no conclusive answer, for although there is evidence of companies pressing the acceptance of further credit to people already over-committed, little is known of the social consequences of debt, or of the likely effectiveness of measures that might prevent it. The numbers having some form of credit problem are substantial, while the more serious money problems are less common but concentrated within vulnerable poor groups. They are not easy to investigate because of the sensitivity of the subject.

Many poor people pay more for credit than is necessary or justified. The poorest tend not to use banks, the cheapest source of credit. Instead they rely on a limited range of expensive credit facilities chosen because of custom, recommendation, convenience and consideration of whether the weekly payment required will fit into the weekly budget.

A question of particular interest is whether debts, which are relatively small but not easily repaid, can spiral because illegal money-lenders, the 'bank of last resort' for poor and desperate people, operate in such a way that debt becomes overwhelming. Evidence is sparse but the occasional reference to excessive debt, the depositing of child benefit books as security, and the use of 'heavies' to ensure repayment, leads to conjecture that there may be a small but significant amount of illicit debt amongst poor people.

The extent to which low income consumers are persuaded if not pressurised into purchases they don't want or can't afford has not been studied in the UK. There is no research comparable with that of Caplovitz in the US. He noted how the style of marketing was adapted to meet and often exploit the circumstances of poor customers.

Anecdotal comment suggests that there may be some strong marketing pressure in the UK particularly amongst ill-informed and low resistance groups in society. Such pressure may lead to overcommitment or to poor value or both.

Poor value and additional costs arise for a variety of reasons. The inflexibility which goes with having little or no capital and a low weekly income prevents cheaper large-scale purchase, does not permit the buying of economical household equipment and tends to lead people to make 'bad buys'. Having no spare cash or savings frustrates cost effective preventive measures. Low income, combined with inadequate capital and restricted access to credit, leads to an inability to pay bills at the time they are presented which can force families to resort to action that eventually can be costly. Ignorance and lack of sophistication lead to faulty judgement affecting value obtained for money. Market factors causing poor value are defective goods and limited shopping scope.

Money management
Money management is a topic with a minute literature. The occasional references are mainly about families with acknowledged social problems which happen to have a financial component. The lack of research into styles of money management, relating them to temperament and comparing their effectiveness at different levels of income, deprives the topic of a basic framework of reference which would facilitate analysis of the particular problems of managing on a low income.

The essential preservation of liquidity is difficult for low income families with no savings, and budgeting, in the sense of conscious allocation, requires strong discipline, perpetual juggling of commitments, and frequent reassessment of priorities. For those with the lowest incomes, the pressures are disproportionately great.

Some low income families cope rather than budget. To do so, they adopt a variety of strategies, occasionally developing a noticeable skill in deploying them. Bills may be paid or ignored only after careful selection, and those, who control discretionary sources of income may be manipulated. People having the most difficulty in coping – and even perhaps failing – are at the extreme end of the continuum of money management. Some belong to the group commonly known as problem families. These are an ill-defined group who have drawn attention to themselves by requiring help, sometimes of an extensive nature. There is general agreement that they often live in a state of financial chaos, but the reasons for it are disputed. However there is evidence that, on becoming adult, some children of problem families may adopt different patterns of behaviour.

The timing of income receipts and bill presentation rarely matches, and foresight is necessary if money problems are to be avoided. Several studies suggest that it is lacking amongst vulnerable families. Relatively little is known about the importance of budget cycles, but some vulnerable families undoubtedly have fairly inflexible weekly cycles which do not easily adjust to monthly or quarterly bills.

One particular aspect of money management, maldistribution within the family, is of particular interest because it directly affects living standards. As a research topic, it presents formidable difficulties which is perhaps a partial explanation of its relative neglect. Family relationships and maldistribution within the family interact on each other and, as might be expected, much of the evidence of serious maldistribution comes from studies of battered wives and lone parents. Maldistribution can lower individual living standards more than any other factor because so long as she lives with her husband, a wife is not eligible for the safety net of SB.

An Australian study indicated that, amongst the general population, the husband's personal expenditure is often considered to be committed in the same way as are urgent bills. The amount tends to be related less to a family's income level than to community norms. Wives usually manage the family money but have much less say in its control. Some researchers have argued that direct involvement by the husband in the paying of the expenses of the household is likely to reduce the risk of budgetary problems while the contribution made by working children to household expenses has been criticised as often being very inadequate.

Debt

The majority of British families use credit to buy goods of all kinds including houses. They are all debtors in the sense that they owe money. However the term 'debt' is more commonly used for the situation that arises when agreed repayments are not being made. Debt of this kind is thought to be a growing problem, although its precise size is unknown. Approximately 200,000 people are sued annually in the county courts of England and Wales (1980 figures) for defaulting on hire purchase and other money loans. Less formal collection methods are applied to an unknown number of other defaulters.

Debt is a subject on which strong views are held. Debtors are regarded by some as culpable and by others as unfortunate; and the evidence is insufficient to say which is the more accurate view. For many years, little has been known of the causes and consequences of debt. But in the late 1970s and early 1980s pioneering work by the

Scottish Law Commission and research related to the use of credit by other bodies, in particular the National Consumer Council, have produced much valuable information.

Debtors tend to be married people with children and low incomes. The elderly generally manage to avoid getting into debt, while families with the lowest incomes and where neither parent is working are particularly prone to it. Vulnerable families include those who pack their commitments too tightly into a weekly budget. Unexpected calls for expenditure, even for small amounts, can quickly transform a just manageable situation into a spiral of debt.

A fall in income, such as that arising from unemployment or illness, is generally accepted as the most important precipitating cause of debt. Voluntary overcommitment, personal characteristics, irresponsible behaviour and the failings of the creditor are additional causes but their importance is not easily assessed. Surveys have had low response rates and, with such a sensitive topic, replies have to be assessed with caution.

Debt recovery measures, with the exception of Scottish ones, have been little investigated. Scottish evidence suggests that creditors generally protect their interests reasonably satisfactorily, but for debtors the recovery procedures can be harsh. Where there is genuine misfortune, debt repayments can entail excessive cutting back on other expenditure; if the debt recovery process is carried to its conclusion, there can be disproportionate personal hardship and public humiliation.

Living with money problems
The major DHSS studies provide a mass of factual material about the way of life of many on low incomes, while smaller case studies give a more personal view. Overall the picture that emerges is one of a depressed life. Home environments tend to be drab, household possessions limited, food and clothing in short supply and 'cutting down' is common. Many of the poor face an acuteness of choice which diminishes only if income rises comfortably above SB levels. The more significant indicators of a restricted life may be the less tangible aspects of living although the picture is impressionistic. Some studies emphasise the exhaustion and stress felt by mothers struggling to manage on their money. Others refer to debt sometimes leading to excessive anxiety or withdrawal and living in a fantasy world. Physical and mental health and personal relationships are affected by shortage of money. An atmosphere of despondency and low expectation pervades some families, with those who have lived on low income for a period of time being particularly vulnerable. However the available studies do not

permit a thorough assessment of either the incidence or the precise nature of the effects referred to. Situations that tend to coexist with money problems are often the main focus of the studies and with the present state of knowledge it is difficult to disentangle the complex relationship between them and money problems.

Fertility

Fertility is relevant to money problems for two reasons. High fertility may contribute to money problems, and the style of living associated with them may enhance fertility. There is no doubt that money problems are more likely the greater the number of children, but on the second point the evidence is ambivalent. It is argued that motherhood gives a sense of value to the restricted lives of poor women, yet survey evidence shows that many births to mothers in low income groups are unintended, although a far smaller proportion are regretted. The underlying factors determining the desired size of the family appear complex, are little understood and are likely to vary with social and economic change. But increased access to contraception has undoubtedly helped mothers to have no more than the number of children they wish.

12 Social Policy Implications

This literature review has ranged over a wide area, covering some well researched topics and others that have been relatively neglected. For some topics the implications for social policy are clearly signposted, whereas for others, only general guidelines are indicated.

The incomes of families with money problems
Resources which are inadequate relative to requirements are, by definition, the root cause of money problems. The simple solution of providing more cash is rarely a realistic option, so scarce resources have to be targeted onto chosen priorities. The literature reviewed indicates the groups most in need of help and suggests areas where social policy intervention would be most useful.

Level of income directly determines the capacity of families to cope with crises or to carry any extra financial load, and it indirectly affects many factors that modify money problems such as value obtained for money, credit status, savings, stocks of household equipment, and personal possessions. Some people with high incomes get into financial difficulties, but inevitably low incomes are more conducive to serious problems.

Tautologically all families defined as poor have low incomes which lead to restricted expenditure and low living standards. More usefully, the hardship arising from restricted expenditure varies amongst people, all of whom may be described as poor. The usual poverty definitions cover a fairly wide range of income, and at this level small differences are important. Several different poverty levels are in common use, and amongst people all judged to be poor some are much worse off than others. Incomes at or below short-term SB are small compared with 140% of long-term SB. Those with the lowest incomes would be expected to have more problems. But the literature shows repeatedly that, compared with those a little better off, the poorest have very many more problems and often the pressure is excessive. If hardship is to be identified and priorities determined, the distinction between the poor and the very poor needs to be drawn and stressed. It should however be noted that accurate assessment of the income that actually determines the living standard is not easy because some of the cash and kind additions to income are officially disregarded, and are therefore easily overlooked.

Poverty is notoriously difficult to define or measure, but apart from facility, the common use of SB levels as a measuring rod has little to commend it. The SBC (1978b) was not in favour, arguing that a poverty line should relate to the level of earnings. As the SBC implied, a poverty line should be a measure of relative hardship. It should not be influenced by what the government of the day feel is an appropriate level. On practical grounds, the two SB levels differ significantly (the higher rate being 125% of the lower one in 1982) and confusion easily arises over which is being used. The only advantage of using SB provision as a poverty line is that it is, to some extent, an equivalently adjusted measure. But the SB dependency allowances are the result of judgements rather than equivalence estimates; and in relation to actual costs, the allowances for children, and in particular for teenagers, are almost certainly too low.

Adjustments for equivalence are only a step towards a true reflection of hardship. With the exception of Townsend (1979), few have attempted to devise more sophisticated measures, almost certainly because of the conceptual and practical difficulties. Expenditure surveys report the consumption levels of basic items such as food, fuel, clothing and housing, but they give little indication of the pressures arising from the dynamics of family life, individual circumstances, peer group pressure and social mores.

The more detailed the analysis of poverty and hardship, the more resources the analysis requires. Nevertheless it is surprising that, since over £20 billion (SSAC, 1982, 1980/1 figures) of public money is paid out in social security expenditure designed in part to relieve hardship, the tools of measurement should be relatively so rough and ready. No doubt this is because other factors are thought to be more relevant than hardship; and, on the whole, the public have not shown undue concern about the hardship of poverty.

Through a wide range of income maintenance schemes the state is closely involved in determining the level of income of those in the lowest ranges of the equivalent income distribution. But it does not aim for equality of standard of living for those dependent upon it. Tradition, and the assumed values and preferences of society, lead to some getting more than others, although the size and distribution of the social security budget responds to new information and changing circumstances. There is a known variation in the public attitude towards the state support of certain groups (H. Parker, 1980). Some circumstances are considered to be worthy and deserving of help. Others are regarded as blameworthy, thus meriting only limited, or even no, response from the state. These attitudes affect whole families because the social security status of the parent determines the standard of living of the dependants.

This review is interested in the position of families with children, and the public attitude towards them has been ambivalent. It has not been disputed that people dependent on social security need some extra cash for a dependent child. Nor was the principle of child tax allowances questioned by the general public although it was by specialists in the field. But the current main provision for children, a cash payment of child benefit, although naturally appreciated by the mothers receiving it, has not been given the same public support as other benefits such as pensions or disability allowances. This may be because of a traditional feeling that it is parents who should take the major responsibility for supporting their children. It is probably also because of an unawareness of the extent to which the presence of children lowers material living standards. For example, it is not generally appreciated that those with the lowest living standards (income in the bottom quarter of the equivalent income distribution) are more likely to be members of families with children than they are to be elderly; and, as this review has shown, of those on means tested social security or low wages, families with children are the worst off.

One method of improving the position of the worst-off families with children is to encourage the mothers to work. The additional income undoubtedly relieves poverty, but it is unlikely that more mothers will be able to work unless both job opportunities and additional child-care facilities are available. When there is high unemployment, the former, seems unlikely; and, as Piachaud (1982) pointed out, there are no signs of improvement in the child-care services.

Government cash help for families with children is given through the social security system, using universal or means-tested benefits. The latter is cheaper, even though means-testing can be administratively expensive, but it has stigma and take-up disadvantages. Another method is to devise clawback procedures so that better off families benefit little if at all. The options cannot be properly assessed except in the context of help given to all groups by government, whether in the form of tax allowances or cash benefits. The tax allowance form of help is attractive to governments partly because it does not appear in expenditure figures. But although less visible, it has the same effect as cash benefits on the balance of government income and expenditure.

Whether changes are minimal or substantial, universal or restricted, decisions have to be taken about priorities and the direction of change.

The evidence of this review suggests that it is the largest low income families with working or self-employed heads, some lone parent families, and the long-term unemployed who are most vulnerable to the greatest hardship, and, on this criterion, they have the priority need for help.

Donnison (1980) commented, 'It is the working poor whose living standards impose a political ceiling on what you can do for people out of work.' But their living standards are also important in their own right, for it is the working poor who form the majority of poor families.

Government support of the living standards of these families has declined in relative importance in the post war period, as the SSAC (1982) pointed out. Between 1946 and 1981, average earnings doubled in real terms, and most major benefits generally matched that increase. But the real value of child support in the form of tax and family allowances and later child benefit changed only marginally. At best, it increased by about 13% for families with one child, and at worst it declined by about 7% for families with three children.

As a percentage of the married couple's retirement pension, child support fell from 57.1% in 1948 to 22.2% in 1981. Although there are other advantages, in terms of value, the replacement of family allowances and child tax allowances by child benefit has not been helpful, except for poor, non-tax paying families; and because of the decline in the tax threshold there are very few of these. Overall the real value of child benefit declined by 8% between April 1979, the end of its phasing in, and November 1981. In addition, its introduction brought a serious drop in the real value of child support for families with older children because of the abolition of age-related child tax allowances (SSAC, 1982).

Pressure groups such as the Child Poverty Action Group have argued strongly for an increase in child benefit. Help given in this form does not carry with it the disadvantages of means-tested benefits. But with approximately 12 million children in the population, the cost is high. Each additional 10 pence a week increase in child benefit is estimated to cost £55 million a year net of savings on other social security benefits (SSAC, 1982). A worthwhile increase of say £1 a week would therefore cost over half a billion pounds. Only a relatively small proportion of any additional expenditure would reach those in poverty.

No more than 13% of families getting child benefit were found by the DHSS Family Finances Survey (OPCS, 1981) to have low incomes (below 140% of SB levels). But a larger proportion of children would benefit because poor families are disproportionately large. Also the disadvantages of means-testing cannot be ignored. But the most important consideration is that child benefit should not be judged by a simple cost evaluation. It is, above all, an effective way of smoothing out a major life-cycle variation in income. Since children, on becoming adults, pay taxes to provide benefit for the next generation of children (as well as paying for the state pensions of their parents and childless couples), child benefit can be thought of as a 'pay as you go' system of anticipating a child's future earnings, which benefits all families, today's and tomorrow's.

If improvement in the level of child benefit has to come slowly, priority should be given to large families who are the most severely affected by the gap between child benefit and the cost of a child. They could be helped effectively by following the European practice of increasing the level of child benefit for dependent children after, say, the third or fourth. Such a policy would also increase work incentives for large families who, under present provision, are generally the least financially disadvantaged by being out of work.

The relationship between low earned income and depressed living standards is not a simple one because of the many factors involved. The relative decline in universal benefits has highlighted the importance of means-tested benefits available to low income working families. Of these, FIS is the most important because of both its amount and because it gives an automatic right to other benefits. Between 1979 and 1981, the FIS prescribed amounts were increased ahead of inflation, and to the greater benefit of the larger families. The SSAC (1982) argued that FIS should be seen as a 'crucial integral part of the social security net'. However it has not been a benefit that has been widely welcomed, mainly because it is means-tested. But so too is SB, and there is no obvious reason why, in principle, means-testing should be less acceptable for the working than for the non-working poor. In practice, the situation may be different. Those for whom a means-tested benefit, such as FIS, provides a topping-up income have a greater financial ability to reject it, because of their dislike of means-testing, than have those with no other source of income – which is the position for many on SB.

A major difference between SB and FIS is the level of take-up – 74% for SB and 51% for FIS in 1977 and 1978/9 respectively (SSAC, 1982). FIS will only become a generally acceptable benefit when its take-up reaches a level that shows that it is broadly meeting the need for which it is intended. If low take-up is mainly the result of stigma, that level is unlikely to be reached. But if it is the result of a failure to recognise eligibility which Corden and Bradshaw (1982) found was the most important cause of delay in claiming, attempts to 'push' FIS, which Corden and Bradshaw called for, might help to change the present unsatisfactory situation.

The financial position of many lone parents is unsatisfactory, in part because they form a heterogeneous group and there has been a varied public attitude towards them. In general, fathers are expected to provide for their children. Only when a father dies, does a mother get a non means-tested state benefit as a right. Unmarried mothers, separated and divorced wives and widowers get no state income specifically as a consequence of their state of lone parenthood. They are entitled only to more generous benefits, allowances, and SB disregards, in addition to their general right, shared by most heads of household, to claim SB. Although the higher earnings disregard gives lone parents a slight advantage over others on SB, reliance on the means-tested benefit inhibits any substantial additional earnings and imposes a ceiling on the family income. Nearly 40% of lone parents depend on SB, so it is not surprising that Layard, Piachaud and Stewart (1978) found that 58% of lone parent families have incomes below 140% of SB level.

Discussion of the level of appropriate provision for lone parents is complicated by three factors. Their personal financial resources vary considerably; most of them are women, the majority of whom have an earnings potential well below that of the average male worker; and when one parent fills the role of two, additional costs are inevitable.

The pattern of family life in Britain has changed significantly. Only about a quarter of households are now of the stable nuclear family type with breadwinner Dad, housewife Mum and two children (Study Commission on the Family, 1980). About one in eight children live in one-parent families at any given moment and as many as one in five is likely to do so before he or she is 16. (Study Commission on the Family, 1981). Although not the norm, this type of family structure is now very normal. The change has yet to be fully acknowledged by social security provision and taxation policy. Circumstances that are either near universal, such as old age, or have serious consequences, such as widowhood or sickness, have gradually attracted some level of universal non means-tested state income. The evidence suggests that lone parenthood needs special consideration, but it has not yet attracted a state income. When it does, there may be anomalies, in the sense that some lone parents are already comfortably off, but then so too are some widows.

The improvement in take-up following the renaming of the one-parent benefit shows the importance of the nature of benefits being readily understood. Greater visibility is one argument for abolishing the special one-parent tax allowance and using the resources to enhance the one-parent benefit. Another is that a unified benefit of reasonable size gives support to the legitimacy of the claim of one-parent families to a state income, and it provides a foundation for it.

Social change has been the driving force behind the increasing number of lone parents, whereas economic change has caused the rise in the number of long-term unemployed. Their low living standards, particularly for families with children, to which attention has been so frequently drawn by the SBC, is overshadowed in the public and political mind by resentment of scrounging and a belief in strong work incentives. Nevertheless if a high rate of long-term unemployment persists, state provision of a low level of SB income will be increasingly hard to justify. The argument that it is necessary for the preservation of the work ethic will undoubtedly decline in force. Although apparently firmly rooted in the attitudes of the majority of the British public, the work ethic is being more readily questioned by academics, trade unionists, and a few politicians. Technological development, in so far as it transforms patterns of employment, may eventually also transform the work ethic.

High unemployment was a factor in the riots that occurred in Brixton and Liverpool in 1981, and there has been frequent comment on the likely social consequences of persistent high unemployment. The level of benefit is an obvious factor affecting the response of young people to unemployment. Equally important but less visible is the eventual effect of benefit levels on children. In post-war Britain few have had unemployed parents for most of their childhood, but that may change. If so, the children will spend their formative years with a life-style constricted by the lowest family income that social security provides.

On grounds of hardship, there is no case for denying the long-term rate of SB to all the long-term unemployed. Until this is done, the policy of giving the long-term rate to those aged 62 and over who withdraw from the labour market could with advantage be extended. The Social Security Advisory Committee (1982) recommended that priority should be given to unemployed families with children on the grounds that they are amongst the worst off of all claimants, and that children should be spared as much as possible of the deprivation caused by unemployment.

Practical help for families with money problems

Money problems differ greatly in their form and seriousness. They range from the major problems suffered by the very poor or the financially irresponsible to the lesser difficulties of those who have a temporary financial stumble. In between is an array of problems involving people with different temperaments, abilities and circumstances. The type of help useful to some is not necessarily effective for others.

Amongst the most serious problems are those of the problem families. They are also the most intransigent. The causes can be so complex and deep-rooted that most forms of help merely alleviate and do not resolve the difficulties. Fortunately the number of problem families is relatively small, and they may not be as self-perpetuating as was once thought. It is also possible that the problems may appear greater to observers than they do to the families themselves.

Some of the characteristics of problem families, such as irrationality, ignorance, and difficulty in understanding are common amongst others with money problems, and they can cause particular difficulty over the provision of help.

French research carried out for the Caisse Nationale des Allocations Familiales (1979) into the perception of rights and effectiveness of claims by a sample of families eligible for benefit showed that nearly a third of the clients had little or no understanding of the system and needed personal help. The research found that the assumption that clients are 'normal' reduced the effectiveness of administrative procedures, and it did so in particular for the cumulatively disadvantaged because they tended to have the most difficulty in understanding.

Assumptions about the normality or otherwise of clients need to be made with much caution. Although convenient, use of the words 'normal' and 'abnormal' in this context may be offensive in principle, and undesirable in practice. Nevertheless the French research makes a valuable point. The traits and weaknesses of a person being helped have to be explored – although not presumed – if the help provided is to take the appropriate form. Otherwise, its value can be appreciably diminished. But diagnosis needs to be as sensitive in this area as in the medical field and an individual approach is essential.

The delicacy of touch required for effective intervention was further indicated by another French study for the Caisse National des Allocations Familiales by Pitrou (1981). Her qualitative survey of 160 families whose circumstances made them vulnerable to crises showed the sensitivity of feelings about seeking institutionalised help. The families instinctively did not want to become a 'case'. They felt it was not worth sacrificing their independence particularly when the help could be inconvenient, fragmented, incomprehensible or slow to arrive.

Similarly Hesketh (1978), researching into fuel debts, found many families reluctant to seek advice or any kind of conditional grant to help them out of their financial difficulties. Constrained by what seemed to them to be a hopelessly inadequate income, they clung as long as possible to the freedom of choice which the handling of their own money in their own way still gave them.

Inability to cope with money can be a serious social and economic disability. The literature suggests that where there are personality and intelligence problems, the understanding of them is limited and help of an effective kind is rarely given. Sometimes, as with rent arrears, people are reluctant to accept that human frailty can contribute to or be a cause of money problems. This may be a reaction to the readiness of others to do so. It may also be because of fear that such an admission could undermine the case of rent arrears being primarily attributable to money shortage. Unfortunately this view leads to socially sensitive problems being ignored when possibly they could be relieved, given specialised attention and sufficient resources.

Budgeting and Budgets

Over a million people annually fall behind with their rent, have their fuel supply disconnected, or are taken to court for defaulting on commitments. Many more households cannot find the money to pay bills when the first demand is made. In only a superficial sense is this evidence of a large-scale failure in budgeting because there are many causes of delay and default with comitted payments. Nevertheless weakness in budgeting is almost certainly a factor. In a few instances it can be a direct cause of delay or default; in others, it contributes. Making a payment by incurring debt provides no additional long-term resources, while the interest charges, which are often high, deplete existing ones which are already insufficient. If budgeting skills can avoid or reduce debt, they are of obvious value.

The movement away from frequent bills for small cash payments to infrequent demands for large ones has not helped those who find budgeting difficult. Goldring's comment, already quoted, is particularly pertinent. 'By their habits of mind and because of the practical realities of their situation, they [FSU families] cannot think in terms of saving money for a contingency three months in the future.' The number of families to whom this description applies is unknown, but many low income families rely on a weekly budget cycle.

Significantly the movement away from the weekly cycle is strongest among monopoly suppliers who are the best able to disregard the preferences of their customers. Firms anxious to sell generally accept weekly payments where it is wanted. But many local authorities are charging rent fortnightly, and, on the income side, the DHSS is experimenting with some fortnightly payments and is changing child benefit from a weekly to a four-weekly payment except for families on benefit or in hardship.

Government-sponsored market research related to payment intervals for child benefit found that 70% of mothers would find it very easy
or fairly easy to manage with payments every four weeks (Hansard, 31
March 1981, vol. 2, col. 79). Taking the converse, 30%, a significant
proportion, presumably would have difficulty in managing without
weekly payments. The Government subsequently proposed that all
existing claimants could choose between weekly and monthly payments, and as many as 63% opted for weekly payment (Hansard, 21
June 1982, vol. 26, col. 24W). Of new claimants, only lone parents and
those receiving SB or FIS had an automatic right to choose, although
the right could be claimed on the grounds of hardship. DHSS made it
clear that this would not be interpreted as convenience or preference.
The Social Security Advisory Committee (1982) regretted the limitation of the option, feeling it should be open to all future recipients, a
view which the findings of this review support.

As already noted, the essential requirement for successful budgeting
is 'a basic understanding of the interrelationship that exists between
the long term, the medium term and short-term commitments, all of
which have to be met from the weekly wage packet or monthly cheque'
(Blamire, 1977). In practical terms this implies some form of controlled short-term savings.

For those on SB, the SBC (1977a) suggested that some part of a
claimant's entitlement should be held back, and paid as a lump sum of
right every six months. Because the money could be anticipated, it
would permit payments to be made to those in urgent need without
discriminating against those able to manage. For claimants, the scheme
would provide a form of short-term saving. The reports of difficulty in
affording items such as clothes and the high number of ENPs that have
been given for them suggest that many would find it helpful. A disadvantage is that unless the scheme were made voluntary, it would
diminish the individual's right to control his or her own money.
Nevertheless the SBC proposal has a prima facie appeal and merits
further discussion.

For those with income obtained from work there are no obvious
similar solutions. What research there has been suggests that families
having money difficulties need a savings system that is delicately
poised between imposing an external discipline and permitting a
flexible response to the circumstances of the moment. For families
with incomes that are very low relative to requirements, such a system
is not easily found. Possibly the monthly payment of child benefit
may have advantages as well as the disadvantages already discussed.
Having to let the benefit accumulate may encourage some families to
treat it as their regular source of short-term savings.

Caplovitz (1963) commented 'It seems ironic that merchants in low income areas . . . are more prepared to organise their services to fit the special requirements of the consumer than are public agencies to deal with their troubles.' In some areas, his remarks apply to the SBC. The levels of benefits and discretionary payments are thoroughly considered, but the manner and timing of payments are given little attention. That the subject merits increased discussion is shown by the NCC's (1976b) criticism of SBC policy of paying heating allowance at the same rate throughout the year and Marsden's (1969) comment that lone mothers feel out of tune with the life of the community because they get their income at a different time from most families.

However, firm suggestions for change cannot be made because there has been little research into family budgeting. Little is known about its practice, and the relationship between successful budgeting and family circumstance and temperament is not understood. The views of people with practical experience of helping with budgeting difficulties need to be disseminated, and the whole area explored.

A related but different aspect of budgeting is the analysis of the different goods and services bought by people at different income levels. The OPCS (1981) survey of the financial circumstance of low income families provides much valuable information, but inevitably the qualitative detail is missing. Remarkably there have been no contemporary case studies of poor peoples' budgets. Reeves's classic 1913 study *Round About A Pound a Week* showed how such studies can increase understanding and complement statistical studies. Reeves demonstrated the poverty of people she studied by her finding that, even with the greatest economy, they had only 1*s*.2*d*. (6p) a week to feed each mother and each child. At that time 4*s*. (20p) was the sum allowed in the workhouse.

An approximate equivalent to the budget study has been Piachaud's (1979, 1981, 1981c) work on the level of the dole and the cost of a child. Using his own judgement and FES studies, he provided a realistic picture of the implications of current levels of unemployment pay and SB rates for children. Work such as his, but preferably based on real life budgets, needs to be developed. The detail of a family's expenditure delineates its life-style. It indicates its view of its needs and aspirations, and provides diagnostic clues to problems it may have.

Advice with Money Problems
Advice on handling debt is not a universal panacea because it can do little to resolve problems arising from an inadequate income. Nevertheless, where it is effective, it has obvious advantages for both debtors and creditors. Each benefits financially and the debtor may be spared

the social effect of prolonged debt recovery procedures (Scottish Law Commission, 1980e). In her report for the Scottish Law Commission, Millar estimated that only 25–30% of debtors seek help with debt problems. Not all debtors need advice or would benefit from it, but Millar suggested that the proportion seeking help is low because of the stigma attached to debt. For maximum use, debt counselling services need to be approachable and for this reason, Millar recommended that the considerable need for debt counselling assistance in Scotland should be met by general agencies such as the Citizens Advice Bureaux in addition to Local Authority Social Work Departments. The NCC (1980) took a similar view with its recommendation that money advice in general should be seen as part of CAB work. It acknowledged the success of the Birmingham Settlement Money Advice Centre but felt it was due to the 'almost evangelical success' of those who run it.

The Birmingham Centre does not claim to possess a new mystique (Blamire, 1973). It merely applies a systematic and logical method to debt counselling which lays particular stress on early advice. 'An incorrect move in the early stages can lead to a compounding of the situation and eventual disaster' (Blamire and Izzard, 1978). A basic requirement of successful counselling is communication which is not easy for many of the people who have money problems. The difficulty in communication is illustrated by the fact that 90% of debt cases in the county courts are undefended, even though, as Borrie (1973) stressed, this is to the disadvantage of the debtor. The personality traits that cause communication difficulties are probably a part explanation of the slight use of advice bureaux noted by Ison (1979) and the NOP survey for the Crowther Committee (Department of Trade and Industry, 1971b) although the limited amount of advice available and unawareness of what is available are other obvious factors.

The Maloney (Board of Trade, 1962) and Crowther (Department of Trade and Industry, 1971a) Committees favoured the development of nationwide expert advisory services to supplement CABs and specifically designed for low income consumers. Yet there has been no government action and because of the shortage of money the spread of money advice centres or the alternative of specialist workers attached to CABs has been slow. The relatively slight pressure for the extension of advisory work related to money problems reflects past lack of interest in the social consequences of debt despite the comment of the Crowther Committee that 'the country cannot remain indifferent to the magnitude of the social problem created by thousands of people whom it lures into shouldering a burden of debt which they can't sustain'.

One of the few examples of commitment rather than indifference is the New Cross Debt Clinic, which gives help with immediate problems and tries to secure a more lasting solution by advising on budgeting and the assessment of priorities. In 1979 the clinic got a Docklands Urban Programme grant to pay an outworker to tour schools and housing estates giving advice and setting up self-help groups. In the long run the Director, Katy Ritchie, would like to see local authorities assume responsibility for education in money matters.

Local authority social workers have an uncertain role in helping with money problems. Stevenson and Parsloe (1978) in their detailed study of the work of social service departments found that although most social workers gave practical help, including advice with budgeting to clients, it did not appear to be either an important or welcome part of their work. Of a sample of social workers in three areas of Yorkshire and Humberside interviewed by Spencer and Crookston (1978) 72% accepted that it was part of their task to teach budgeting to bad managers even though it was considered to be difficult and 'nobody was keen to do it'. The ambivalent reaction of social workers arose for several reasons. Some felt it interfered with their major task. They were reluctant to become involved with what were considered to be personal matters, and they hesitated to advise on managing an income which was below the level they thought necessary. Attempts to increase the level of income or to supplement it from various sources seemed more common than advising on budgeting, which some believed to be a hopeless task.

There is however ample evidence that advice is needed. Donnison (1980) suggested that 'in the social work profession we have to focus more attention on money [and] management of it. . . .' But the evidence suggests that social workers may not be effective teachers of money management. The French emphasis on teaching rather than treating and their greater use of specialist social workers (Rodgers, 1979) might usefully be copied. It is unrealistic to expect that families with severe difficulties can be formally taught budgeting, and there will be difficulties with motivation, but the work of bodies such as the Family Services Unit and family groups has shown that skills can be improved. Those organised by the London Voluntary Service Council have budgeting in the background of many of their activities, and the leaders, although not giving formal advice, steer discussion in the appropriate direction. The work of such groups was encouraged by the establishment in 1980 of an independent voluntary 'Cope' whose purpose is to foster the development of the family group method within the country. Such methods hold promise of helping people with the severest or most intransigent money problems.

Newspapers, magazines, radio and television have taken a growing interest in money matters and consumer problems. ITV's programmes such as *Money Go Round*, *Moneywise*, *For What It's Worth*, and BBC radio programmes such as *Money Box* provide valuable advice, although often at a fairly sophisticated level, while *Checkpoint* and *You and Yours* regularly include items which should make the listener more wary. But once again there is the problem of making contact, and it is doubtful if these programmes are watched or heard by the most vulnerable groups. The quality newspapers have for years given the kind of financial advice their readers want. The *Mail* and the *Express* have developed a similar service, but there is, as yet, little money advice for the person short of money rather than with a slight surplus.

Debt arises from a mixture of budgetary failure and inadequate resources as well as from budgetary failure alone. Effective help therefore needs to include welfare rights advice. The incomprehensibility of complex welfare provisions is particularly damaging to poor people, as was shown most strikingly in Harvey's (1979) study of rent arrears, even though the sample was unrepresentative.

There are no indications at present that welfare rights provision will improve in the 1980s; and, as already noted, the introduction of unified housing benefit makes it likely that some, and possibly many, people will be inadequately advised by over-burdened local authorities. As a result they may fail to claim their 'topping-up' benefit, and consequently lose the important 'passport' advantages (i.e. an automatic entitlement to other benefits) of SB.

Money problems inevitably increase in times of recession. If the recession of the early 1980s persists, there will be an exceptionally heavy need for money advice and welfare rights provision. If government does not respond to it, the distress of those in difficulty will be unnecessarily intensified.

Education in Money Matters
It is ironical but perhaps inevitable that people most in need of money skills are the ones most difficult to reach. Schools have an important role, for it is here that a basic framework of money literacy can be established before the pressures of low income living stifle initiative and interest. There are several indications of a growing awareness of the role of schools in this field. Aspects of money management are scattered throughout the curriculum, but the pattern is gradually changing and the subject is developing an identity of its own. The Business Education Council (BEC), which started its first school-based one year course in 1978 had 200 schools taking it by 1982, while the Schools Council Industry Project involving 150 schools has included money management within its more general brief. Other

developments include a £150,000 research programme at Manchester University looking at ways of combating economic illiteracy amongst teenagers, a pilot scheme run by the Scottish Money Management Association, established in 1980, to investigate the teaching of money management in primary schools and the way it is handled in secondary schools, and a consumer education schools pack announced in 1980 and sponsored by the Department of Trade. There are examinations taking in personal and business finance at all levels – GCE/CSE, RSA and BEC.

Despite the relatively small number of schools involved, there appears to be a welcome number of developments in the field, although *The Times Educational Supplement*, which noted them in its review 'Money Management' (28 May 1982), described the revolution as 'still patchy' and in some areas 'very vulnerable'. It commented that despite the increasing amount of material available, what happens in the classroom is 'very uncertain'. Some teachers are concerned about the use of commercially designed material because of fears that it is intended to invoke client loyalty. One teacher in the TES review complained that the material was designed for everyone but suited 'very few'. Nevertheless the developments are encouraging. They should be monitored, and, where appropriate, given greater publicity, so as to encourage reluctant heads to involve their schools.

Maldistribution of Income within the Family
A sensitive area for intervention is that of maldistribution within the family. Although difficult, it is possible for a government to have a marginal influence. For example the government decided which parent should receive child benefit, and the controversy that arose when the benefit was first introduced illustrates the sensitivity of the issue although the circumstances of the time were somewhat special. Only when a marriage formally breaks down does the law intervene in the sharing of family income. Legislation to cater for women still married is theoretically conceivable, but the practical problems would be immense and public opinion almost certainly hostile. The difficulty of finding appropriate remedies should not, however, lead to a dismissal of the subject, which would benefit from public discussion, as did the issue of battered wives in the 1970s. Over time, changing attitudes towards the relationship between men and women are likely to be the chief instrument of change. But the state could influence these and give practical help to some of the worst cases by ensuring that entitlement to SB guarantees a minimum standard for both man and wife, with the wife being given some rights over the SB allowances for herself and her children.

It is often argued that the married man's tax allowance should be abolished and the resources used to increase child benefit. The political response has been cautious, no doubt because of the large number of married couples without children who would lose by the change. Should the proposal eventually be adopted it will give wives control over a greater proportion of the family income, which will benefit those unfairly treated by their husbands.

Apart from counselling, the most effective form of practical help that can be given to wives deprived of money by working husbands is for local authorities more readily to provide accommodation for the wives wishing to separate so that they can claim SB in their own right.

Modifications to the money environment
One of the most striking findings of the literature is the high degree of inequality that can exist between two parties to a money transaction. The consumer or debtor can be unsophisticated, uncertain, gullible, nervous, unintelligent, illiterate. He or she can be involved in making an infrequent transaction with a person or business representative who is sophisticated, confident, knowledgeable, articulate, and backed up by skilled professionals as he performs, what is for him, a routine task. These descriptions are extreme, but aspects of them apply to many people with severe money problems, and they need to be borne in mind when the money environment is assessed.

That they are often forgotten is shown by the unintelligibility and complexity of many consumer measures, the disconcerting formality of financial procedures and the legal processes, and the class gulf between specialist advisers and some who need advice. Recognition of the frailties of some consumers and debtors does not automatically lead to suggestions for the reform of the money environment. The problems they pose are not easily resolved, and the position of others has also to be considered. But as Ison (1979) showed, recognition of human frailty is an essential part of constructive discussion of how to give more equal protection to debtors and creditors, and to consumers and suppliers.

Consumer Protection
Consumer protection, as a public issue, is heavily dependent on the sound and detailed work of the National Consumer Council, the Consumers' Association, and the Office of Fair Trading. Perhaps because the problems that arise are relatively invisible and rarely if ever assume the proportions of a public scandal, consumer protection has not captured the public nor political imagination, although the establishment of a Minister for Consumer Protection is a useful step

forward. For financial and organisational reasons, the industry lobby is likely to remain stronger than the consumer one. To offset the balance, the consumer organisations have to increase public interest and involvement. Yet despite extensive use of the media to get publicity, consumers appear to be relatively indifferent to efforts to protect their interests.

From the point of view of low income consumers, relatively extensive government intervention has provided only marginal protection. Significantly Painter (1978) noted that the growth of consumer practice law had not been because of a desire to protect under-privileged customers. The major pieces of legislation have come about because British trade and industry wanted them. Ison (1979) commented on the imbalance of lobbying pressure which has led to the Government making untenable compromises and not ensuring adequate enforcement machinery, thereby weakening useful legislation.

The Office of Fair Trading is an important instrument of the Government in this area, and it has many powers, but whether it has adequate resources to progress vigorously and quickly in its efforts to protect consumers is more questionable. For example the OFT has the major responsibility of licensing those providing credit, yet Ison argued that it does not have the resources to check the honesty and accuracy of replies received from applicants even on a sample basis.

In questioning the adequacy of the resources, Ison makes a valid point. The staff of the Office of Fair Trading numbered 306 in December 1981, and in his Annual Report for that year (OFT, 1982a), the Director General drew attention to the manpower demands put on Government and local authorities by the implementation of the Consumer Credit Act. The Director General added that 'If, therefore, governments wish to continue to develop the protection available to consumers in their often unequal struggle with trader or manufacturer . . . consideration might be given . . . to alternative, more flexible arrangements than those provided by the civil and criminal law in its present form.'

A more flexible response was strongly advocated by Ison (1979). He criticised the adversarial system of the courts and their formal customs for being inappropriate and failing to give equal protection to people who had different capacities to function within the legal system. For small consumer claims, Ison called for arbitration by a single judge who would operate in a flexible and personal manner to establish, in whatever way he chose, the validity of the complaint before him.

Credit Boundaries and Debt Recovery

The position of credit boundaries is a part of the important but controversial issue of the excessive encouragement of the use of credit. The checking of credit status is one factor influencing the position of the boundaries, and Doig and Millar (Scottish Law Commission, 1981c) showed how variable the creditors' attitude is towards it. Many creditors, including those who requested detailed information, felt that the granting of credit was an art as much as a science. In so far as it is an art, the process rests on individual discernment, and the literature shows that this carries a risk of personal bias leading to unfair treatment. A scientific assessment of credit status is based on the probability of various factors causing default. Once again, as the Director General of Fair Trading pointed out in relation to 'red lining' and 'credit scoring', the individual can be unfairly treated. There is an inherent conflict between fairness for every individual and generalised attempts to limit the credit granted to people likely to become overcommitted. A balance has to be struck between the two.

Preventing an increase in indebtedness is obviously in the interest of both creditors and debtors. Credit reference agencies can be helpful, but their effectiveness depends on the use creditors make of them. Some of the more intractable cases of debt default result in court-awarded administration orders. These do not prevent the debtor from obtaining further credit unless a provision to that effect is specifically written into the order. Excessive debt would be more effectively restricted by the proposal of the Insolvency Law Review Committee (Department of Trade, 1980b) for a new order, the Debts Arrangement Order (DAO), under which the debtor would be prevented from obtaining further credit beyond the figure applying in bankruptcy (then £50) without disclosing to the creditor that he was subject to a DAO. Any credit facilities obtained in this way would then have to be reported to the court.

The other approach is to limit the effectiveness of sanctions which creditors have against debtors. If debt is not easily and relatively cheaply recovered, creditors, as commercial enterprises, will be cautious about granting credit to those who cannot afford repayments. This method was favoured by Ison (1979). He was highly critical of the British system suggesting that the courts merely act as collection agents for creditors. Ison argued strongly that a just balance of power between creditor and debtor would result from abolishing retailers' legal claims for debt with repossession of goods and adverse reporting being the only sanctions against debt. The literature indicates that hardship arising from the overextension of credit is borne disproportionately by the debtor and not by the creditor, and Ison's proposal merits consideration.

The Scottish research showed the harshness of some sanctions against debt. It illuminated the problems that arise for both debtors and creditors and the researchers made many constructive suggestions for improving recovery procedures. If the creditors interviewed by Doig and Millar (Scottish Law Commission, 1981c) are typical, there is a willingness to show practical sympathy towards debtors with genuine problems. Revised payment arrangements were commonly offered, and in some cases, as long as six years was allowed for the clearance of debts of about £300. But the creditors interviewed repeatedly drew attention to 'their lack of a crystal ball' in identifying debtors' financial problems and Doig and Millar urged that debtors should be encouraged to contact creditors rather than 'hoping the problems will disappear in time'. The subtlety of approach required was shown by the experience of one firm which, finding that many people could not compose letters for themselves, successfully prepared a pre-written one for debtors to complete.

Debtors also do not have a 'crystal ball' and, although creditors are generally willing to agree alternative payment arrangements, debtors are not made aware of this at an early stage or in any detail. If this were done, Doig and Millar felt that more satisfactory settlements would be reached.

Improving communications may appear to be an obvious and somewhat mundane recommendation, but the Scottish research programme makes its importance clear. It is the essence of many of the specialised points made by Doig and Millar (Scottish Law Commission, 1981c) in the final Scottish report. In some cases, there will not be any effective communication unless creditors take the initiative. They have not only to pass on relevant information but also to make sure that it is understood, if necessary by providing names and addresses of helpful agencies such as the Citizens' Advice Bureaux.

Major reform, rather than modification was proposed by Adler and Wozniak (1979), on the grounds that Scottish diligence is an ancient and unsophisticated coercive system, which takes account neither of individual circumstances nor of the factors giving rise to the debt. By contrast, in the English attachment of earnings system, the court, not the creditor, decides the terms for repayment, and it does so after considering the individual circumstances.

Adler and Wozniak rejected a legal approach to debt repayment, and they were critical of an overall welfare model because it would require debtors to become social workers' clients, and would favour social security claimants. The arbitration model, Adler and Wozniak proposed, would not involve the courts unless the debtor denied his debt. The arbitrator would decide the appropriate level of repayment, taking into account all the circumstances. Counselling, money and social services advice would also be offered where appropriate. As Adler and Wozniak pointed out, their proposal rests on the belief that the debtor is 'unfortunate' rather than 'inadequate' or an 'amoral calculator', a belief which, in general, the research evidence supports.

A prime cause of debt is acknowledged to be a drop in income with illness and unemployment being major reasons for this. Insurance cover would ease the problem and two-thirds of Americans are covered when debt is incurred for amounts greater than $200. Doig and Millar (Scottish Law Commission, 1981c) found that only three out of the 55 creditors they surveyed had compulsory insurance policies and these operated for only part of their business. The lending organisations generally offered optional schemes, giving protection against illness, personal injury, and death; and in one case, redundancy was included. Of those interviewed in the NCC survey (1980) 65% would like insurance cover and 26% would not. The estimated cost would be to increase the instalment by 7%. The NCC noted that the Birmingham Settlement Money Advice Centre supported compulsory insurance. The NCC itself favoured insurance as a genuine option with all contracts recommending it and pointing out the advantages but without compulsion (NCC, 1980). Compulsion would of course make it cheaper for people who need insurance because of the subsidy from those who don't.

Fuel Debt

Fuel debt is a serious and intransigent problem. Accumulating evidence leaves no doubt that many poor people have great difficulty in paying for fuel. Current government help is linked to those in special categories and does not allow for houses that are particularly hard to heat. With fuel taking such a high proportion of the expenditure of low income families, a rational and broadly based government scheme for helping poor consumers cannot be indefinitely deferred, however great the pressure on resources.

The undoubted preference of the fuel boards is to secure payment by active use of the sanction of disconnection, and this suggests that undesirable levels of disconnection will not easily be reduced. Berthoud's main proposal that disconnection should be replaced by the compulsory installation of a meter has a great deal to commend it. It would ensure some fuel supply for consumers and would prevent the accumulation of unmanageable debt. The fuel boards would benefit from the loss of their unwanted welfare role. No doubt there would be additional costs, but avoidance of bad debt is a necessary business cost, and should be treated as such.

Excessive Debt

Repayment of debt excessive in terms of resources available for repayment is an issue meriting special attention. Whilst fraud and deception should never be encouraged, it is also undesirable for the burden of unrepayable debt never to be relieved. The Interim Report of the Insolvency Law Review Committee (Department of Trade, 1980b) noted that an aim of policies should be 'to provide for his [the debtor's] rehabilitation in due course if the circumstances of his case are appropriate'. The Committee recognised, as have so many before, that 'in an appreciable number of cases . . . [the consumer debtor's] insolvency is attributable . . . to a general irresponsibility and muddle in his past and an inability to cope with his position'. As already noted, the Committee proposed an improved version of the present administrative order procedure, which it titled a Debt Arrangement Order (DAO). Aspects that helped debtors included the court's right to discuss applications where there are no realisable assets or no available surplus income, and to forbid further enforcement against the debtor without court leave. Such a debtor could be prohibited from obtaining further credit. Additionally the court would have power to make orders resulting in payments of less than 100 pence in the pound, and at the end of the period of the order the debt would be considered discharged. Such a procedure, if adopted, would provide relief to those otherwise unable to become free of debt. However the Government's Consultative Document 'Bankruptcy' (Department of Trade, 1980a), published simultaneously with the Committee Report, ignored the problems for aiding consumer debtors, focusing only on bankruptcy procedures that would reduce government expenditure.

Berthoud's cautious but welcome proposal for a 'once only' pay-off of part of the very largest fuel debts as the only solution to a practical problem is another recognition of the undesirability of leaving large consumer debt as a personal millstone for life.

The 'Lenders of Last Resort' for Low Income Families

The Crowther Committee (Department of Trade and Industry, 1971a) drew attention to the position of money-lenders who are at the end of the credit line for those in 'most urgent, even desperate, need of money as often as not to pay off debts incurred by other means'. The evidence of this review suggests that the position at the end of the credit line is taken by illegal money-lenders whose activities are, by definition, unregulated and unsupervised. The hints of intimidation and exploitation are strong enough to merit an investigation of the extent and consequences of illegal money-lending.

The Crowther Committee went on to argue that there appears to be room in society for an organisation catering for low income groups, and pointed out that existing institutions did not cater for them except at very high cost.

In Canada, a Special Senate Committee on Poverty (1971) was more specific and recommended the establishment of a joint government–industrial scheme to provide insured loans to high risk borrowers for essential requirements. The indications from the literature, that spiralling debt may be trapping some families almost permanently in the hands of illegal money lenders suggest that these families need help. The ease with which debt can spiral and the ensuing oppressive consequences should be publicised. Encouragement to resolve debt problems early is very desirable. Help in doing so is important, and on some occasions financial assistance may be appropriate. Serious debt is a sign of the breakdown of the system, and this inevitably results in costs whether they be borne invisibly by individual families or by the state. If families cannot cope, early state help might, in the end, be less costly.

Empirical work and academic discussion related to social aspects of debt are mainly of recent origin and in some areas they are relatively slight. However, interest in the subject is growing. The work of the Scottish Law Commission, Ison, Rock, and Parker has made it clear that prevention and help with debt are important subjects. The real but barely visible difficulties of those submerged by debt show the need for further investigation of the social consequences of debt.

Money problems and deprivation

The literature indicates the variable nature of money problems. Some develop into crises, creating distress and hardship to a serious but unknown extent, while others, of a more chronic nature, lead to a restricted life-style which, in its most acute forms, could fairly be described as deprived. As has been indicated throughout this review, it would be unrealistic to expect the literature to establish a precise causal link between money problems and deprivation, and it does not do so. But the involvement of one with the other is clearly indicated.

Debt is one of the more specific aspects of money problems. Minor debt may be no more than a salutary experience, an unpleasant way of learning that in the end budgets have to balance. But it can spiral into serious debt; or a sharp sudden adverse change of circumstance can of itself produce debt of a serious nature. The effects may then be severe. Enforced repayment, as described by the Scottish Law Commission reports of 1980 and 1981, resulted in short and medium-term reductions in living standards well below poverty levels, and this may have contributed to the accompanying high incidence of marriage breakdown, with long-term consequences for the children.

As already noted, debt can sometimes – and the extent to which this happens is unknown – develop into an intractable long-term if not lifetime problem. With present knowledge, one can only speculate on the depriving effect of a life-style that is dominated by the presence of large and perhaps spiralling debt. The resignation and fatalism to which Berthoud (1981) referred are predictable, but they are not conducive to a resolution of the debt problem nor indeed to coping with any of the other problems of living.

A standard of living well below that normal in society is the more common aspect of money problems, affecting millions rather than thousands. The way of life of poor people has frequently been described, generally with sympathy and occasionally with passion. A common feature is the shortage of consumer goods and services compared with the rest of the population. In extreme cases, for those with the lowest incomes or the largest families, the shortage becomes a dearth, and the standard of living can fall to a very low level. Equally striking, in descriptions of extreme poverty, is the atmosphere of stress resulting from the struggle to manage. Sometimes it goes with a dogged cutting back; often there is resignation or indifference; and on other occasions desperation. Wilson and Herbert (1978) criticised Lewis (1967) for suggesting that the culture of poverty had a variety and richness within its own limitation. They put a contrary and depressing view, saying that 'the variety of life-style encountered amongst these [large] families contains a tragic aspect. The draining of human energy and potential outweighs all.' Their comments appear applicable to others in extreme poverty.

Yet deprivation does not fully equate with poverty. Deprivation arises in an unpredictable manner from the blending of poverty with other circumstances and with personal characteristics. But, the greater the poverty, the more likely it is that the end result will be deprivation. Similarly there can be no certainty about the extent to which current deprivation is transmitted across generations, for transmission operates through the moulding of personalities and attitudes as well as through the limiting of opportunities. But it seems probable that, for example, children brought up by mothers who are as exhausted, stressed and despairing as those described by Wilson and Herbert (1978) will bear some scar from the experience. On the other hand some children of problem families have been reported as being appreciably happier than those of the reference group (Tonge et al., 1979). The human spirit is resilient and a few examples of those who have triumphed over appalling difficulties can always be cited. But it would be unwise to presume that the vast majority will easily or always overcome the stresses induced by extreme deprivation in childhood.

The consequences of money problems will be more predictable when there has been further investigation of both their obvious and less obvious effects. For example, inept money management will lower a standard of living. But does it bring with it a perpetual sense of crisis damaging to family stability, or is it just a reflection of temperaments which tolerate or even enjoy living in confusion or crisis? How does severe debt affect a family's way of life, and what are the long-term consequences? In what circumstances does debt spiral to an intolerable level? To what extent does consumer practice or malpractice effectively reduce living standards? How important are poverty-induced costs? How great is the incidence of income maldistribution within the family and what are the effects on the children? There are at present few answers to any of these questions, yet they would add to the understanding of the interplay between money and deprivation, and perhaps to new policies.

Research into the relationship between money problems and deprivation is intrinsically difficult, because neither of the concepts lends itself readily to operational definition, and the concept of deprivation is unusually controversial. Bias is not easily avoided because willingness to be questioned may be affected by the degree of deprivation. A longitudinal study is the obvious research method for the assessment of the long-term depriving effects of money problems. But apart from cost considerations, the most severely deprived may not be equally available for such studies as those in a non-deprived control group.

The general approach to exploring the nature of deprivation has to be pragmatic, for the development of society is becoming wayward and uncertain. The factors encouraging and restraining deprivation in 10–15 years may well be different from those that do so today, just as today's are different from those of the past. The force of intergenerational transmission is particularly difficult to assess, for it can be overshadowed by the circumstances of the moment. Tonge *et al*'s (1979) study of adults who had been children in deprived families showed that current pressures are quite capable of outweighing the moulding influences of past ones.

Severe deprivation may be likened to chronic illness. There is no equivalent of surgical treatment to bring rapid relief to the sufferers and most remedies are likely to be of only marginal benefit. Nevertheless what remedies there are should not be discounted. They are valuable to people living at the margins of poverty. Moreover the reasons for their success or failure are of particular importance because the greatest gain will come from understanding the nature of deprivation and developing preventive measures.

Annotated bibliography

Adler, M. and Wozniak, E. (1979) 'More or less coercive ways of settling debts', Unpublished paper, Department of Social Administration, University of Edinburgh.
An account of methods used to settle debts in Scotland, which draws attention to those which operate by shocking the debtor into settling.

Aird, A. (1977) 'Goods and services' in Williams, F. (ed.) *Why the Poor Pay More*, Macmillan.

Alpren, L. (1977) *The Causes of Serious Rent Arrears*, Housing Centre Trust.
A study of rent arrears in a district of a large South London borough based on a stratified random sample of 42 tenants.

Ashton, T.C. (1956) 'Problem families and their household budgets', *Economics Review*, **48**, July, p. 95.

Askham, J. (1975) *Fertility and Deprivation*, Cambridge University Press.
A retrospective study of attitudes to fertility of women in samples of small families (two children) and large ones (four or more children) in class V and class III families in Aberdeen. 90 women interviewed out of 126 selected.

Bagley, C. (1969) *The Cost of a Child: Problems in the Relief and Measurement of Poverty*, Institute of Psychiatry.

Baldwin, S. (1973) 'Credit and class distinction' in *The Year Book of Social Policy*, Routledge & Kegan Paul.

Baldwin, S. (1977) *Disabled Children – Counting the Costs*, Disability Alliance.

Beckerman, W. (1979) 'The impact of income maintenance payments on poverty in Britain 1975', *Economic Journal*, **89** (354), June, 261–79.

Bennett, S. (1981) *Pulling the Plug on the Poor*, North Lewisham Law Centre.
A study of 12 electricity consumers out of 38 who went to the Law Centre with fuel debt difficulties.

Berthoud, R. (1980) *Review of the Code of Practice on Fuel Debts*. Policy Studies Institute.

Berthoud, R. (1981) *Fuel Debts and Hardship: Review of the Electricity and Gas Industries' Code of Practice*, Policy Studies Institute.
A review based on statistics supplied by the fuel industry and a survey in 1980 and 1981 of customers and debtors in four electricity and four gas areas. There were four major sample groups and four special ones. Over 2000 people were interviewed, an overall response rate of 51%, but only 21% for the survey of the long-term disconnected.

Birmingham Settlement Money Advice Centre (1979) *Notes for Guidance*.

Blacker, C.P. (ed.) (1952) *Problem Families: Five Inquiries*, Eugenics Society.

A survey of problem families in five areas; selection of the families carried out by local authorities on the grounds that the families presented intractable problems to one or more social service departments. The five inquiries were not uniform.

Blamire, J. (1973) 'Money advice – the method explained'. A paper given at a conference on consumer debt, 30 November 1973, at the University of Aston, Birmingham.

Blamire, J. (1977) *Budgeting: a guide to the art of making ends meet*, Birmingham Settlement Money Advice Centre.

Blamire, J. and Izzard, A. (1978) *Debt Counselling*, Birmingham Settlement Money Advice Centre.

Board of Inland Revenue (1981) 123rd Report for the year ended 31 March 1980, Cmnd 8160, HMSO.

Board of Trade (1962) *Final Report of the Committee on Consumer Protection* (Maloney Committee), Cmnd 1781, HMSO.

Borrie, G.T. (1973) 'Consumer credit and the law'. Paper given at a conference on consumer debt, 30 November 1973, at the University of Aston, Birmingham.

Bowen, J. (1980) *Consumer Attitudes to Electricity*, Electricity Consumers' Council.

Bradshaw, J. (1974) 'The family fund' in Newman, N. (ed.), *In Cash or in Kind*, papers delivered at a conference held in Edinburgh.

Bradshaw, J. (1975) *The Financial Needs of Disabled Children*, Disability Alliance.

Bradshaw, J. (1978) 'A review of research on variations in fuel expenditure'. Social Policy Research Unit, Department of Social Administration and Social Work, University of York.

Bradshaw, J. and Hutton, S. (1981) 'Tariff tilting', Social Policy Research Unit, Department of Social Administration and Social Work, University of York (unpublished).

Brenner, M.H. (1973) *Mental Illness and the Economy*, Harvard University Press.

Brenner, M.H. (1979) 'Mortality and the national economy: a review and the experience of England and Wales 1936–76'; *The Lancet*, 15 September 1979, 568–73.

British Association of Settlements (1975) *A Right to Fuel*, BAS.

British Association of Settlements (1977) *Supply and Demand; The Policies of the National Right to Fuel Campaign*, BAS.

Brown, G. and Harris, T. (1978) *The Social Origins of Depression*, Tavistock.

Brown, M. (1964) *Problems of Homelessness*, Manchester and Salford Council of Social Service.

A report of a consultation group set up in Manchester in 1954 to consider the problems of homelessness and to undertake a project involving preventative and remedial measures such as intensive case work and help with budgeting.

Burghes, L. (1980) *Living from Hand to Mouth*, Poverty Pamphlet 50,

December. Family Services Unit and CPAG.

A survey of 65 families, containing over 200 children, who were all in contact with a Family Service Unit. Interviews took place in May or June 1980. The families were larger on average than all families on SB, having about three children rather than two. Additionally, they were more likely to be long-term claimants.

Caisse Nationale des Allocations Familiales (1979) *Famille et Droits Sociaux. Les modalites d'acces aux prestations familles*.

Research carried out by the Fondation pour la Recherche Sociale for the Caisse Nationale des Allocations Familiales.

Caisse Nationale des Allocations Familiales (1981) 'La vie precaire des familles face a leurs difficulties' (by A. Pitrou).

Research carried out by the Laboratoire d'Economie et de sociologie due Travail.

Calderbank, P. *et al*. (1977) Unpublished DHSS survey of the circumstances of a sample of 654 disabled men receiving SB in 1972.

Canadian Special Senate Committee on Poverty (1971) *Poverty in Canada*.

A report of a committee set up in 1968 to make a comprehensive survey of the problem. The Committee argued that services were wasted if the basic level of income was inadequate, and it recommended a guaranteed minimum income based on a negative income tax.

Caplovitz, D. (1963) *The Poor Pay More*, The Free Press.

A study of the consumer practices of low income, mixed race families in a deprived area of New York: 464 families were interviewed, representing a response rate of 82%. A carefully documented account of the adaptation of a market to the poverty of its customers resulting in shoddy merchandise and increased costs.

Caplovitz, D. (1974) *Consumers in Trouble: a study of debtors in default*.

A record of interviews in 1967, with 1331 default debtors obtained by sampling court records in four US cities. A high percentage of missing persons contributed to a low average response rate of 61%.

Cartwright, A. (1970) *Parents and Family Planning Service*, Routledge & Kegan Paul.

Cartwright, A. (1976) *How Many Children*? Routledge & Kegan Paul.

A study of family size and spacing in England and Wales in 1973 based on a random sample of legitimate births in 25 local authorities. Interviews with 1473 mothers and 263 fathers.

Cartwright, A. (1978) *Recent Trends in Family Building and Contraception*, Studies in Medical and Population Subjects No. 34, OPCS, HMSO.

Central Policy Review Staff (CPRS) (1981) *Cashless Pay*. Alternatives to cash payment of wages, HMSO

Clark, M. (1978) 'The unemployed on supplementary benefit: living standards and making ends meet on a low income', *Journal of Social Policy*, **7** (4).

A national survey of 1535 unemployed men on SB in October 1974, aged 16–64, 0.6% of the total. The objective of the survey was to see how the families coped in real terms as well as in relation to their living standards when in work and to those of the rest of the community.

Coates, K. and Silburn, R. (1970) *Poverty: The Forgotten Englishman*, Penguin.

An account of the style of living in a very poor area of Nottingham in 1966/8, including comparisons with life on a council estate.

Colledge, M. and Bartholomew, R. (1980) 'The long-term unemployed: some new evidence', *Employment Gazette*, **88** (1).

A survey of research initiated by the Manpower Service Commission to provide information about the characteristics of the long-term unemployed, their potential for work and training, the factors affecting their ability to take these up, and their attitude towards various MSC programmes. The research involved a large-scale structured survey of 1698 long-term unemployed people, randomly selected, and 50 in-depth interviews.

Consumers' Association *Which?* (1980) 'Fuel prices', September.

Consumers' Association *Money Which?* (1969) 'The credit jungle', September.

Consumers' Association *Money Which?* (1979) 'Credit terms', September.

Consumers' Association (1980) *The Which? Book of Money*, Consumers' Association.

Corden, A. and Bradshaw, J. (1982) 'Why people don't get FIS', *New Society*, 22 July.

Cranston, R. (1978) *Consumers and the Law*, Weidenfeld.

Cutwright, P. (1971) 'Family income, family size and consumption', *Journal of Marriage and the Family*, February.

Daniel, W.W. (1974) *A National Survey of the Unemployed*, Political and Economic Planning.

A nationally representative survey of 1479 unemployed men drawn from the registers of the Department of Employment in 1973 at a time when the unemployment rate was 2.3%, a response rate of 67%.

Daniel, W.W. (1981a) 'Why is high unemployment still somehow acceptable', *New Society*, 19 March, 495–7.

Daniel, W.W. (1981b) *The Unemployed Flow*, Stage 1, Interim Report, Policy Studies Institute.

An interim report based on Stage 1 interviewing of a national cohort of nearly 8000 people who became unemployed in one week in May 1980. The interview took place some six weeks after registration, by which time about one-third had found jobs. The gross response rate was 68%.

Daniel, W.W. and Stilgoe, E. (1977) *Where Are They Now*, Political and Economic Planning.

A follow-up survey of the 1973 survey of the unemployed by Daniel: 932 out of the 1479 were traced and interviewed, a 63% response rate. Of those interviewed in both years 38% were in work in the later year.

Department of Employment Gazette (1979) 'The impact of rising prices on different types of households', **87** (2), February.

Department of Energy (1976a) *Energy Tariffs and the Poor*, HMSO.

Department of Energy (1976b) *Review of Payment and Collection Methods for Gas and Electricity Bills* (Oakes Committee Report), HMSO.

Amongst the many recommendations of the Committee was one of 'no disconnections', but the Government disassociated itself from the recommendation.

Department of Energy, (1978) *Energy Policy – A Consultative Document*, Cmnd 7101, HMSO.

Department of Energy (1980) *Tariff Restructuring and Poor Consumers*.

Department of Environment (1978) *Rent Arrears – Local Authority Housing*, HDD Occasional Paper 1/78.

Department of Health and Social Security (1974) *Report of the Committee on One-Parent Families* (Finer Committee), Cmnd 5629, HMSO.

Department of Health and Social Security (1978) *Social Assistance. A Review of the Supplementary Benefits Scheme in Great Britain*. DHSS, July.
An analysis by a team of DHSS officials of the Supplementary Benefits Scheme. It formed the basis of the subsequent 1980 simplification.

Department of Health and Social Security (1980a) *Income During Initial Sickness: a New Strategy*, Cmnd 7864, HMSO, London.

Department of Health and Social Security (1980b) *Inequalities in Health*, Report of a Research Working Group, DHSS.

Department of Health and Social Security (1981a) *Prevention and Health: Drinking Sensibly*. A discussion document, HMSO.

Department of Health and Social Security (1981b) *Payment of Benefits to Unemployed People* Report of the Joint DE/DHSS Rayner scrutiny, 1980.

Department of Trade and Industry (1971a) *Consumer Credit. The Report of the Committee* (The Crowther Committee), Cmnd 4596, HMSO.

Department of Trade and Industry (1971b) *Consumer Credit* (Surveys).
Surveys carried out by NOP Market Research Ltd for the Committee on Consumer Credit. Two stage stratified probability sample of adults 76.5% success rate, 3275 interviews.

Department of Trade (1980a) *Bankruptcy. A Consultative Document*. Cmnd. 7967, HMSO.

Department of Trade (1980b) *Bankruptcy. Interim Report of the Insolvency Law Review Committee*, Chairman, Sir Kenneth Cork, GBE, Cmnd 7968, HMSO.

Dilnot, A. and Morris, C.N. (1981) 'What do we know about the black economy?', *Fiscal Studies*, London, March.

Donnison, D. (1980) 'For whose benefit', a discussion with Ruth Lister, *Community Care*, 23 October.

Duncan, S. and Kirby, K. (1981) 'Rent arrears: causes and effective recovery', *Housing*, May.
A small-scale pilot study of 50 tenants in arrears in Enfield, an Outer London borough. Tenants were selected to represent the whole range of recovery procedures used in the borough, so that the data are weighted heavily towards those in more serious arrears.

Edwards, M. (1981) 'Financial arrangements within families', *Social Security*, December, (Australia).

Eisenberg, P. and Lazarsfeld, P. (1938) 'The psychological effects of unemployment', *Psychological Bulletin*, **35**.

Evason, E. (1973) 'Measuring family poverty', *Social Work Today*, **4** (3), May.

A study of the circumstances and subjective needs of 71 households on a Northern Ireland Housing Executive estate in West Belfast. Comparisons are made of the problems of families at three different low levels of income.

Evason, E. (1980) *Ends that Won't Meet. A Study of Poverty – Belfast*, Poverty Research Series 8, June, CPAG.

A report of the Belfast Welfare Rights Project which had four objectives: to increase take-up of cash benefits; to assess reasons for non take-up; to try out different strategies to encourage take-up; and to collect data on the dynamics of poverty. 1142 households living in four poor areas of Belfast were interviewed. The majority of families had incomes below the poverty line.

Fagin, L. (1981) *Unemployment and Health in Families*, DHSS.

A report of 22 interviews with two-parent families where the male breadwinner had been unemployed for at least 16 weeks, and had been employed throughout the previous year. The sample was mainly obtained from the DHSS nationwide cohort study of the unemployed. 45.5% of those contacted responded.

Feige, E.L. (1981) The United Kingdom's unobserved economy . . . a preliminary assessment', *Journal of Economic Affairs*, July.

Ferri, E. (1976) *Growing Up in a One-Parent Family: a long-term study of child development*, NFER Publishing Co.

A study of the effect of family situation on the development of children using data from the National Child Development Study and from a follow-up study in 1972 when the children were aged 14.

Ferri, E. and Robinson, H. (1976) *Coping Alone*, NFER Publishing Co.

A follow-up study of 202 children, motherless at the age of 11, in the National Child Development Study, 168 of whom were traced, interviewed at the age of 15, and compared with a similar size sample of those who were fatherless at 11.

Fiegehen, G.C., Lansley, P.S. and Smith, A.D. (1977) *Poverty and Progress in Britain, 1953–73* The National Institute of Economic and Social Research, Cambridge University Press.

A statistical study of low income households: their numbers, types and expenditure patterns, based on analysis of the 1971 *Family Expenditure Survey*.

General Household Survey (1978) OPCS Social Survey Division, HMSO.

Gershuny, J.I. and Pahl, R.E. (1980) 'Britain in the decade of the three economies', *New Society*, 2 January 1980.

Gingerbread (1978) Evidence to the RCDIW. *Selected Evidence submitted to the Royal Commission for Report No. 6: Lower Incomes*, HMSO.

Goldring, P. (1973) *Friend of the Family. The Work of the Family Service Units*, David & Charles.

A report of the work of the FSU at the time of its 25th anniversary, based on case histories, reports and discussion with FSU workers.

Goldthorpe, J.H. and Llewellyn, C. (1977) 'Class mobility: intergenerational and worklife patterns', *British Journal of Sociology*, September.

Gravelle, H.S.E., Hutchinson, G. and Stern, J. (1981) 'Mortality and unemployment: a critique of Brenner's time series analysis', *The Lancet*, 26 September 1981, 675–81.

Gray, A. (1981) *On the Black Report*, Health Economics Research Unit, University of Aberdeen.

Gray, A.M. (1973) 'The rent supervision scheme in Portsmouth', Social Sciences Research and Intelligence Unit, December.

Gray, A.M. (1974) 'Family budgeting systems: some findings from studies in Edinburgh and Portsmouth' in Newman, N. (ed.) *In Cash or in Kind*, papers delivered at a conference held in Edinburgh.

A survey of the budgeting experiences of the 97 manual workers in Edinburgh 1968–9, and of 100 families in rent arrears in Portsmouth.

Gray, M. *et al*. (1977) *A Policy for Warmth*, Fabian Society.

Greenwood, W. (1933) *Love on the Dole*, Jonathan Cape.

Hakin, C. (1981) A talk to the British Association for the Advancement of Science, September.

Hall, J. (1976) 'Subjective measures of quality of life in Britain: 1971 to 1975. Some developments and trends', *Social Trends* 7.

Hamill, L. (1978) *Wives as Sole and Joint Breadwinner*, Government Economic Service, Working Paper no. 13, Economic Advisers Office, DHSS.

Harbert, W.B. (1965) 'Who owes rent?', *The Sociological Review* 13 (2), July.

A study of 87 families in serious rent arrears with Southampton City Council. 76% of the families had three or more children.

Harris, A.E. *et al*. (1971) *Handicapped and Impaired in Great Britain*, OPCS, HMSO.

A survey of handicapped people aged over 16 living in private households. It provided the first reliable estimate of their numbers based on preliminary stratified random sampling of 250,000 households.

Harvey, A. (1979) *Remedies for Rent Arrears*, Shelter.

A study of rent arrears in the London Borough of Camden where arrears at the time of the study were three times the national average. Forty-six cases, mainly referrals and not randomly selected, were interviewed. One objective was to help the tenant when possible.

Hawthorn, G. and Carter, H. (1977) *The Concept of Deprivation*. A paper prepared for the DHSS/SSRC Joint Working Party on Transmitted Deprivation.

Henry, S. (ed.) (1981) *Can I Have It in Cash?*, Astragal Books.

Hesketh, J.L. (1978) *Inside the System: how an electricity board deals with fuel debts*, Family Welfare Association of Manchester, Manchester.

Heywood, J.S. and Allen, B.K. (1971) *Financial Help in Social Work*, Manchester University Press, Manchester.

A study of the use of Section 1 payments in four areas – two county boroughs and two counties.

Hill, M. and Laing, P. (1978b) *Money Payments, Social Work and Supplementary Benefit: a study of Section 1 of the 1963 Children and Young Persons Act*. Occasional Paper no. 1, University of Bristol School for Advanced Urban Studies, Bristol.

A study of 432 Section 1 payments made in six boroughs throughout the country for a period of seven months.

Hill, M.J. & Stevenson, O. (1976) *From the General to the Specific*, Oxford University Press.

42 in-depth interviews with men aged less than 40, who had been unemployed for at least 26 weeks.

Hinchcliffe, B.R. (1953) 'Review of "problem families: five inquiries" ',
British Journal of Sociology, **4**, March.
A highly critical comment on the book edited by Blacker.

Hoggart, R. (1957) *Uses of Literacy*, Chatto & Windus.

Hollingshead, A. (1954) 'Class differences in family stability' in Bendic, R. and
Lipset, S.M. (eds.) *Class, Status and Power* Routledge & Kegan Paul.

Holman, R. (1970) *Unsupported Mothers and the Care of their Children*,
Mothers in Action.
A report to a questionnaire sent to 114 members of Mothers in Action, to
which 95 replies were received.

Houghton, P. (1973) 'Money advice – the theory and the message'. Paper given
at a conference on consumer debt on 30 November 1973 at the University of
Aston, Birmingham.

House of Commons Public Accounts Committee (1979) Evidence of Sir
William Pile, 26 March 1979.

House of Commons Public Accounts Committee (1980) Evidence of Sir
Lawrence Airey, 4 June 1980.

House of Commons Public Accounts Committee (1981) Evidence of Sir
Lawrence Airey, 6 April 1981.

House of Commons Social Services Committee (1980) *Perinatal and Neonatal
Mortality*, 663–1 HMSO.

House of Commons Treasury and Civil Service Committee Sub-Committee
(1982) Evidence of Board of Inland Revenue, 26 May 1982.

Hunt, A. *et al*. (1973) *Families and their Needs*, HMSO.
An inquiry carried out in 1970 by OPCS for the DHSS in five areas of the
country, which looked at the circumstances of samples of fatherless, motherless
and two-parent families.

Hutton, S. (1981) 'Household fuel expenditure: the 1978 Family Expenditure
Survey', Social Policy Research Unit, Department of Social Administration
and Social Work, University of York (unpublished).

Ilersic, A.R., Christopher, A. and Mydelton, Davies, C. (1979) *Tax Avoison*,
Institute of Economic Affairs.

Irvine, E. (1954) 'Research into problem families', *Journal of Psychiatric
Social Work*, May.

Irvine, E. (1967) 'The hard to like family', *Case Conference*, **14** (3).

Isherwood, B.C. (1978) 'Equivalence scales, a review of estimation methods',
an unpublished paper prepared for the DHSS seminar on equivalence scales,
27 January, Economic Adviser's Office, DHSS.

Isherwood, B.C. (1979) An unpublished paper on fuel expenditure given at a
SSRC seminar, 23 March.

Ison, G.T. (ed.) (1968) *The Responsibility for Consumer Protection*, Proceedings of a conference sponsored by the University of British Columbia
and the British Columbia Credit Union League.

Ison, G.T. (1979) *Credit Marketing and Consumer Protection*, Croom Helm.
An examination of integrity in marketing and its relationship to the law

based on a survey of the purchases of major consumer durables. A random sample of 1540, mainly pre-selected and clustered at 60 sampling points by means of a two-stage probability sample, was used. 30% of households were rejected because no major purchase had been made; 51.5% gave acceptable interviews relating to 1226 purchases of durable goods.

Jahoda, M., Lazarsfeld, P.F., and Zeisel, H. (1933) *Marienthal*, Tavistock 1972, (first published, 1933).

A careful study of every family in a small Austrian village, population 1486, at a time of very high unemployment in 1931. Information was obtained in many ways – statistically, case studies, observation, and from the involvement of the researchers in the community in various ways. Impressions for which there was no objective support were discarded. The thesis of the study was that prolonged unemployment leads to a state of apathy in which even the few opportunities left are not utilised.

Knight, I.B. (1976) *Two-parent Families receiving Family Income Supplement in 1972; a follow-up survey a year later*. Statistical and Research Report Series no. 13, DHSS, HMSO.

A follow-up study of the 614 two-parent families receiving FIS interviewed in 1972. 521 were reinterviewed a year later, by which time 47% of the 521 were still receiving FIS.

Knight, I.B. and Nixon, J. (1975) *Two-parent Families in receipt of Family Income Supplement*, 1972 Statistical and Research Report Series no. 9, DHSS, HMSO.

A study of the circumstances of two-parent families receiving FIS based on a sample of 800, of whom 614 were interviewed, a response rate of 77%.

Land, H. (1969) *Large Families in London*, Bell.

A study in depth of the living standards of 86 London families with five or more dependent children. 150 London families randomly selected from family allowance records were contacted by post, and after a reminder, 86 were interviewed, a response rate of 57%. The study provides descriptive evidence of the characteristics and problems of large families and gives indications of the problems that are eased if income is greater than the average.

Layard, R. Piachaud, D. and Stewart, M. (1978) *The Causes of Poverty*, Background paper no. 5 to Report no. 6, RCDIW, HMSO.

An examination of the distribution of income relative to needs based on the 1975 GHS survey which provided usable data on 8586 households in Great Britain. The study looks at the roles different types of income play in the total income of households and families in different parts of the distribution, and it considers the main groups at risk of poverty.

Levin, P. (1980) *In Debt to the LEB*, CPAG.

Lewis, O. (1967) *La Vida*, Secker and Warburg.

Liffman, M. (1978) *Power for the Poor: The Family Centre Project, an experiment in self-help*, Allen & Unwin.

A description of an innovative, experimental anti-poverty programme for chronic aid seekers. Established in 1972, the Family Centre Project in Australia experimented with new methods of involvement and support, including an income supplement scheme. An objective of the project was to show that changes in economic and social conditions and in opportunities are pre-conditions for other change and for effective social work. The history of the project and the discussion is relevant to many aspects of anti-poverty inter-vention.

London Borough of Hammersmith (1975) 'Rent Arrears – Survey of London Boroughs', Hammersmith Housing Utilisation Review Sub-Committee.

Lord High Chancellor's Office (1969) *Report of the Committee on the En-forcement of Judgement Debts* (Payne Committee), Cmnd 3909, HMSO.

Lord High Chancellor's Office (1981) *Judicial Statistics: Annual Report 1980* Cmnd 8436, HMSO.

Low Pay Unit (1977) Evidence to the Royal Commission on the Distribution of Income and Wealth for *Report no. 6, Lower Incomes*.

Low Pay Unit (1980) *Sickness. Who Pays?* Low Pay Unit, London.

A pamphlet commenting on the Green Paper *Income During Initial Sick-ness: a New Strategy*.

Macafee, K. (1980) 'A glimpse of the hidden economy in the national accounts', *Economic Trends*, **316**, February.

McClements, L. (1975) 'Equivalence Scales for Children', DHSS mimeo, July.

McClements, L. (1978) *The Economics of Social Security*, Heinemann, London.

Marsden, D. (1969) *Mothers alone: poverty and the fatherless family*, Allen Lane.

A detailed and perceptive account of the lives led by lone mothers and their children living on National Assistance in two towns in the North and South of England. 116 families were interviewed in 1966 from 215 whose names were randomly selected by NAB officials.

Marsden, D. and Duff, E. (1975) *Workless*, Penguin.

A study of the life-style of men without work in their prime of life, based on interviews recorded over time with twelve selected families, approximately four-fifths of those approached.

Marshall, R. (1972) *Families Receiving Supplementary Benefit*, HMSO.

An investigation, on a comparative basis, into how equitably SB met the needs of six groups of families. Six equal samples, two with fathers unemployed and sick, and four with mothers unmarried, separated, divorced and widowed, were matched for time on SB, size and age structure of families, and type of area. The families were obtained from eight local offices, and half had been on SB for six months to two years, and half for longer than two years. 384 interviews were hoped for, and 348 were obtained.

Masey, A. (1977) 'Savings, insurance and credit' in Williams, F. (ed.) *Why the Poor Pay More*, Macmillan.

Merseyside Child Poverty Action Group (1977) *Cut-off and Cold*, CPAG.

Merseyside Right to Fuel Action Group (1980) *Heating or Eating? A review of the code of practice*.

A survey of 20 out of 29 households with fuel debts who approached a local welfare rights agency in 1979.

Midlands Electricity Consultative Council (1979) 1978/9 *Annual Report*.

Ministry of Social Security (1967) *Circumstances of Families*, HMSO.

A government survey of a sample of 2500 families with two or more children. 2409 were interviewed by officials of the National Assistance Board. The purpose of the study was to establish the extent to which the resources in families with children were less than requirements.

Moore, P. (1980) 'A pledged order book', *New Society*, 14 February.

Morris, P. (1965) *Prisoners and Their Families*, Allen & Unwin.

Research report based on interviews with 824 prisoners and 588 wives. 200 of the prisoners were in prison for the non-payment of debt or arrears of maintenance. A detailed study was made of the families of 100 prisoners to permit a more dynamic view.

Muellbauer, J. (1974) 'Prices and inequality: the United Kingdom experience', *Economic Journal*, **84**, March.

Muellbauer, J. (1977) 'Testing the Barter model of household composition effects and the cost of children', *Economic Journal*, **86**, September, 1–28.

Muellbauer, J. (1978) *Evidence in Selected Evidence submitted to the Royal Commission for Report no. 6, Lower Incomes*. HMSO.

Nairn, M. and Tait, J. (1963) 'A study of 283 families with rent arrears', *The Medical Officer*, March.

A study of 283 Aberdeen families in rent arrears. 70% had three or more children.

National Consumer Council (NCC) (1975) *For Richer, for Poorer*.

National Consumer Council (NCC) (1976a) *Behind with the Rent – A Study of Council Tenants in Arrears*.

A discussion of rent arrears including survey material from a non-representative sample of 70 tenants, 31 from Inner London boroughs, 19 referrals from the Birmingham Settlement Money Advice Centre and 20 from miscellaneous sources. Two-thirds were unemployed.

National Consumer Council (NCC) (1976b) *Paying for Fuel: an interim report*.

National Consumer Council (NCC) (1976c) *Paying for Fuel*, HMSO.

National Consumer Council (NCC) (1977) Williams, F. (ed.) *Why the Poor Pay More*, Macmillan.

A collection of articles which relate the concept of detriment, i.e. reduced value for money, to a wide range of consumer services.

National Consumer Council (NCC) (1980) *Consumers and Credit*.

A response by the NCC to a request from the Secretary of State for Prices and Consumer Protection for suggestions for ways of improving the use of credit and for the identification of unfair practices and barriers to the efficient use of credit. The response was based on three reports: (1) A survey of 915 adults in early 1979 in Huddersfield and Southampton. The response rate of 65% was low mainly because of refusals to participate. (2) A series of group discussions and in-depth interviews with people likely to have problems with credit. (3) A report on the credit experiences of clients of the Birmingham Settlement Money Advice Centre by G. Parker.

National Council for One-Parent Families (1979) Annual Report, NCOPF.

National Council for One-Parent Families (1980) Annual Report, NCOPF.

Nicholson, J.L. (1949) 'Variations in working class family expenditure', *Journal of the Royal Statistical Society*, Series A.

Nicholson, J.L. (1976) 'Appraisal of different methods of estimating equivalence scales and their results', *The Review of Income and Wealth* Series 22, no. 1, March.

North Tyneside Community Development Project (1978) *In and Out of Work*, NTCDP.

A small-scale local study of unemployment in North Shields based on follow-up interviews with 50 of the 90 unemployed men interviewed by Sinfield in 1963/4, together with interviews in 1976 of a new sample of 100 unemployed men and 88 who were in work.

North Tyneside Community Health Council (1981) *Unemployment and Health* (by M. Colledge) NTCHC.

Office of Fair Trading (OFT) (1975) *Annual Report of the Director General of Fair Trading for 1974*, HMSO.

Office of Fair Trading (OFT) (1976) *Annual Report of the Director General of Fair Trading for 1975*, HMSO.

Office of Fair Trading (OFT) (1979a) *Annual Report of the Director General of Fair Trading for 1978*, HMSO.

Office of Fair Trading (OFT) (1979b) *NOP Market Research Consumer Credit Survey 1977*, OFT.

Office of Fair Trading (OFT) (1981a) *Annual Report of the Director General of Fair Trading for 1980*, HMSO.

Office of Fair Trading (OFT) (1981b) *Review of the Price Marking (Bargain Offers) Orders*. A report by the Director General of Fair Trading.

Office of Fair Trading (OFT) (1982a) *Annual Report of the Director General of Fair Trading for 1981*, HMSO.

Office of Fair Trading (OFT) (1982b) *Credit Scoring: a consultative document*.

Office of Population Censuses and Surveys (1980) *Survey on Drinking in England and Wales*.

Office of Population Censuses and Surveys (1981) *Family Finances* (by Ian Knight). Occasional Paper 26, OPCS Social Survey Division.

A methodology report of a survey of low income families and their financial circumstances with a brief descriptive summary of results.

O'Higgins, M. (1980) *Measuring the Hidden Economy*. A review of evidence and methodologies. The Outer Circle Policy Unit.

Pahl, J. (1979) 'Patterns of money management within marriage', an unpublished paper, University of Kent.

Painter, A.A. (1978) *A Guide to Consumer Protection Law*, Barry Rose (Publishers) Ltd.

Parker, G. (1980) 'Birmingham Money Advice Centre clients' in *Consumer and Credit*, NCC.

Parker, G. (1981) 'Money management and consumer debt. A review'. An unpublished paper prepared for the Welsh Consumer Council.

Parker, H. (1979) 'Why we should work at family budgets', *New Society*, 24 May.

Parker, H. (1980) *Goodbye Beveridge*, The Outer Circle Policy Unit.

Philp, A. (1963) *Family Failure*, Faber.

A study of the characteristics and difficulties of problem families accepted by Family Service Units for long-term case work. With the help of the more experienced case workers and with advice from a psychiatrist, a social history guide to the cases was built up and used as the basis of the research. The aim was to identify some of the major factors creating difficulties for the families and to consider their interrelationship.

Philp, A.F. and Timms, N. (1957) *The Problem of the Problem Family*, Family Service Units.
   A review of the literature on problem families.

Piachaud, D. (1974) *Do the Poor Pay More?* Poverty Research Series 3, CPAG.

Piachaud, D. (1976) *Prices and the Distribution of Income*. Evidence submitted to the Royal Commission on the Distribution of Income and Wealth. LSE mimeo. December.

Piachaud, D. (1979) *The Cost of a Child*, Poverty Pamphlet 43, CPAG.
   An estimate of the cost of children of different ages based on a modern minimum set of requirements intended to reflect prevailing social attitudes. After making allowance for means-tested benefits, the prevailing SB scale rates were calculated to be 65–78% of the estimated cost of children, the percentage varying with the age of the children.

Piachaud, D. (1981a) 'Peter Townsend and the Holy Grail', *New Society*, 10 September.

Piachaud, D. (1981b) *The Dole*, Discussion Paper no. 89, Centre for Labour Economics, London School of Economics.
   An examination of the level of income provided for the unemployed in relation to requirements, spending patterns, financial hardship, replacement ratios and international levels of provision.

Piachaud, D. (1981c) *Children and Poverty*, Poverty Research Series 9, CPAG.
   An updating of earlier work on the cost of a child, and an estimate of the cost of a teenager based on views of minimum need from a sample of 116 teenagers. The minimum cost was twice the SB rate. Also estimates of the number of children in poverty using actual SB rates and adjusted ones with the children's rates increased by 50%.

Piachaud, D. (1982) *Family Incomes Since the War*, Study Commission on the Family.

Pond, C. (1977) 'Inflation' in *Why the Poor Pay More*, Williams, F. (ed.), Macmillan.

Radford, D. (1980) 'Rent arrears: how serious? how soluble?', *Housing* April, 4–7.
   'Rent arrears: a basis for comparison', *Housing*, May, 15–17.
   'Rent arrears: comparing local control policies', *Housing*, June, 10–12.
   Three articles giving the main results of the National Survey of Rent Arrears carried out amongst local authorities in England and Wales in 1979. The information relates to the financial year ended March 1978 and is based on a response rate of about 74%.

Rainwater, L. (1974) *What Money Buys: Inequality and the Social Meanings of Income*, Basic Books.

An examination of the relationship between income, personal well-being and membership in industrial society. Several different sources of data used, including the Boston Social Standards Survey, involving 600 interviews in 1971 in the Boston Metropolitan Area.

Rainwater, L. and Weinstein, K.K. (1960) *And the Poor get Children: sex, contraception and family planning in the working class*, Quadrangle Books.

A study of the psycho-social factors involved in the family planning and contraceptive practices of working class men and women. Interviews with 100 working class respondents obtained by quota sampling.

Ramsden, S. and Smee, C. (1981) *Employment Gazette*, **89** (9) September.

Reeves, P. (1913) *Round about a Pound a Week*, G. Bell & Sons Ltd.

Rein, R. and Rainwater, L. (1978) 'Patterns of welfare use', *Social Service Review*, University of Chicago, December.

Richardson, P. (1978) *Fuel Poverty*. Papers in Community Studies no. 20, Department of Social Administration and Social Work, University of York.

A report based on sample surveys of 248 households in low income centrally heated council estates in Leeds and York in 1976; a response rate of 86%.

Rock, P.E. (1973) *Making People Pay*, Routledge & Kegan Paul.

A study of debt enforcement procedures from a sociological point of view and as instruments of social control. Included is a survey of the attitudes of 119 people randomly selected from the two electoral districts of London with the highest and lowest frequency of county court judgements.

Rodgers, B.M. (1979) *The Study of Social Policy: A Comparative Approach* Allen & Unwin.

Includes four case studies of social work and the personal social services in Britain, France, Israel and Australia.

Rowntree, B.S. (1901) *Poverty; a Study of Town Life*. Macmillan.

Royal College of Psychiatrists (1979) *Alcohol and Alcoholism*, Report of a Special Committee, Tavistock.

Royal Commission on the Distribution of Income and Wealth (RCDIW) (1977) Report no. 5: *Third Report on the standing reference*, Cmnd 6999, HMSO.

Royal Commission on the Distribution of Income and Wealth (RCDIW) (1978a) Report no. 6: *Lower Incomes*, Cmnd 7175, HMSO.

Royal Commission on the Distribution of Income and Wealth (RCDIW) (1978b) *Selected Evidence submitted to the Royal Commission for Report no. 6: Lower Incomes*, HMSO.

Royal Commission on the Distribution of Income and Wealth (RCDIW) (1979) Report no. 7: *Fourth Report on the Standing reference*. Cmnd 7595, HMSO.

Salmon, J. (1974) *Resources for poor families: an experimental income scheme*. A research report for the Australian Government Publishing Service.

A report of the financial circumstances of poor people being helped by the experimental Family Centre Project in Melbourne, Australia, the help including the provision of an income supplement.

Scottish Law Commission (1980a) Research Report no. 1. 'The nature and scale of diligence' (by B. Doig).

212   MONEY PROBLEMS OF THE POOR

Scottish Law Commission (1980b) Research Report no. 2. 'The characteristics of warrant sales' (by A. Connor).

Scottish Law Commission (1980c) Research Report no. 3. 'Debt recovery through the Scottish Sheriff Courts' (by B. Doig).

Scottish Law Commission (1980d) Research Report no. 4. 'Arrestment of wages and salaries – a review of employers' involvement' (by A. Connor).

Scottish Law Commission (1980e) Research Report no. 7. 'Debt counselling. An assessment of the services and facilities available to consumer debtors in Scotland' (by A.R. Millar).

Scottish Law Commission (1981a) Research Report no. 5. 'The origins and consequences of default – an examination of the impact of diligence (summary) (by M. Adler and E. Wozniak).

Scottish Law Commission (1981b) Research Report no. 6. 'Survey of defenders in debt actions in Scotland' (by J. Gregory and J. Monk) OPCS, HMSO.

Scottish Law Commission (1981c) Research Report no. 8. 'Debt recovery – a review of creditors' practices and policies (by B. Doig and A.R. Millar).

Smee, C.H. and Stern, J. (1978) *The Unemployed in a Period of High Unemployment*, Economic Adviser's Office, DHSS mimeo.

Smith, A. (1981) 'The informal economy', *Lloyds Bank Review*, July.

Smith, D.J. (1980) 'How unemployment makes the poor poorer', *Policy Studies*, **1** (1) July, 20–6.

An article based on a national survey of the registered unemployed carried out by the Policy Studies Institute in 1979 for the Department of Employment. The purpose of the survey was to make comparisons between members of minority groups and white people living in the same areas. The sample of white unemployed people is considered to be not substantially different from white unemployed people generally.

Social Security Advisory Committee (SSAC) (1982) *First Report of the Social Security Advisory Committee*, 1981, HMSO.

Social Trends (1979) no. 10, 1980 edition, HMSO.

Social Trends (1981) no. 12, 1982 edition, HMSO.

Spencer, J. and Crookston, E. (1978) *The Relationship between Local Authority Social Service Departments and the SBC*, Department of Social Administration, Manchester University (unpublished).

A study of the relationship between social service departments in three different areas in Yorkshire and Humberside, using samples for three different types of cases.

Stephens, T. (ed.) (1946) *Problem Families*, Victor Gollancz and the Pacifist Service Units.

A case history study of 62 poor Liverpool families helped by the Pacifist Service Units. An early and eloquent description of the life-style and difficulties of problem families.

Stevenson, O. and Parsloe, P.(1978) *Social Service Teams: The Practitioner's View*, HMSO.

An examination of the task of the field worker in local authority social service departments. Teams from eight different areas studies, 1975–6–7.

Strathclyde Regional Council (1978) *Annual Report of the Head of Consumer Protection for the year 1977–8.*

Study Commission on the Family (1980) *Happy Families.*

Study Commission on the Family (1981) *Families in Focus* (by L. Rimmer).

Supplementary Benefits Commission (SBC) (1976) *Annual Report 1975*, HMSO.

Supplementary Benefits Commission (SBC) (1977a) *Annual Report 1976*, HMSO.

Supplementary Benefits Commission (SBC) (1977b) *Low Incomes*, Evidence to the RCDIW Supplementary Benefit Administration Paper no. 6, HMSO.

Supplementary Benefits Commission (SBC) (1978a) *Annual Report 1977*, HMSO.

Supplementary Benefits Commission (SBC) (1978b) Oral evidence to the RCDIW in *Selected Evidence submitted to the Royal Commission for Report no. 6 Low Incomes.*

Supplementary Benefits Commission (SBC) (1979) *Annual Report 1978*, HMSO.

Supplementary Benefits Commission (SBC) (1980) *Annual Report 1979*, HMSO.

Supplementary Benefits Commission and Local Authority Social Service Departments (1976) *Assistance in Cash.*

Sutherland, I. (1980) 'Moneylenders soaking the poor', Across the Borders Supplement, *Community Care*, 28 February.

Tenants Rights Information and Research Unit (TRIRU) (1982) *Unable to Pay. Low Incomes, Rent Arrears and Council Housing Policy in Brent*, The Brent Federation of Tenants and Residents Associations.

Thatcher, A.R. (1974) 'Year to year variations in the earnings of individuals', *Journal of the Royal Statistical Society*, Series A, **134**.

Tipping, D,G. (1970) 'Price changes and income distribution', *Applied Statistics*, **19** (1).

Tonge, W.L., James, D.S. and Hillam, S.M. (1975) *Families Without Hope: a controlled study of 33 problem families*, British Journal of Psychiatry Publication no. 11.

Tonge, W.L., Lunn, J.E., Greathead, M. and McLaren, S. (1975) An unpublished follow-up of the adult sons and daughters of a sample of Sheffield problem and comparison families, reported to the Joint Working Party on Transmitted Deprivation in 1979 (originally reported by Tonge, James and Hillam in 1975).

Townsend, P. (1974) 'Poverty as relative deprivation: resources and style of living' in Wedderburn, D. (ed.) *Poverty, Inequality and Class Structure*, Cambridge University Press.

Townsend, P. (1979) *Poverty in the United Kingdom*, Allen Lane.
A comprehensive book which seeks to define, measure and in part explain the extent of poverty in the United Kingdom. The full data was obtained from a representative national stratified sample survey carried out in 1968–9, involving 2050 households and over 6000 individuals, and from four supplementary surveys covering an additional 4000 individuals in Glasgow,

Salford, Neath and Belfast. The evidence suggested that if a 'relative deprivation' standard was adopted, 26% of the population should be said to be living in poverty.

Townsend, P. (1981) 'Peter Townsend replies', *New Society*, 17 September.

Treasury (1942) *Social Insurance and Allied Services* (Beveridge Report) Cmnd 6404, HMSO.

Treasury (1980) *The Taxation of Husband and Wife*, Cmnd 8093, HMSO.

Trinder, C. and Clark, S. (1976) *What Price Fuel*, British Association of Settlements Rights to Fuel Campaign.

A critical response to the Government document *Energy Tariffs and the Poor*.

Ungerson, C. and Baldock, J. (1978) *Rent Arrears in Ashford*, University of Kent.

A study based on interviews with households in Ashford in Kent. From 657 replies to letters sent by the Housing Department to 1250 randomly selected tenants, two samples of 60 were chosen from the 545 not in arrears, and the 112 in arrears. 35 of the former group and 45 of the latter one were those interviewed.

United States Bureau of Labor Statistics (1960) 'Estimating equivalent income or budget costs by family type', *Monthly Labour Review*, November. US Department of Labor.

Van Ginneken, W., Join-Lambert, L. and Lecaillon, J. (1979) 'Persistent poverty in industrial market economies', *International Labour Review*, 118 (6).

Van Slooten and Coverdale, I. (1977) 'The characteristics of low income households', *Social Trends*, 8, Central Statistical Office, HMSO.

Walker, G.L. and Church, M. (1978) 'Poverty by administration: a review of supplementary benefits and scale rates', *Journal of Human Nutrition*, 32 (1), February.

Walker, R. (1978) 'Rent arrears recovery' in *Housing*, July.

Welsh Consumer Council (1981) 'Money management and debt problems', a report of proceedings of a seminar held in Cardiff on 12 March.

Wheeler, E.F. (1979) Letter in the *Journal of Human Nutrition*, June.

Whyte, W.F. (1943) *Street Corner Society: the social structure of an Italian slum*, University of Chicago Press.

Widdowson, E.M. (1947) *A Study of Individual Children's Diets*, UK Medical Research Council Special Report Series no. 257, HMSO.

Williams, F. (1977) 'Introduction' and 'Conclusion' in F. Williams (ed.) *Why the Poor Pay More*, Macmillan.

Wilson, H. and Herbert, G.W. (1978) *Parents and Children in the Inner City*, Routledge & Kegan Paul.

A report of research seeking to explore the development of two children in two-parent families with five or more children living in deprived inner city areas, and known to the local authority children's department. Of the 185 families first contacted, 86 failed to fulfil the criteria, and 56 were finally interviewed.

Wynn, M. (1970) *Family Policy*, Michael Joseph.

A study of the economic cost of rearing children and the social and political consequences.

Young, M. (1977) 'Housekeeping money' in Williams, F. (ed.) *Why the Poor Pay More*, Macmillan.

Index